T0287804

Additional Praise for
## *ENERGY LEADERSHIP*

"As humans, we are able to accomplish anything we set our minds to, but we also can be our own worst enemy. *Energy Leadership* enables all of us to reach our highest potential and aspirations, because once your energy is aligned to your aspiration and intent, anything is possible."

—STEPHEN BADGER, Former Chairman of Mars,
Incorporated; Producer, Muscle Shoals

"As a coach, I am often asked to create awareness of how people show up as leaders. I can say, as a 20-year expert leadership coach and trainer, the secret answer is energy. This book offers step-by-step actions you can take to raise your energy level in the moment. Want more energy? Read this book, apply the concepts, and be prepared for instant impact."

—JOE ILVENTO, Chief Learning Officer,
Executive Coach, Commvault

"A truly enlightening book revealing how to change yourself and your business from the inside out. Worth gold."

—DR. JOE VITALE, author, *The Attractor Factor, Zero Limits,*
and *The Awakened Millionaire*

"The principles from Bruce's book helped me reframe my perspective from frustration and victimization to opportunity and action. I was so motivated that I landed a new role with a Fortune 100 company and continue to see endless possibilities for my professional future. This book is a must-read for anyone wanting to take control of their thoughts and energy!"

—DELPHINE SMITH, Senior Business Advisor, USAA

"A powerful guide to elevating your energy, whatever your starting point. Bruce Schneider has created a masterwork."

—LC GRANGER, Board of Directors, Women in Film

"Reading Bruce D Schneider's book radically changed the way I think about leadership and energy, two concepts critical in my field. Even better: discovering, understanding, integrating, and practicing Core Energy Coaching™ skills transformed how I choose to show up as a leader and how I choose to connect and respond to situations and people as an executive, as a father, as a husband, and . . . yes, also as a motorbike rider."

—FABIO PARACCHINI, Chief Strategy and
Innovation Officer/Head of Health, The Embassy

"*Energy Leadership* presents many fascinating ideas. Put what you learn from this book into practice to help you, the people around you, and your organization make a more positive difference in our world."

—MARSHALL GOLDSMITH, Executive Leadership
Coach and author, *Triggers, MOJO,* and *What Got You Here
Won't Get You There*

# ENERGY LEADERSHIP

# The 7

## LEVEL FRAMEWORK *for* MASTERY IN LIFE *and* BUSINESS

# ENERGY LEADERSHIP

## SECOND EDITION

## BRUCE D SCHNEIDER

WILEY

Published by John Wiley & Sons, Inc., Hoboken, New Jersey.
Published simultaneously in Canada.

For general information on our other products and services or for technical support, please contact
our Customer Care Department within the United States at (800) 762-2974, outside the United
States at (317) 572-3993 or fax (317) 572-4002.

Wiley also publishes its books in a variety of electronic formats. Some content that appears in print
may not be available in electronic formats. For more information about Wiley products, visit our web
site at www.wiley.com.

*Library of Congress Cataloging-in-Publication Data:*

Names: Schneider, Bruce D., author.
Title: Energy leadership : the 7 level framework for
    mastery in life and business / Bruce D Schneider.
Description: 2nd edition. | Hoboken, New Jersey : Wiley, [2022]
Identifiers: LCCN 2022016666 (print) | LCCN 2022016667 (ebook) | ISBN
    9781119899549 (cloth) | ISBN 9781119899471 (adobe pdf) | ISBN
    9781119899464 (epub)
Subjects: LCSH: Organizational change—Psychological aspects. |
    Leadership—Psychological aspects. | Emotions—Social aspects. |
    Motivation (Psychology)—Social aspects. | Employees—Coaching of.
Classification: LCC HD58.8 .S365 2022  (print) | LCC HD58.8  (ebook) | DDC
    658.4/092—dc23/eng/20220518
LC record available at https://lccn.loc.gov/2022016666
LC ebook record available at https://lccn.loc.gov/2022016667

Cover Design: Wiley
Cover Image: © bgblue/Getty Images, Rings: Wiley

SKY10034445_061722

# Contents

# Acknowledgments

With Unlimited Gratitude to . . .

Joan Ryan, the most fascinating human being I've ever known. Thank you for sharing your life with me.

Liz Fisch, for being a wonderful friend and partner. It's always a delight to have you contribute your gifts throughout much of my work, including this one.

Monica Coleman, Luke Iorio, and my daughter Erica Schneider, for being my partners and a few of my favorite teachers.

A special thank-you to my other partners, friends, and family members, as well as iPEC's outstanding leadership team, trainers, staff, mentor coaches, and success coaches. There are too many to mention each one by name here, but they are all in my heart as well as my writing. A few of them include:

Chris Miller and the other Eureka team members, Craig Schneiderman, Paul, Maria, and Gianina Monroe, Sherri Gerek, Simone Noordegraaf, Heather Doyle, Amy Everhart, Cindy Gardner, Lisa Kaplin, Tonya Echols, Tommy Acierno, John Bond, Steve Coleman, Deb Van de Grift, Gary Fisch, Paul and Kathy Mummolo, Hanna VanKuiken, Larry Gerek, Bill Bent, Zack Lemelle, Susan Stone, Jerry Schneiderman, Joyce Schneiderman, Ed Abel, Gary Kamen, Kellie De Ruyter, Jessica and Carlos Beltran, Brandon Dunn, Eleni Flescher, Kim Connor, Matt Hogan, Walter Aguilar, Maddie, Nate, and Owen Ryan, John Neral, David Scoggins, Barbara Curatolo, Jennifer Potthoff, Lynn Waldorf, Mary Jo Rathgeb, Don Madura, Caesar Salazar, John Petrillo,

Micheline Germanos, Lisa Te Slaa, Ascanio Pignatelli, Nate Coleman, Tom Kress, and the talented team at Wiley—Brian Neill, Shannon Vargo, Deborah Schindlar, Donna J. Weinson, and Premkumar Narayanan.

Finally, a huge thank you to the tens of thousands of iPEC Coaches who help raise the consciousness of the world, one person at a time.

# Introduction to the Second Edition

My introduction to the concepts in this book came during iPEC's very first Energy Leadership graduate coach training program in January 2007. My coach training experience at iPEC the previous year had been life-changing, but the Energy Leadership framework truly took it to the next level.

Shortly after finishing my graduate work, I had the chance to share the material with a new client who had recently suffered a major loss and was unable to move forward. Two weeks later, we met for our next session. My client told me that the Energy Leadership concepts had inspired and motivated him, and he recounted a list of accomplishments that had eluded him for months. *Hmm,* I thought, *this stuff really works!*

I was hooked. So hooked, in fact, that I became a partner at iPEC, spending 12 years working with Bruce on creating and refining our coach training and client programs, as well as helping with his 2018 book, *Uncovering the Life of Your Dreams* (a fictional deep dive into the highest level of energy).

Though I retired in 2019, when Bruce asked me about helping with the new edition of *Energy Leadership*, I jumped at the chance.

Nearly 15 years after its publication, the story and its lessons are still incredibly relevant. Even though written in the context of a small business, the concepts are applicable to everyone in all walks of life. Though that sounds cliché, I can attest that it is true, having had exposure to thousands of life, business, executive, and corporate coaches and hearing their clients' success stories.

In addition to updating the original book, we've added a Part II, where Bruce introduces advanced, yet very accessible, explanations of what actually influences and forms our energy in the present moment and shows how to use that information to achieve high performance and high consciousness.

Bruce's and iPEC's mission is "raising the consciousness of the world, one person at a time"; reading this book will certainly do that for you.

There is so much fear and divisiveness in our world right now. My hope is that the information in this book helps achieve a kinder world that's filled with curiosity, open-mindedness, and optimism.

Liz Philips Fisch, PCC, CPC, MEd
February 2022

# Preface

This is not another leadership book. In fact, it's not even a book about leadership in the sense that most people think of leadership. It's a book about energy – our most valuable, personal resource – and how to raise and use yours. The results are manifold and life-transforming, and one of them is becoming a better leader – the leader of your own life and, regardless of whether you are in the boardroom, classroom, or living room, a leader who inspires and motivates everyone around you.

The book is entitled "Energy" Leadership because it is energy that defines a great leader. What exactly is energy? The answer is simple: everything. Everything you see, hear, smell, taste, touch, and even think is made up of vibrating, living energy. Energy is about the way you "show up" in and to the world. Most of us are unaware of the type of energy we embody and how that plays out in our lives. Energy Leadership will not only help you to become aware of your current energy level but will also give you tools to make important energetic shifts that will change your world as you know it.

The Energy Leadership process could have been demonstrated by using parents, teachers, or any other type of leader, from any aspect of life, as the storyline example. I chose to use a small corporation, as I believe it most clearly demonstrates the value of the Energy Leadership concepts not only for personal development, but for where change is often cited as most needed: in the workplace. This book tells the story of my coaching relationship with Richard O'Connell – a partnership that produced great and lasting changes. And it began this way . . .

*Richard O'Connell drummed his fingers on his desk. He checked and re-checked his e-mail, trying to distract himself from the impending appointment. He was anxious but also oddly indifferent, as if it didn't matter how the appointment went. His eyes felt heavy. His face sagged. He slumped in his chair and felt the weight of his guilt and desperation pressing on his back. At 52, he had invested his heart, soul, and no small amount of capital into his company, put his name on the masthead, grown it into something he could be proud of – and then watched it get creamed by the competition. After 15 years of being a successful and profitable consulting business, the last year and a half had seen the once robust company sliding further and further toward bankruptcy. He had seen his staff members get restless, and what had previously been predictable squabbles escalate into full-scale turf wars. A few people had quit already. In the midst of it all, he was amazed that one person had even asked for a raise.*

*Richard had implemented various efforts to respond to the changes in the industry and decline in clients. New marketing initiatives were put in place, cutbacks were made wherever possible, updated services were offered to current clients – but still, the profit-and-loss reports for the last few quarters reflected a clear and consistent prognosis: O'Connell Consulting had about nine months to live.*

*After trying everything he could think of, Richard felt like he had nothing left to lose. He had called me the week before to set up today's appointment. He was candid with me when we spoke, telling me that someone had told him about business coaching, but that, in truth, he didn't think it would help. Richard admitted that he thought it was going to take more than a pep talk to pull this company out of its rut – in fact, he wryly told me that he believed it would take some kind of business version of those heart defibrillator paddles they use in emergency rooms.*

*We spoke for a while during that initial phone call. Richard was very honest with me, telling me that he kept asking himself certain questions over and over again: "What is wrong with these people? Can't they see the shape we're in? Can't they just get past all this pettiness, pull together, and help get us all out of this mess? What's wrong with this industry? What are we doing in this business, anyway? Why has it become so cutthroat? Why is it that every time I turn around another one of our accounts has been stolen right from under our noses?"*

*And the kicker: "With all my experience, great contacts, killer ideas, and how much I care about the people I work with and for . . . what is wrong with me that I can't make this business a thriving success?"*

Although it might have felt that way to him, Richard wasn't alone. A relentless stream of questions like his runs through the minds of many businesspeople, from those working in struggling entrepreneurial enterprises to those in apparently flourishing global companies. Let's call it the Stream of Unconsciousness, a negatively based "what's-wrong" perspective that erodes morale, dulls productivity, and deeply cuts into profit.

It may look as if these kinds of questions are the result of a crushing business climate, but they are actually part of its cause. Indeed, within any individual or company, there is a direct relationship between the what's-wrong attitude stream and the flow of finances and personnel.

As a coach who helps people deal with everything from personal difficulties to corporate mayhem, I have seen firsthand how deeply ingrained the what's-wrong way of thinking has become. No wonder the majority of people in business, from seasoned CEOs to the newest hire, feel unsatisfied and unfulfilled, and that keeping and motivating talented and dedicated people presents an organization with its most challenging and important task. Despite best efforts, and as a result of the what's-wrong perspective that arises when businesses face obstacles, most staff members see their leaders as uncaring, uninspiring, and unfit to lead. The what's-wrong attitude isn't limited to business, unfortunately – it's found in schools, families, nonprofit organizations, in our relationships, and in our perceptions of ourselves.

What does it take to reverse the pressure and negativity that surround not only our business ventures and corporations but also our personal lives and the state of our communities?

What will help employees to be productive and content, and to have a positive view of both their organizations and coworkers?

What will turn around people like Richard, who may indeed have the foundation for success but lack some essential ingredients integral to achieving it?

It requires a critical understanding of the tenets offered in this book on Energy Leadership that are essential to uncovering the answers to these questions. It takes authentic leaders who commit to developing their skills, sophistication, and versatility. It demands that even those who don't view themselves as leaders recognize that everyone leads, either intentionally or by default. It necessitates people becoming aware of how powerful they are and can be in the workplace, at home, and in the world at large. In sum, the way to become a powerful leader – who leads both oneself and others to achieve extraordinary things – is to understand the power of energy.

For the first time, *Energy Leadership* codifies and clearly articulates a theory and practice of leadership – for the workplace and for home – that can address today's unique challenges. The story in this book will . . .

- Convey seven distinct levels of energy and leadership, as well as engagement and consciousness, in life and within the workplace.
- Point out the difference between "catabolic" and "anabolic" leaders. Ideal leaders are anabolic leaders, meaning they create and automatically attract success. You may be shocked to learn that the vast majority of all leaders have a great deal of catabolic energy, thereby destroying the energy and momentum of the people around them and their companies and families as a whole.
- Present the "Energetic Self-Perception Chart," which has been shared with hundreds of thousands of people to help them make transformations in their personal and professional lives. This chart depicts the seven unique levels of energy that, when understood, can alter the way people think about themselves and the world around them.
- Offer you a clear vision of your own level of energy and engagement, not only on the job, but also in everyday life.
- Help you recognize your energy around any specific situation or task and learn how to optimize it to get the results that you seek.
- Reveal proprietary processes for shifting energy that anyone can use in any leadership situation, whether that means leading yourself or others, in small groups or large, at home or at work.

The book chronicles the coaching process as it unfolds in O'Connell Consulting, and it describes the transformation and business turnaround that takes place as each person assumes the mantle of energy leadership.[1] It traces the path commonly followed by the people I coach and includes the principles and lessons crucial to developing an expanded consciousness. This expanded consciousness can lead to greater employee retention, higher productivity, and increased profits, as well as more personal satisfaction and a sense of purpose.

When you've finished reading *Energy Leadership*, you will have traveled this path with Richard and his staff, and you will understand how it can apply to your own business and personal life. Based on decades dedicated to research and application, this book illustrates techniques that can help individuals recognize what drives and engages people and provides specific developmental strategies to help leaders motivate and inspire others.

People who master and use the concepts of Energy Leadership arm themselves with the knowledge and skills to become effective leaders who inspire themselves and others to do much more than they would have on their own. The system creates a true win-win for leaders, their staff members, their family members, their friends, and their organizations.

What transpired in a small consulting firm is nothing short of miraculous.

---

[1]Among the characters of Richard and his staff, some are composites, and in every case, names and identifying characteristics have been changed to protect the individuals' privacy.

# ENERGY
# MATTERS

# 1 | Thank God It's Monday!

*A leader doesn't just get the message across – a leader is the message.*
—Warren Bennis, authority on organizational development, leadership, and change

Things just *felt* different.

When I walked through the doors of O'Connell Consulting, a familiar face caught my eye. I approached her desk and noticed how the mahogany gleamed. The crisp sign on it read *Christina Suarez, Executive Assistant.*

Christina welcomed me: "Good morning, Bruce." She looked bright, relaxed. "You're here early. Can I get you anything?"

Of all the changes I had seen in this company, none could match the transformation Christina had made. Her hangdog expression I had encountered on my first visit had vanished and her air of resignation and "why bother?" was history. Even her workspace was different – the boxes of unfiled folders cluttering the entryway were gone and the old, scuffed reception desk had been replaced with one much more aesthetically pleasing and inviting.

Christina spoke animatedly, without a trace of the mumbling I experienced when I first met her. She made me feel welcome, the way someone would greet you at a casual party. It was delightful to see her new and improved demeanor – a powerful indicator of the revitalization that had taken place here.

"I don't need a thing, Christina. It's great to see you, though," I remarked, returning her warmth with my own. "You make it such a pleasure to be here," I said, and meant it from the bottom of my heart. There was that smile again as she briefly turned away from me to tell Richard O'Connell, the company's chief executive officer, that I'd arrived.

When Richard and I began our work together six months earlier, the company he had created, nurtured, and loved for 15 years was uncomfortably close to bankruptcy. The nerves of the staff were frayed, the management team was at each other's throats, the support staff whispered their contempt for the whole organization, and almost everything seemed lost.

Today, a mere six months later, everything *was* different.

Richard was waiting for me, Christina reported, so I made my way toward his office. In the hallway, a confident, upbeat, impeccably dressed woman strode in my direction. "Well, good morning, Bruce. You're looking dapper," Tonya Swanson said and extended her hand. Another remarkable change: When I'd first met her, Tonya had been the most negative member of Richard's inner circle, despite being a highly talented vice president in charge of operations. Now, she exuded creativity and positive energy in whatever she did. Instead of avoiding Tonya, people now flocked to her. Tonya's transformation from "drain to gain" was one of the most important reasons that O'Connell Consulting recorded its highest revenues ever the quarter following my work there.

I said good-bye to Tonya and continued down the corridor. Soon I passed Don Taylor's office, and there he was, diligently tapping on his keyboard. His expression was so different from the "old Don": He looked positively absorbed. When he glanced up and caught me staring at him, he winked and got back to what he was doing. I interpreted that to mean he was, indeed, fully engaged. As I stood there a few seconds longer, I remembered all too well having seen him "working" too hard and constantly frustrated with nearly everyone he was managing. Now, he was more efficient, effective, and finally enjoying his job, as if it was no longer drudgery. He also enjoyed leading the staff members who reported to him, whom he now referred to as his *partners.*

Only six months earlier, when Don's energy was incredibly volatile, no one would have believed that he would become the company's most inspirational figure and a driving force behind the company's success.

Almost at Richard's door, I was nearly trampled by Kyle Pennington, who was about to fling open the door to his boss's office.

"Sorry, Bruce. Didn't mean to cut in front of you," he said, as he continued to dash ahead of me. "But I've got some good news for Richard. Won't be but a minute."

While I waited outside the office, through all the commotion and "positive energy" welcoming me, I noticed Kyle's predecessor was nowhere to be seen. His wasn't among the many smiling faces greeting me today. *That's about right,* I thought. In my time there, I didn't recall ever seeing that man smile or get excited about anything.

Kyle zipped out of Richard's office almost as quickly as he entered, which meant it was my turn to see the boss.

My client sat at his desk, reading the first-quarter report that Kyle just handed him. Richard already knew the results, so the enthusiastic perusal I witnessed was an acknowledgment of the dramatic success his company had achieved.

"Grab your chair, my friend," he said.

For a moment, both of us remained quiet, each unwilling to interrupt with words what we both were now experiencing: an easy yet electrified silence filled with anticipation and no small amount of wonder.

"How does it look?" I finally asked Richard as I sat down, nodding at the report and grinning at him. But we both knew I meant much more than that.

Richard was visibly excited and half-ready to jump out of his chair. But his response was understated: "It looks really good, Bruce. In fact, I'm tempted to say it's almost perfect."

Today was the date we had decided on at our first meeting to review our progress and celebrate the company's dramatic turnaround; a day we hoped would come. It served as a testament to a few simple and important facts: Richard's company still existed, was still viable – and was *prospering*. From here on out, a whole new world of possibilities opened up for him, as well as for every one of his employees. And employees like Christina, Tonya, Don, and Kyle were clearly aware of it.

Now it was my turn to play: "So what else is new?" I asked rather casually.

"Very funny," Richard replied. He looked out his window, which opened on a lush green hilltop. But his gaze seemed to stretch much farther. "Where should I start?" he asked, as much to himself as to me.

Richard began by telling me that the past six months had been the most challenging, revealing, and intriguing of his career. O'Connell Consulting had gone from nearly having to close up shop to now making record profits. He reminded me that six months ago he'd thought he'd have to replace his management team or go under and lose the company and dream he had worked so hard to create. Instead, the management team had become a powerful force for guiding people and change. The fear of closing shop was not even an option. His team was now fully invested and engaged in helping him grow the business and consistently creating a work environment that was highly positive.

Richard paused, as if he needed a moment to fully take in what he had just shared. Then his review continued: "My support staff is not only productive, but they communicate and solve problems together. I'm not just guessing when I say that they're fully engaged and happy, too. I can see it on their faces and feel it in the air."

The fact that he mentioned this last observation demonstrated a significant transformation in his own level of awareness. In the past, Richard would have been so absorbed with his own "stuff" that he wouldn't have even put his feelers out or concerned himself with others' level of engagement. He would have just assumed that people were slacking off, taking him and the company for a ride, causing trouble, and making his job impossible.

Nowadays, he said, he was meeting with every one of his staff regularly. The staff had changed, too, of course. Instead of using him as a dumping bin for problems, his people now were proposing solutions, reviewing objectives achieved, and setting new goals for the future.

"Our entire organization is finely tuned. In fact, we're experiencing – no, we're *creating* new growth in a competitive marketplace," he said.

Richard wasn't finished. Looking me in the eye, he said that the most important change, however, was not within his company. It was within himself. He told me he now knew who he really was: "I'm an effective leader who's crafting a purposeful and powerful life."

Richard seemed almost surprised to hear himself say it. He then disclosed that he thoroughly enjoyed coming to work each and every morning these days.

"Oh, there's one more thing: My wife," he added, smiling, "says I should give you more money."

We both sat back, amused. Although it was a lovely sentiment, we both knew I was not the source of this company's turnaround or of the differences his wife was seeing at home.

What had happened in Richard's company to account for the changes he reported? Was it his coming into the office earlier, so that he didn't feel rushed to catch up right from the start of his day? Was it the individual attention he gave his employees each morning, or the weekly updates he was now receiving promptly from everyone? Was it his employees' "thank-God-it's-Monday" attitudes that seemed to open a world of limitless possibility?

In our work together, we had implemented various processes, and I had helped him gain some critical new understandings about how people work together. This and many other factors had led to what he was describing to me. Yet none of these was the main cause of the miraculous transformation in Richard's business over the past six months. These positive developments were actually *effects* of the change, not causes.

What really changed? It was Richard himself.

**Six Months Earlier . . .**

When I first walked into Richard's office for our initial coaching session, I had to avoid a minefield of boxes as I made my way to the first person I saw. Patiently, I waited for the mystery woman behind the tall, cluttered reception desk to address me. She ignored me and continued to type, so I entertained myself by imagining I was invisible. For what seemed like several minutes, I got lost in a reverie, picturing all the amazing things I could do if no one could see me. Alas, she finally spoke.

". . . help you?" the woman whined, barely audible. She sounded like she had been anesthetized and was dreading her impending operation.

I told her my name, and she turned her back to me to contact Richard to let him know "Bruce Somebody" was there. She said nothing more but did manage to point in the direction of his office, for which I was most grateful.

Richard greeted me with a level of enthusiasm that exceeded the receptionist's, but not by much. (If you haven't figured it out, the whiny woman was none other than Christina Suarez.) Numb and barely communicative, Richard's energy was more like that of a patient in the recovery room, hardly able to speak coherently. After some disengaged pleasantries, he made his desperation clear. He told me that if he didn't do something radical to turn his company around, it wouldn't be in business much longer.

Richard made it clear that I was his last resort: "I don't know what else to do. A coach seems like as good an idea as any. When I heard about you, I decided I'd give it a try. At this point, we really don't have much left to lose."

---

**Get This**

You can become a powerful leader of your company and your life. To get you started immediately, I'd like to introduce you right now to the first of five "energetic principles" that shape every interaction in this book.

The first principle is so powerful that discovering and applying it can change your entire life.

## Energetic Principle #1

**Life offers neither problems nor challenges, only opportunities.**

Let that sink in: **There are no problems. There are no challenges.**

That may sound like unvarnished positive thinking, but it goes deeper than that. Consider this: Problems and challenges are *creations of a fear-based perspective* on life. When we transcend fear, what remains is *opportunity*.

Okay. You may still be thinking, *That's it?* Yes, sort of. The secret is that the principles I'll be sharing with you *energetically resonate* at a level of success. And remember that conceiving something isn't the same as believing. And believing isn't the same as *implementation*, something every businessperson knows already.

The real power comes in living a principle like this *as truth*.

This is why, although Richard's situation seemed bleak at the outset of the story, I was still more than willing to go forward and see what might be created out of what he perceived to be a mess – the mother of all business failures – his own personal code red.

One thing was piercing through his cloud of condemnation: O'Connell Consulting was poised for a miracle.

## Why Bother?

I have encountered entrepreneurs before when they reach the point where they wonder what on earth could possibly help, and doubt that there's even an answer. I let Richard know that his feelings were normal. Even though our current situations were far different, I could see myself in him, and I felt an eerie similarity.

Although it seems as if it was a past life, I, too, remember thinking that nothing I did made a difference. This was back in my teen years, a time when I felt like I had no direction or purpose in my life. I alienated myself from all groups and social cliques. To be honest, I stayed away from almost anyone who breathed. I felt quite different from others and angry at virtually everyone else for being what I desired to be: noticed. I created a world that demanded violence and defied authority, and then I staged a complete revolt against any type of spiritual practice. (I now believe this was my way of trying to generate whatever attention I could muster.)

Just before I started college, a drunk driver killed himself and nearly killed me as he got on a highway in the wrong direction and drove into oncoming traffic. The head-on collision left me badly broken and barely breathing. Later, one member of the ambulance team told me of the astronomical odds against my surviving that accident, and when word got out about it, I became known as a "living miracle" in my hometown of North Brunswick, New Jersey.

All the attention I could ever have desired was then available to me. Oddly, that powerful experience taught me that I didn't need it. The attention and accolades meant nothing, and I turned away from them and toward something much more meaningful. I knew then something that I always remembered since: everything I do matters, and everything I am matters even more.

In 1978, I was given the gift of life for the second time. At that point, I decided to make it a life worth living.

The accident became the impetus behind the eventual creation of all the work I do, and much of what I would share with Richard over the time we'd work together. It had taken decades to develop.

As I told him, what you're about to learn is not just some training to implement with employees; it's a way of life.

# 2 | What Energetic Level Are You?

*We do not see things as they are. We see them as we are.*
                                        —Attributed to various sources

"What, exactly, do you do?" Richard asked me.

"That's a reasonable question," I acknowledged. "But before we jump into that, I would like to ask a favor of you. You said I was your last resort, yet I don't believe what I'm going to share with you is a last-ditch approach. It is vital information for every business in the world, regardless of what shape it's in. In fact, it is vital information for every person in the world.

"The favor I'm asking is for you to have an open mind. I'm also asking that you have faith, even though you feel hopeless. What do you say?"

"Faith? I don't know about that. I'll do my best, and I will at least keep an open mind," Richard promised.

"Fair enough. Before we get into the true potential my work holds for you, let's cover a few important concepts." I handed Richard a page of definitions of keywords and phrases as a quick reference for him as he became more familiar with the Energy Leadership process. (See Appendix A.)

11

"So, Richard, take a look at those definitions later, when you can take your time with it. Right now, I want to show you something else. It's part of what I do – the cornerstone of it, really." I pulled my Energetic Self-Perception Chart (Figure 2.1). "See this? It's a diagram of the seven levels of energy, or consciousness. We can call it the I Chart for short, since it's really all about seeing *yourself* clearly. Unlike the eye chart opticians show

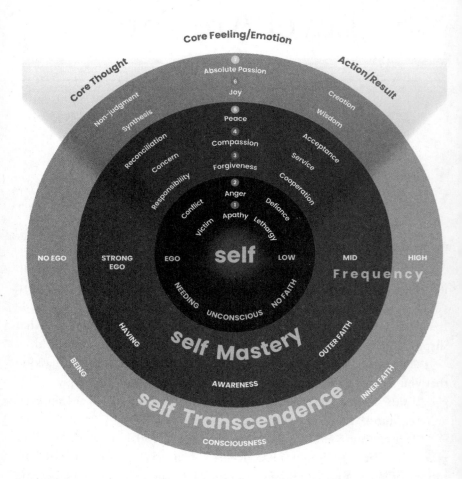

**Figure 2.1   Energetic Self-Perception Chart (I Chart)**
© Bruce D Schneider 1999, 2006, 2022.

you, which helps them figure out how well you see what's outside, the I Chart helps us figure out how well you see what's *inside*. Keep in mind that everything you think, say, and do is generated by some preconceived sense of 'I' – that's you, Richard. Am I making sense?"

"Uh . . . huh. Let me see that chart, okay?"

I turned the chart so he could see it.

"Huh," he said again.

"Let's take a walk," I suggested. Getting out of the office and its energy and environment to discuss the I Chart made sense. It was an apt metaphor for moving Richard out of the life he had lived so far to discover a potential new reality.

He agreed, mentioning that we could head for Giuseppe's, a local Italian restaurant, and get lunch. *Interesting.* We were both probably hungry, but I wondered if Richard thought he always needed to be going "somewhere." This efficiency is often typical of executives, whose preference is to kill two birds with ONE stone. While they sometimes accomplish multiple goals, they often miss the deeper journey.

*Never mind,* I thought. That is a subject for another day. I wanted to get Richard into the "I" Chart, and since we actually did need to eat, I agreed to his request.

"Let's go," I said.

★ ★ ★

A couple of blocks away from the O'Connell Consulting building, I motioned to two facing benches with a stone table in between.

"Let's sit here for a minute, okay?" I offered. Opening my notebook, I again handed Richard the Energetic Self-Perception Chart, and asked him to take a second look.

As Richard sat down and reviewed the chart, I couldn't help but be curious about whether he had any inkling that it held the blueprints to a dynamically different future for O'Connell Consulting – and for his own life.

*No time like the present to find out,* I thought to myself. "Take a look at this, Richard, and I'll explain a bit more to you. Feel free to ask me questions.

"Your level of energy determines your success. The more you have, the better you'll do. Your self-perception, and by extension your concept of the world around you, is based on your energetic level. This level determines what you attract and what's reflected back to you. Most important, it determines how effective you are as a leader.

"To increase your energy, you first want to know where in the chart you currently are. Know that your overall energy is affected by spiritual, mental, emotional, physical, social, and environmental factors. Understanding these factors is advanced work – for now, all that's important to know is that the I Chart is a dynamic tool that can help you understand how you 'measure up' energetically. It does this by illustrating the seven levels of consciousness, so that you can learn more about who you are today and who you can be tomorrow."

I pointed to the three circles and the seven levels of energy on the chart and explained,

- Each of these three circles represents a general level of awareness or consciousness.
- The seven numbers represent more specific, and ascending, energy levels.
- The first circle of awareness (the innermost circle) contains energetic Levels 1 and 2. This is called the circle of *self*. The second, which I call the circle of *self-mastery*, contains Levels 3, 4, and 5. In the outermost circle, Levels 6 and 7 appear. This is the circle of *self-transcendence*.

I explained to Richard that Christina was a good example of someone with a lot of what I call Level 1, or victim energy, and pointed out that the inner circle on the chart was not unlike the inner circle in his organization, a place where Level 1 energy is prevalent. Just in our brief interaction earlier, it appeared that Christina saw the world, or at least her workplace, as a pretty hopeless place. As a result, she attracted people and situations that supported this viewpoint, and also expressed that energy to coworkers and clients.

## Are You a Victim?

Chances are, you don't think of yourself that way. Most people think of a victim as someone who is being physically or verbally abused, perhaps someone that suffered as a result of a crime.

Let's ask it another way. Do you have any victim energy? You may be surprised at the true answer. What most people don't know is that there is Level 1 victim energy in everyone. When your thoughts, beliefs, emotions, and perceptions work against you, don't serve you well, or stop you from doing something, then you are being a victim to those thoughts, feelings, or circumstances – the things that hold you back.

I asked Richard to tell me about any other employees he found challenging. Without a moment's hesitation, he began to complain about Don and Tonya, two executives who were constantly battling it out, whether in the middle of a Zoom meeting, standing in the hallway, or collaborating behind closed doors, yelling so loudly that everyone could hear them anyway.

He told me that Don was a seasoned marketing man and Tonya was a former (and formidable) corporate lawyer. Both had strong opinions about what was right for O'Connell Consulting and just who was holding them back. What had started out as the usual in-fighting and finger pointing ("Every business has people who butt heads," Richard assured me) had turned decidedly ugly as the business declined.

"I don't know what to do with them," Richard admitted.

"It sounds to me as if Don and Tonya see the world as filled with people who are competitive, angry, and aggressive – people who behave like they do," I began. "That's Level 2 conflict energy."

Because of their Level 2 energy, I pointed out, they not only demonstrated these qualities on a regular basis, but also expected everyone else to behave this way, as well.

Now I had Richard's attention.

"Yes, I can see that," he said. "Don and Tonya go at it constantly, and everyone else in the office is either defensive around them, snipes behind their backs, or just avoids them altogether because it's so tense. It's as if they are always ready to attack . . ." He was considering the ripple effect of their anger.

"So Don and Tonya get their view of the world confirmed by other people's behavior around them," I continued for him.

Then I asked why he thought it might be tough for any of his employees to change. Or for anyone to change, for that matter.

He deliberated for a while, seeming to soak in the midday sun. "It's probably hard to face the friction we feel from new and uncomfortable energy," he said, laying the chart down on the table.

"Mm-hmm. That makes sense. *People are sometimes more willing to accept the pain they know than to face the fear of things they don't.* But that doesn't mean people can't change," I assured Richard. "They just need the right tools for the job.

"Take a look at this." I picked up the chart, slid my finger across the top of it and showed him the words *Core Thought* and *Core Feeling/Emotion.* Then, when I pointed to *Action/Result,* Richard leaned forward.

"I'm all about results," he assured me.

"Well, your results are all about you," I responded. "Your thoughts determine your feelings and emotions, and your feelings and emotions shape your actions. Based on what you think and feel about yourself and the people around you, you create your world. *Although your world is totally real to you, there's no 'reality' to it, except how you personally define what you see.*"

Richard understood what I was saying. He'd seen this principle in action in the office. Each one of his employees had expressed, and stuck to, his or her own perspective about the events of the past few quarters. Each perspective came from the individual's energetic frame of reference.

"Each of us has an Average Resonating Level of energy," I stated and checked to see if Richard was still following. He had a curious look on his face, concentrated and kind of pinched. I decided to forge ahead with a metaphor I knew he'd appreciate.

"This level can be related to a stock in the market. Stocks fluctuate during the trading day and close at new prices that reflect the day's activity. The more people who buy or sell a particular stock, the higher or lower it closes. Looking at the day's trading as a whole, we see the average price at which the stock traded.

"As human beings," I continued, "we're like stocks with our energy going up and down on this chart all day long. Based on simple math, you can determine your average level. Thoughts and feelings such as nonjudgment and joy raise the price of your stock. Their counterparts, like victimization and anger, can easily lower stock value.

"At any given moment, Richard, you're somewhere within these seven levels. I said before that your thoughts lead to your emotions and actions. But where do your thoughts come from? All thoughts come from your level of consciousness, which is your self- and world-perspective. *Your current state of consciousness is composed of your existing energetic makeup, which encompasses every thought, feeling, and emotion you've had today, as well as your recent actions.* It also includes every thought, feeling, and emotion you've *ever* experienced, and every action you've taken in your life. These experiences are etched in you like data is etched into a computer chip.

"Your Average Resonating Level is somewhere between one and seven. No one vibrates at an average of one, at least not for long, and no one can sustain a Level 7. In addition, your level can be on or between any two numbers."

Realizing I had just given Richard a lot of information and was covering some new territory for him, I reminded Richard to jump in with questions or comments whenever he felt like it.

Richard smirked. "I'm working on them," he said, and then he nodded for me to go on.

## The First Circle of Awareness – Levels 1 and 2

"Let's make this real for you. I told you why I perceive Christina as having a lot of Level 1 energy. This doesn't mean that's her 'average,' although it could be, but it's certain that Level 1 energy is influencing her at work, or at least it was this morning. Look on the chart, and you can learn more about what she was feeling. First, some part of her thinks she's a *victim*. And with enough victim-oriented thinking, people lose all sense of meaning and purpose. Her emotions and her senses have become dulled, and she's sliding into growing *apathy*. Since Christina imagines herself a victim and may well feel apathetic, she won't have much energy to take action. As a result, she'll remain *lethargic*."

"No wonder those boxes are still piled up around her desk," Richard interjected. "I swear they've been there for months."

"Right," I encouraged him.

Next, I offered Richard a possible explanation for what was happening between Tonya and Don, too. Both resonated with a lot of Level 2 energy. The only way they knew how to communicate was to use anger (loudly) to "clobber" others with their views: *It's a dog-eat-dog world,* they'd say. *Bite or be bitten.*

Richard had said that most people held Tonya, especially, in contempt and at arm's length, probably feeling cornered by her fury. They protected themselves either directly, by behaving in ways that Tonya described as insubordinate, or indirectly, by spreading gossip about her.

For people like Christina experiencing a great deal of Level 1 victim energy, Level 2 behavior like Tonya's just makes them go into hiding.

As I addressed his comments and helped him understand how the different levels of energy came together to create the chaos that was taking place within the company, Richard began to understand his subtle role there as well. When he reacted to conflict by burying his head in the sand, he admitted, he was relating to his employees – and to himself – primarily from a Level 1 perspective. He was aware that while changes needed to be made throughout the company, unless he became a visible and powerful leader, his office and his future had no solid foundation. Unless he took the steps to bring his own energy level up, he realized, the downward spiral would continue, or worsen. His company would surely be lost.

Richard was staring at the ground, looking discouraged again. I reminded him that the first step in making positive changes is being aware of the changes that can be made.

"*That's* what I do, exactly, Richard: I help you expand your awareness."

\* \* \*

Seeming to forget our restaurant plans, Richard was feeling another kind of hunger. "I'm determined to make sense of everything you're telling me, if it takes all day," he said, now seeming to be rooted to his bench. "All of this is a little overwhelming."

My stomach grumbled on cue. "How about if we walk some more and then talk over lunch," I suggested, quickly scanning the shops on the street ahead of us.

Just as we rose from our seats, Richard's cell phone rang. It was Don. Richard said nothing while Don tersely demanded a meeting. "Okay, let's talk when I get back to the office," he told Don.

Apparently, Don wanted to talk to Richard about "something vitally important."

"Well, it looks like I'm not going to be able to avoid this confrontation," Richard surmised.

It was normal for Richard to assume the worst: His was a typical Level 1 reaction. I let him know he was doing this. I also asked if he'd be willing to deal with whatever was going to happen when it did happen, and not before, so we could shift our concentration back to the subject at hand. He agreed. It remained to be seen how effective his focus could be.

\* \* \*

We asked for a booth at the restaurant so we could have a private place for our dialogue.

Richard studied the menu, and I studied Richard. His eyes darted away from the bill of fare often, suggesting more was on his mind than the daily specials. To help focus his attention on our lunch together, I offered to sit in on his meeting with Don, if he thought it would help.

"Okay, thanks," he said. "Thanks a lot." The gesture was just what he'd needed to relax.

"The fish is great here," Richard added. We both ordered it, and he suggested we get back to the chart while we waited for our food to arrive.

Now Richard was very focused, indeed. We continued breaking down the chart, circle by circle. As I pointed to the first circle of awareness and the word *ego*, I explained how much this kind of consciousness seemed dominant for people like Tonya and Don. This circle of awareness includes people who need to control others in order to feel in control themselves. I asked Richard if he had ever heard this quote from the book, *A Course in Miracles*: "Do you prefer that you be right or happy?"

Richard laughed the way people do when you hit a little too close to home.

"When operating at Level 2," I explained, "we prefer to be right. We think that will make us happy."

The first circle also contains the word *need*. People at this energy level are convinced they lack the things they want in life, so they look to others to meet their needs.

"What do you think happens then?" I asked.

"We pressure people to give us what we think we need," Richard answered. "Like money or respect or even love, I would guess."

"And what happens then?"

This was an important question, and Richard impressed me with his answer: "They say that your real needs – the security that money would give you, and the respect and love you want – can only come from within. If you try to have these needs fulfilled by others, you'll be disappointed."

Well, hello, Richard! He surprised me by being more self-aware than I expected. I took this as a cue to carry on and delve deeper.

Expanding on the chart's implications, I noted that people in the first circle are largely *unconscious*. When you live in this circle, you move through your day as if you're just going through the motions, simply trying to survive. You have *no faith* in anything or anyone. You resonate at a low rate of energy.

Any person, partnership, or company that has an Average Resonating Level of energy consistently in the first circle of awareness is in crisis. If "disease" has not already erupted, it is rumbling right beneath the surface. Anyone in a company who resonates at this level needs immediate intervention.

While Richard slowly sipped his tea, I asked him, "What questions do you have brewing?"

Richard said he didn't really have questions right then. But as our food arrived, he focused on something within that first circle of awareness on the chart and lamented, "I was just thinking how 'self' is a sad state of being."

"Hey, Richard, nothing in this chart is either good or bad. Those are judgments you are imposing," I said.

I pointed out that the purpose of the chart is not to make anyone feel one way or another. It is simply a tool to help people see who and where they are right now. Then, they can choose consciously who they would like to become and where they want to be in the future.

"That's good," Richard blurted out, then quickly rolled his eyes. "Oops! Sorry," he said, "'Good' is a judgment. Right, sensei?"

"Yes, grasshopper, it is a judgment," I confirmed, laughing. "Nicely done."

---

### The Power of Choice

As a leader, the best thing Richard could offer his staff was what I offered him in that restaurant: options and possibilities. I was hoping that by the end of our conversation, he might envision choices he'd never imagined.

Most people glimpse things from only one perspective, but just by sharing the I Chart with Richard, I was offering him seven perspectives for viewing anything. With choice comes freedom.

---

★ ★ ★

As we polished off our fish, which was delicious, Richard brought up a point that had occurred to him earlier. While he understood how someone's energy could attract "like" energy in other people, he wondered how that fit with the widely held notion that opposites attract.

Once again, Richard demonstrated that he could be attentive. Even more, he was a gifted critical thinker. When he chose to focus, he missed very little.

I told him that to most people, right and wrong, happy and sad, even blue and orange might appear as opposites, but they actually contain exactly the same resonating energy. *One person's abuse and another's acceptance of that abuse are similar energies, akin to fuel and a fire.* Both attraction and conflict occur when energies match, not when they don't.

The true opposite of the color blue isn't orange; it's the absence of color. The true opposite of being happy isn't being sad; it's a lack of emotion. By the same token, the real opposite of wrong isn't right; it's our abstaining from making any judgments. Energetically, things like good and bad aren't opposites, because they're both judgments.

"The opposite of our seeing things as either good or bad is not making judgments about them at all," I said. "How much sense does that make?"

Richard nodded. "A lot. If someone attacks me and I defend, we're still both fighting."

"Now who's the sensei?" I grinned at his insight.

## The Second Circle of Awareness – Levels 3, 4, and 5

When you move from the circle of *self* into the circle of *self-mastery*, you position yourself closer to achieving success. At Level 3, you are prepared to take responsibility for what you think and feel, knowing no one can *make* you feel anything. It becomes your *choice*, and your responsibility, to react or not to react to anything that comes along in your life.

People still do a lot of judging at this level, I told Richard. They continue to blame others when things go wrong. They also start to *forgive* others, as they begin to let the "blame game" subside. At Level 3, you're willing to work with people you like and tolerate those you don't. The result is *cooperation*.

It was essential that Richard understand how moving himself and his staff into this level would completely change the dynamics in his office and would immediately put them on a road that could lead to success. Cooperation is the lifeblood in all organizations, and Richard's company needed an infusion right away.

He grasped this concept immediately. "Okay, how do we do that?" he asked. "I can't just announce that we're all going to start cooperating and expect them to do it. I can't threaten them into it, either, can I?"

"The way to promote cooperation is to release everything that blocks it, so threatening them would definitely be counterproductive. Once people let go of fear, worry, guilt, and especially anger, what they have left is the kind of energy that creates instead of destroys."

★ ★ ★

At Level 4, judgment, anger, guilt, resentment, and other self-directed thoughts and feelings begin to fade and are replaced by a genuine desire to help others. The core thought when operating at this level is *concern*, which leads to *compassion* and *service*. At this level, you no longer take words or actions personally. You don't waste time worrying about what others may have done "to" you. Instead, you consider what each person's current challenge may be, and how you might be of help in fixing it.

"That sounds nice," Richard said, making the word *nice* sound like an insult.

It was becoming obvious that although Richard had some wonderful qualities, he was being held back by some of his beliefs: that business had to be devoid of emotion, that it was a naturally combative environment, and that generosity of spirit implied weakness. I decided to make a note of these beliefs but not address them right away.

"The judgments[1] we make at this level are based on our notions that people need 'fixing' at all. However, any individual or company with a predominance of Level 4 energy will be both happy and successful.

---

[1] For ease of reading, I've used the words judgment and judging interchangeably. Technically, there is a difference. Judgment is really just the discernment of options, while judging is prejudicial and based on past thinking and belief systems. Judging precludes good judgment.

Entire organizations operating at this level will clearly make their mark in the world.

"Okay with you if I press on? My explanation of the next three levels will be brief, and we can make our way back to your office and meet with Don."

"Please," Richard replied.

Quickly, I summed up Level 5: The core belief associated with Level 5 energy is *reconciliation*, specifically reconciling differences, instead of identifying and focusing on them. At this level, you now less frequently view things as good or bad and right or wrong. *Things just are*. Because of this attitude, you're much less afraid. You feel *inner peace*, which leads to *acceptance*.

Richard raised an eyebrow at me, again indicating that such niceties as inner peace and acceptance didn't belong in business.

In response, I raised both my eyebrows at him and finished my thought. "Instead of making you passive, energetic acceptance produces something quite different. You accept the natural process of living that constitutes human existence. As a result, you no longer try to control life, and a paradox now presents itself. Because you've let go of your need for control, for the first time you actually gain it.

"It's like you said, Richard. Real control comes from within, not from something you convince someone else to do for you. At Level 5, you always have the power to make choices. Unlike the levels below, when you vibrate with this high level of energy, you're driven not by fear, but by opportunity and curiosity. Many entrepreneurs and potential leaders have a lot of Level 5 energy but are not sure how to tap into it consistently, usually due to doubt and fear.

"Think about it," I challenged him. "What could you do if you were absolutely unafraid that something negative might result?"

Momentarily taken aback, he didn't answer me right away. "It would be nice," he said finally, this time without irony. "I suppose I could get a lot more done."

So true. What's more, when you resonate within the second circle of awareness, you're relatively happy and secure. You have a *strong ego*. On the chart, this equals a strong sense of self. This means you're not afraid to be who you are. In other words, you're comfortable in your own skin. Your focus is on *having* instead of needing.

*Moving from a perspective where the focus is on needing to one where the focus is on having is a critical step in the transformation of both individuals and organizations.* I told Richard this was something that we would work on further to help him and his staff make the transition.

The remaining terms in the second circle are *awareness*, which refers to your level of knowing that we, rather than the outer events we experience, create our realities. Also, *outer faith* is the belief that someone, somewhere, created us, and for a purpose.

"Listen, Richard," I said, hoping to keep his attention for just a while longer. "The level of energy in this second circle is exponentially greater than that of the first. If Level 2 equaled, say, 200 on an energy meter, Level 3 might measure 2,000. That's how great a difference I'm talking about. And when we go to the last circle, it's an even greater leap."

## The Third Circle of Awareness – Levels 6 and 7

The last circle of awareness is called *self-transcendence*. When you enter this realm, you actually transcend your ego. You succeed in becoming one with everything. This is your highest energy frequency by far, and it can lead to amazing breakthroughs and results.

Within this last circle of awareness are Levels 6 and 7. Level 6 is the level of *synthesis*. You can define this process as combining separate elements or substances to form a coherent whole. When you're able to generate this whole, you experience both *joy* and *wisdom*. Unlike happiness, which can be fleeting, joy is permanent, no matter whatever else you may feel at this level.

At Level 6, you might feel sorrow, for example. But simultaneously, you are still at a level where you can experience joy.

Wisdom is based on a deep and profound sense of knowing, linked to your intuition. When you use your intuition, you tap into your true genius.

Finally, when you reach Level 7, you completely leave judging behind. You are flooded with *absolute passion* for all of life's experiences and are able to tap your talent for being deeply creative. You have now touched the core of who you truly are. At this level, you have the potential to manifest almost anything into your life in an instant. *Most important, at this level, you are able to consciously use any of the lower levels to your benefit.*

The higher your *level of consciousness,* the higher you are on this chart, and the faster you can turn ideas into reality. You can literally make your dreams come true. You can turn your business around and build it into something you haven't let yourself dare to even think about lately.

What was Richard thinking now? I tried to read his expression and see what his body language might tell me. "If you're ready to continue," I said, "this is where we're headed."

He said nothing, and then nodded slowly. "If I'm getting all this," he ventured, "because my energy level is around 1 − I'm beaten down and desperate − all those around me might be reflecting this energy back. If I shift higher up the chart, it's likely that they'll follow?"

My response was indirect − and to the point. "It's time to re-create your life, my new friend."

Richard's gaze had gone slightly flat. "This is all fascinating," he responded. "I get it. I also realize some of the implications. But, frankly, right now my head is spinning."

"Let it spin," I advised him. "When it stops, you'll see the world from a different perspective."

"That sounds . . . right," Richard said.

★ ★ ★

## Back to the Grind

Lunch ended around 3 p.m. It had been a productive day, but a long one, and it wasn't over yet. We still had Richard's meeting with Don to deal with. But first I wanted Richard to create an assignment for our next session. As we strolled back into the street, I asked Richard what he thought he could work on before our next session.

Richard reflected and then said that he would like to think more about each person in his company, including himself, and measure everyone's actions against where he thought they fell on the chart. To set a good example, he said he would try to let go of making judgments, as well as some anger and fear.

"Your choices sound promising," I said. "Many of my clients find it helpful to keep a 'judgment journal,' recording in it any judgmental thinking that they find themselves engaging in. This is valuable because it is easier to change a behavior if you are aware that it is happening." Richard nodded enthusiastically.

When we entered the O'Connell Consulting building, the difference between the energy outside and the energy inside was palpable. Could he feel it, too? Don met us at the door and asked if I would wait while he spoke to Richard privately. Richard nodded, and they disappeared into Don's office.

Only moments later, Richard emerged and beckoned me toward his own office around the corner. As we settled in, Richard broadcast the latest news. Evidently, we missed another blow-out between Don and Tonya. So Don had just declared to Richard that he was fed up with Tonya's antics and presented an ultimatum.

"Get rid of Tonya, or I will leave."

Don did not set a deadline, but he made it clear that something needed to happen – soon.

## Keep a Judgment Journal

To find out how often you're falling into the trap of labeling people, experiences, behaviors — what have you — as either "good" or "bad," start a two-column journal.

In the left column, write any "positive" judgments you make during the day. In the right column, write any of the "negative" ones.

Pay attention to all the variants of "good" and "bad" that you may use, such as "hardworking" and "lazy," "valuable" and "worthless," "right" and "wrong." Just observe your own thoughts, and any time you notice that you are either praising or criticizing someone, including yourself, or something else, make a quick note in your journal.

# 3 | Just Give It Six Months

*Our role is not to teach [people] to think as we do but rather to teach them, by example, the importance of taking a stance that is rooted in rigorous engagement with the full range of ideas about a topic.*
— bell hooks, author, feminist, and social activist

Richard was understandably distraught and obviously trying to keep a lid on his anger. "See what I have to deal with," he grumbled.

When I did not respond immediately, he sighed, explaining that he had had enough for the day and needed some time alone. I said I understood and scheduled our next session for one week later, quickly adding that he could call me to talk about anything, including his dilemma with Don.

"Let me just say this before I go," I offered. "I understand you're upset and that you feel the future is tenuous at best. Your company reflects who you are and what you want to achieve. It's normal for you to feel angry, unnerved, and maybe even depressed."

---

## Core Energy Technique

*Validation*

Validation is a technique you can use to help someone release anxiety and truly feel heard. Its main purpose is to normalize emotional responses. A perfect icebreaker, validating someone's emotions begins to shift the energy by letting the other person know they have the right to feel whatever emotions are present.

To do this, you must become aware that any emotional response is *always* normal. The response arises from whatever someone's experiencing at that moment. Responses are also linked to temperament, personality, frame of reference, and perspectives on life – and based on all those, whatever someone thinks and feels is normal for that person.

---

"Thanks," Richard said, sounding chided. "You're right. I wish I could look at this situation as 'just business.' But I can't seem to get past my emotions to see things clearly."

I gave him a pat on the shoulder, "Listen, Richard. You don't have to get past these emotions. They are perfectly normal in this situation, and, honestly, I'd be very concerned if you weren't disturbed."

"I'll take your word for that," he said, seeming relieved. He thought for a moment and then went on, "So what do I do about it? Am I just stuck here?"

"Of course not. *Normal* doesn't mean *necessary*. If you can, just try to accept what is going on right now and know that we're engaged in a process to help you change your thinking about 'bad' situations and what they really mean. That's all you need to do about it for today."

"Right again," Richard agreed.

"I understand. How about I send you a few questions to ponder between now and next week's meeting?" Richard nodded.

I told Richard that I would continue to challenge him in the future in order to raise his awareness. I let him know that we would partner to design goals and the actions to stretch him to reach those goals. Most important, I told him that if he agreed to get something done, we'd build in accountability methods so he could keep his word.

---

### Core Energy Technique

*Designing Action Steps*

It's true: I never *tell* anyone what to do. Instead, I partner with people to take action, with the actions specifically tailored to the coaching session we've been involved in. Partnering enables them to share their ideas and choose what they feel inspired to do, which can solidify their buy-in.

In addition, it's vital to remember that all goals and actions will support the potential results they want to achieve. When people choose to commit to a course of action, they give their verbal agreement and energetic commitment to meet mutually accepted goals. And if they do not follow through with those actions, it's important to circle back to determine why and to come up with new ones.

---

"What questions do you have before I go?"

"Mm-mmm." Richard shook his head to indicate there were none.

"And you can call me if you need anything, remember."

"Thanks, yes. I'm fine."

Richard didn't look fine, but I said my good-byes and left him to his thoughts.

## Richard's Assignments

- See if you can pinpoint other people's energy levels by using the I Chart as a guide. (This was Richard's assignment to himself.)
- Answer the following questions without concerning yourself with the "right" answers (because there simply aren't any).
    - Put yourself forward in time six months from now. Covering as many areas of your life and business as you can, what must have happened for you to believe a miracle had occurred?
    - Again, thinking six months down the road, what would be the most unexpected benefit you could receive from our working together?
    - How do you see yourself as a leader today, and how would you like to see yourself as a leader tomorrow?
    - If an alien approached you and asked you to describe humanity and the condition of the world, what would you say?

★ ★ ★

"Who the hell do you think you are . . . ?!"

As I walked through the doors of O'Connell Consulting a week later, I could hear shouting coming from the corridor off the front desk. As Christina seemed oblivious to the noise, I assumed this was commonplace.

Tonya, the former corporate attorney, was dressed as she might be for a court appearance. This was notable only because the rest of the staff were dressed more casually, and the effect was imposing, which was probably her intention.

A tall woman, she was standing toe to toe and eye to eye with Don.

"Who do *I* think *I* am? What do *you* think *you're* doing?! How many times are you going to allow this crap to happen? Just how many times does someone get to screw up before it's 'game over' with you?" exclaimed Tonya.

Practically growling, Don told Tonya she was completely clueless about what was happening – and not just in this case but far too often around here. Neither seemed overly concerned that a dozen people in nearby offices, including myself, were within easy earshot.

When Richard had first told me about Tonya and Don, I imagined a couple of pit bulls, and it was clear he hadn't exaggerated their animosity. Dog fighting was a good analogy for what was going on in the hallway. I noticed that Richard's door was open, but I wondered if he wasn't in because he didn't intervene. *But he could very well be in there,* I thought, *listening to this and trying to pretend it isn't happening.* As best I could tell, when confrontations arose among his staff, he buried his head.

As if reading my mind, Christina mumbled, without looking up from her desk, "He's in there."

I walked down the hall, entered Richard's office, and closed the door.

★ ★ ★

Richard acted oblivious to the skirmish in the hall. "We're sinking," he began. "In the past 12 months, turnover has been so high that I've thought of installing a turnstile. At least that would make us some money." Morbid, maybe, but he still had a sense of humor.

Setting aside the commotion in the hall for the moment, as well as the way Richard was ignoring it, I asked him to start at the beginning and paint me the full picture of where O'Connell Consulting stood. Continuing his list of complaints (and stating the completely obvious), Richard told me that members of his management team didn't communicate well. Laughing to myself, I wanted to yell, "WHAT? I CAN'T HEAR YOU OVER THE SHOUTING MATCH!"

"I know I need a new core group who knows how to work as a team," he said. "I just can't afford to hire them."

Richard shook his head. He sighed as he described each of his employees, citing major grievances with just about every single one. From Richard's perspective, no one was worth the salary he paid them. He felt that everyone was lacking solid motivation. Employees wanted to milk the company dry – even those who knew full well about the financial crunch threatening to shut down O'Connell Consulting.

"Since I'm not supposed to try to get past my emotions now, I have to say that this kind of behavior really pisses me off!" Richard pounded his desk with a burst of anger.

Little did Richard know that getting pissed off was actually a positive sign, as he was beginning to move from Level 1, victim and passive mode, to Level 2, anger and conflict mode. Anger has much more energy and action than victimization, as it signifies a willingness to fight instead of hide.

"You're pissed off because you believe your employees are selfish and don't understand your challenges," I responded. "You wish that instead of asking for more, they would ask how they could help you more, right?"

"Yes, exactly!" Richard replied, still anxiously animated. "Why are people like that? What 'energy level' is *that?*" Richard was sneering now.

"Why are people like what?"

"Selfish."

So he thought his employees were selfish. Good to know. Yet Richard's true agenda didn't really include why others were or were not the way he perceived them. I knew that I needed to challenge his belief about his employees, and people in general. But it was important first to have him believe in me.

This task was delicate. At this early stage in our relationship, Richard was testing me to see if I was strong enough to lead him. If I appeared weak, he might lose faith that I could help him. To prompt him to positive action, I first had to be the leader he believed I should be, without him telling me what that might entail. So I let my instincts guide me.

In measured tones, I said, "I'm not sure how your people truly think and feel." Then I added gently, "Let's focus on you first. Okay?"

"Okay," Richard said, sounding cowed. "Sorry." He was waffling between the two levels, feeling belligerent one moment and belittled the next.

"There's no need to apologize to me for what you think and feel," I assured him. Since the screaming had stopped, I thought it might be relatively safe to suggest that he show me around and introduce me to a few people. I also wanted to learn what I could by watching his employees in action – or, as Richard might have said, we'd watch his employees' *inaction*.

As soon as we left Richard's office, we met Nate Allen, who was the company's sales manager. His energy, a slow heartbeat above that of a corpse, was at least one possible explanation for the company's reported dearth of new clients.

Nate, who was standing in the hallway where Don and Tonya had raged just minutes before, was probably in his 50s, a man of average height who seemed smaller because his shoulders sagged. He also seemed to be hiding in his clothes, because they looked about a size too big for him. His appearance alone was enough to set off the low-energy meter, but when he opened his mouth, it was obvious.

"Hi . . . Richard. Hi . . . Richard's . . . friend." I think he was trying to be clever, or genial, or something, but it fell flat.

"Nate, this is Bruce."

We shook hands as Richard informed me that Nate was his first employee. "Nate's really stuck with us through thick and thin."

Richard's forced smile looked more like a grimace to me.

"Nice to meet you," I said to Nate, trying to catch his eye. But he didn't look directly at me, although he stared after us as we continued down the hall.

When we were far enough away from Nate that Richard could speak freely, I asked him about Nate's effectiveness.

Richard's reply was tellingly off the mark. "He's a great guy and a great friend," he stated. *Okay, we'll come back to that later*, I thought, making another entry in my growing list of mental notes.

We toured the rest of the office, and I met the people in accounting, client services, and human resources. All the staff seemed to have their noses down, as if that was where they thought they should be: on the proverbial grindstone. However, instead of giving an impression of industriousness, the effect was deadening. It seemed that the sound of keyboard tapping was the most potent energy in the place.

## Home Port

When we'd returned to his office, Richard described the various aspects of his business in greater detail. He also included some insights into his personal life. At home, he was either moody and irritable, or exhausted and, frankly, emasculated. His wife Jodi didn't even try to talk with him about work anymore, and since that was his whole world right now, they didn't talk much at all. She complained that they were drifting apart, losing whatever intimacy they had once shared. The strain on their finances, the absence of communication and connection, and the resulting lack of physical intimacy were starting to make him think he might be headed for a divorce.

He told me that he blamed himself for his troubles at home because his company took all of his energy, and he had little energy left to work on his marriage. He was genuinely embarrassed that he hadn't acted sooner, but now, he said, something clearly had to be done. Cutting costs through layoffs was the only move he could think of that would put a stopper in his sinking ship.

★ ★ ★

As we wrapped up our meeting, I expressed my gratitude for Richard's honesty. "Thanks for everything you've related to me," I said, pointing out the positive wherever I could, even in the face of Richard's self-defeating psychology. Some of his strengths were already evident, and I wanted him to know it. "I appreciate working with people who aren't afraid to lay it all on the line and tell the truth."

In addition to acknowledging Richard's rock-solid honesty, my statement was also a test of how he felt right then. If he responded with a simple thank you, I'd conclude he was ready to move forward. If he ignored my compliment and continued to complain, it would mean he still needed to vent to unpack more of his emotional baggage.

Richard didn't continue complaining. He didn't thank me for my compliment, either. Instead, he swiveled his chair and stared off into space.

"What's your timeframe?" I asked. To get his attention and help him reengage, I was being purposefully vague, but my tone was pointed. I wanted to know when his business would dry up for good.

"Nine months," he said, immediately understanding what I was asking. "That's about how long we have to turn O'Connell Consulting around. If our cash registers aren't ringing regularly within six months, we'll be belly up soon after."

"How do you know?"

He called Christina to bring in the latest financial reports. Without looking at her, he reached for the papers. She stood by, waiting for him either to ask her to stay or dismiss her, but instead he beckoned me close to his desk, and pointed a finger at expenses and receivables. When he told me how much new business was likely down the road, I could see why he envisioned a plunge off the cliff.

As if suddenly remembering Christina was still there, he looked up and told her, "Uh, thanks, Christina. I'll keep these and give them back to you to file later."

She turned and left his office, closing the door behind her. Even without seeing her face, I could tell she was rolling her eyes on the way out.

"You know she had the audacity to ask me for a raise yesterday, right when I was thinking of letting her go? After our conversation about her Level 1 energy, I'm thinking she may be the weakest link. Honestly, I think creating some pink slips is really our best way out," he said.

"I get it," I responded. "If that's the only choice we have, then it's what we'll do. We'll definitely explore shrinking the payroll as an option. Let's not get ahead of ourselves, though, by jettisoning anyone just because they're demonstrating low energy right now.

"Before we get into that, let me applaud you for the careful way you've dealt with each company dollar. Most organizations keep only a few months of reserve capital on hand. You've built a far stronger foundation. Congratulations for being well prepared for bumps in the road."

## IN HER OWN WORDS

**Christina**

I used to like my job. I thought I had a lot to offer in a place like this, to a company like O'Connell Consulting, for a boss like Richard. That's what's so bizarre about the way things are now: when Richard and I first got to know each other, it was obvious that we clicked and would make a good team.

Back then, which was about 10 years ago, Richard and I quickly became compadres, laughing at all the paperwork he had to fill out just to teach an extension studies class for our business school at the university. As the department secretary, I really enjoyed helping him get his feet wet when he first started, and we used to go out for key lime pie at a great little coffee shop across the street from the campus. He had a lot of fire about what he was doing in his business and the successes he was having, and he had a real heart for sharing that with the adults who were enrolled in our certification courses. Most of them were looking for a new career, and I have no doubt Richard convinced quite a few of them that being a marketing consultant was the best profession in the world.

When our department started downsizing because of budget cuts, I knew I was on the chopping block, and I told Richard about it. He was all indignant on my behalf, telling me that I was not disposable, that they didn't know what a gem they had, and that he would hire me in a snap if I'd come to work with him. When I asked him if that was a job offer, he grinned at me like somebody who'd just won an Emmy. I told him it was a great idea, especially since I'd thought all the same things, practically word for word. We took that as a good omen: that we thought so much alike.

So I left the university and started working for Richard as his assistant. At first, it was exciting, and I could see that I was making a big difference in the day-to-day operations. Now I can say I probably know this business as well as anyone else here, including Richard. But something happened along the way. It used to be when there were bumps in the road, Richard and I and the rest of the team would get together, and we always seemed to figure it out. Yet when the company got a little bigger and the dollars started dwindling, everyone in upper management started freaking out and stopped treating the people here like anything other than hired help.

People have lives, you know? It's not just about what we do in this office. I've got to think about my retirement and how I'm going to take care of myself – I'm on my own. Not that I haven't had my opportunities, but I'm not so sure I even want to be married, although Carlos keeps asking about once a year. I just don't want to depend on a man for my security, and that's part of what's so frustrating about this situation. Seems like my future is in Richard's hands, and he doesn't really care about any of that anymore.

Some days, I'd like to go into Richard's office and ask him who's treating his "gems" like trash now? I feel just as disposable today as I did at the university. I know what Richard is thinking; I'm not stupid. Some of us are going to get fired, assuming there's even a company to get fired from.

That's why I asked him for a raise. I know we can't afford it. But I want Richard to have to deal with me. To tell me honestly whether he thinks I'm of any value to this company anymore, or just what. It's like I've become invisible to him. I know I'm partly to blame for that . . . sometimes it just feels more comfortable to blend into the woodwork when everything is so volatile around here. I can tell you this much: it definitely feels better not to care, or at least to pretend that I don't.

"So what's next?" Richard asked me.

"How about your assignments? How did those go?"

Richard blanched. "Oh. Those. Sorry, I didn't get those done."

Richard looked embarrassed, which signaled to me that he understood that his lack of follow-through was serious. I pointed out to him that *sometimes we learn more from what we don't do than from what we do.*

"Tell me about why you didn't do this," I suggested.

He told me that every time he sat down to write his answers, he got "jammed up." Things seemed murky and unclear, and he felt pressure to do something else. "I just couldn't muster the focus or energy to do the thing, and something felt uncomfortable about answering the alien question, mostly because of what I'd say about my world," he told me.

This insight and Richard's inaction revealed a great deal about his energy, which was my objective in asking the questions in the first place. The first three questions had addressed a six-month miracle vision of his life and business, the most unexpected benefit from our work together, and his current and future vision of himself as a leader.

> *Those with Level 1 energy have great difficulty facing current reality and envisioning a future. Even if they can create a future vision, it is usually blurry and obscure. Here's a simple formula: no faith equals no miracles.*

My next question had been about how Richard would describe the world to an alien, and based on his being "uncomfortable" with this question and his potential answer, I sensed there was a very different motive behind his nonanswer. I felt it was actually a sign of Level 3 energy.

> *At Levels 1 and 2, people have few reservations about blurting out a bleak worldview. They would do this as a martyr (Level 1) or with anger and disgust (Level 2).*

Richard was disturbed by the alien question, which told me that somewhere within him, he knew his current view of the world was not accurate. Instead of blaming everyone else for his plight, he could be taking responsibility for his current viewpoint, which is what people at Level 3 do.

After sharing my thoughts with him, I suggested, "Let's take a 10-minute break to walk outside, and then I'd like to discuss how we might work together from here on out."

"Sure." Richard brightened. "I'm open to anything you have to say."

I wondered if that was true. Yet Richard had already let me know that he was at least entertaining the idea of doing the serious inner exploration that would get him where he said he wanted to go.

★ ★ ★

"Here's how I propose we work together," I began. "Let me know how this seems to you."

"Will do," he said.

"You've told me about the challenges you're confronting right now, and many people would think it makes sense to address each one directly. However, that's focusing on *effects*. We want to pinpoint *cause*. If you can be a bit patient, I see tremendous opportunities in what you've already told me. I expect they will radically transform your future."

"You certainly know how to get my attention," Richard replied, his eyes now riveted on mine. "Any opportunities you see in the middle of this mess will be more than welcome to me."

Now it was time to open the first major gateway in our conversation. "You've built a financial safety net so your company could weather a rainy day," I said. "That foresight now gives you the chance to focus on the key element that once made your business thrive. You can use that same element to improve everything you do from this day forward.

"As I mentioned before, this key element is *you,*" I said, leaning in. "The process I propose is one that will have an effect not only on your business life, but on your personal life as well."

Richard's expression once again registered curiosity coupled with calculation. He questioned what I was suggesting, saying that it sounded unusual. He was also concerned that if what I proposed didn't work, his business would certainly go down the drain.

His eyes narrowed slightly. "Even if it does work, people with our kind of consulting services aren't in business for the long haul, anyway. We're positioned to capitalize on the market while it's hot. At the moment, it's barely lukewarm."

Absentmindedly, Richard tapped his index finger on his desk. "It's just not a good industry anymore," he said. "Even if we do everything we can to fix things, the business might fail anyway. Then where will I be?"

Again, I validated Richard's emotions by letting him know that worrying was both understandable and normal. I couldn't make any guarantees, after all, about the future success of O'Connell Consulting, nor was I an expert in his industry. I had, however, already heard several key bits of information he'd provided. Focusing on them could definitely help. And, more important, I knew the power of the process we used, and I had watched it transform companies like Richard's before. In the meantime, I said that as long as he did everything he could to make it work, what I could promise was the success of this process, which is the one thing we can actually control.

"If we do our jobs well," I said, "the benefits of what we do can be extraordinary and lifelong. We might even save this company . . . 'in the process.'"

Deliberating for a moment, Richard smiled. Warily, he asked for more information about "this process of yours."

## The Core Energy Coaching™ Process

The task we were undertaking together would be both simple and complex. It required that Richard and I identify his current energy level and uncover what his strengths were so that we could shift his level higher. Based on all I'd seen, the company was experiencing what I call a *catabolic crunch*. Energetically speaking, that meant it was slowly imploding. The heart of this company was diseased.

"You are the heart," I told Richard. "We need to create ease from disease. This shift will profoundly affect your company and all other aspects of your life."

I began to give him more detail on what we'd be doing together, explaining that we'd be using Core Energy Coaching, a collection of methods I'd developed to help people live at their highest potential. They connect to their passion and then develop specific plans that include action steps to reach a state of success to which only a comparative handful of people actually aspire. The process would help Richard become an inspiring leader who would aid others in becoming notably happier and significantly more productive and successful. He would also learn how to use the Core Energy Coaching process with his own employees by engaging in it with me, and by getting pointers from me as he began to practice the techniques with his core staff.

Core Energy Coaching means getting to the core of the situation and the people involved, helping them from the inside out. This approach isn't for everyone, I told Richard. Some people want a quick fix. Others are in situations so desperate that immediate damage control is the only realistic course of action. Still others are not open to looking within themselves for answers.

"Richard, we'll work together to empower every person you employ. *People find power when it dawns on them that their true success isn't rooted in your helping them. It's grounded in your helping them help themselves.*

"That power gives people a sense of control, and when they feel it, they become engaged in what they do. Once this occurs, employee performance can skyrocket, sometimes in spectacular ways. Your days will no longer be spent dealing with never-ending problems. Instead, you'll have time and energy to craft whole new worlds of excellence for your organization to explore.

"At stake for you," I emphasized, "is a transformation in your energy that can raise your consciousness to a level that you've likely never known before. Ahead of you is the life-changing chance to generate abundant happiness and health, genuine wisdom, and a kind of wealth that could greatly enrich every area of your life."

I asked him to think about how much energy he was spending on worry, fear, doubt, and guilt – and to imagine what it would be like if he could invest all that energy instead in creating and implementing powerful and positive changes.

He put his hand on his chin as he moved toward me. "You've mentioned consciousness a few times. Tell me more about what you mean by that," he requested.

In a more conventional conversation, the corner he had just turned in our dialogue might have seemed insignificant. But given where his own spotlight was now pointing, the question he posed was perfect.

"Consciousness is the process of awareness, and the awareness of the process," I said. I told Richard that we are all going somewhere and are all capable of mastering some extraordinary lessons during our "trip." Once we are aware of this process, we play the game of life differently. We become the rule maker, the coach, the player, and the spectator, all at the same time.

Richard nodded, telling me he would love to be able to make up some new rules for living his own life. He asked how long this "sleight of hand" might take.

For what I proposed, however, there was no trick – and no timeframe, either. Each person's progress and success rate depends on many factors. The most important step in this process is that you encounter it firsthand. Experience requires time.

Why go through all this? Because living through it helps create a conscious leader, someone who makes choices from knowledge, intuition, passion, and power, instead of from fear, worry, and doubt. I explained that once Richard understood and lived the techniques and principles I shared with him, he would become the kind of person who could inspire others and himself to do everything they knew how to do, do it well, and then discover all they can do that they were unaware of – in other words, they would realize their untapped potential.

"Six months," I said, waiting for Richard's reaction. "That's how long I propose we give this process to unfold. Six months from now we'll review our progress. By that time, if we haven't reached our goals, we'll still have time to pull the fire alarm. But if we've turned a corner, you'll be a very happy man."

As we continued, we considered both outcomes that might occur at the end of the next six months. In doing this, I'd provided Richard with an energetic safety net to calm his fears and tweak his courage.

He seemed to hesitate. "Can you really save this company?" he asked, lobbing his most consuming question in my direction.

"Anything's possible," I allowed. "But, as you know, it's not just me who's going to make this happen. I'll do everything I can, Richard. You'll have to do the same."

Richard's expression was determined. "I'm ready," he said. "I have no other choice."

I was ready to let this last remark slide for the moment. "When it comes to bacon and eggs, the chicken is involved, but the pig is committed," I said.

Richard laughed at my delivery of the old joke, and I took this as a good sign.

So I pressed further. "Okay then. On a scale of 1 to 10, the chicken's effort being 1 and the pig's involvement a 10, where are you?"

Richard chuckled again, falling silent as he pondered his response. He'd originally said I was his last resort. Now the time had come to put his belief to the test.

"I'm at a 7," he said.

"Good number," I replied, "and close to what we need to make this agreement to succeed together. What will it take for you to get to an 8 or 9?"

Richard's answer was quick and clear: he wanted some proof from results.

"That makes sense," I told him. "Except I'm not yet asking you to believe in achieving the dream. I'm only asking that you do all you can to make it a reality. That's the part over which you have complete control."

Richard smiled broadly. "If that's the issue, count me in as a 9."

"Okay," I said, "now we're throttling at full force."

To meet our six-month target for change, I proposed we work for a full day either weekly or every other week, based on what we agreed was best. Our time together would include discussion and the chance for me to observe Richard, his employees, and how they related with clients. I planned to use this "observational approach" to discover more precisely what was actually going on. I hoped it would also help me identify important strengths at O'Connell Consulting – assets that were likely taken for granted.

"During our sessions I'm going to stretch you beyond your comfort zone. I'll count on you to tell me when to pull back; otherwise, I'm going to keep the engines at full throttle," I said.

★ ★ ★

Richard's cell phone interrupted our conversation.

"It's Nate," Richard said, "I'd better get it." He pressed a button so that I could hear the conversation, and as Nate started to speak, Richard's entire persona changed. His jaw went slack, and then his shoulders and head dropped in an odd imitation of Nate's own body language.

Nate reported to Richard that he just lost one of the company's key accounts. It seemed that their longtime customer, a legal firm, was being courted by one of O'Connell Consulting's more aggressive competitors, Harris Marketing. I remembered Richard describing Harris as a company that stopped at nothing to steal business from other marketing firms.

"Uh, listen . . . Richard. I talked to, uh, Joe Simpson this . . . morning. He said . . . he wanted . . . well, we've lost the account. The retainer is terminated this month."

"So Simpson and Simpson is history."

"Well . . . right."

"Okay, Nate." Richard took a breath. "See you later."

"Yeah, right . . . okay. Bye."

Amazingly subdued, Richard hung up the phone. To my astonishment, he turned to me and said, nonchalantly, "Sorry about the interruption. Where were we?"

# 4

## "I Want It Now!"

*If you want to build a ship, don't gather your people and ask them to provide wood, prepare tools, and assign tasks. Call them together and raise in their minds the longing for the endless sea.*

—Antoine de Saint-Exupéry, writer and aviator

"Whoa," I exclaimed. "Hold on there, buddy. It must be extremely upsetting to you to lose an important account. Why are you blowing it off?"

Richard was slow to respond. He said he was aware this might happen because Nate hadn't serviced the account properly. It was only when Richard had forced him to do so that Nate had actually visited the client in person. Nate must have gone to Simpson and Simpson not long after we saw him in the hall, and it had obviously been too late to salvage the relationship.

"I'm not blowing it off. It's just that the water's already under the bridge. There's nothing I can do now, and blasting Nate or anyone else won't accomplish anything. Getting mad would just be unprofessional and unproductive at this point. Really, Bruce, there's nothing I can do about this one."

Now we had at least three items on the docket, despite Richard's non-chalance: He was dealing with the loss of a major revenue source, Simpson and Simpson, both from an emotional perspective as well as his firm decision to just let it go without a fight; addressing Don's ultimatum and his continuing brawl with Tonya; and answering Christina's request for a raise. In addition, there were underlying issues, some of which we'd uncovered already and some that remained to be discovered. Our afternoon would be anything but boring.

**From:**     christina@oconnellconsulting.com
**To:**       betty@oconnellconsulting.com
**Subject:**  Re: Can you help?

No idea. R doesn't tell me anything anymore. BTW, they're in there together right now. I do know his name's Bruce something and he's on the calendar for every other Friday *all day* for the next 6 mos.

C

—— Original Message ——

**From:**     Betty Donaldson [mailto: Betty@OConnellConsulting.com]
**Sent:**     Friday, August 11, 2006 9:19 AM
**To:**       Christina Suarez
**Subject:**  Can you help?

Hey, girl. Who's the guy Richard's been meeting with behind closed doors? The natives are getting restless, and everyone's asking me if he's a hatchet man or something. Know anything?
Betty

★ ★ ★

"Tell you what, Richard. Let's order in some food and begin addressing what you're facing right now, starting with personnel."

"Okay, let's get to it," he said. "We've got to start dealing with some of these problems before these people wear me out."

*Richard does look haggard,* I thought, as he messaged Christina and asked her to have some sandwiches delivered for lunch.

It was time to help Richard shift his level of energy up. "It sounds like you've had a trying time of it. We're going to explore all this together," I told him. "Start by telling me something. Since we last met, what's gone well?"

"What's gone well?" he repeated, incredulous. "Nothing I can think of off the top of my head. Isn't it obvious? I didn't get my assignment done. Don and Tonya are still at each other's throats, Christina has asked for a raise and her productivity keeps sinking, and Nate is . . . well, you just heard it: It's *no business* as usual with Nate. Things are pretty bleak."

"I can understand why you feel that way," I said. "But I'd like you to dig a bit deeper, and then see what you can come up with."

Richard looked puzzled and thought for a moment before responding that the only thing that had gone well was some in-depth thinking he had done about the ideas we discussed in our first session, although he hadn't had a chance to put much into practice yet. He wasn't so sure anything could save his company, but he decided that working with me truly was his best course. "If the ship goes down, so be it. I'm the captain. I'm staying on board, and with you, no matter how rough the seas may get."

I had no fear of sinking in the storm. However, that didn't mean his ship couldn't go down, only that I wouldn't be on it if it did. In other words, we were figuratively on two different ships. For his own sake, he'd be wise to change course now. Yet he had chosen not to complete his assignment, even though it was quickly becoming do or die both for Richard and his company. One thing was clear: It would take both of us to create his miracle. By the end of the session, I needed to be convinced of his full commitment to the process, or I'd be gone. I wasn't interested in wasting his time or mine. It was too early for that conversation, though. First, I addressed the noticeable energy shift.

"Good for you, Richard. Considering what you're up against, that's a potent statement." It was indeed a positive sign – evidence of Level 3 energy. Richard was demonstrating the beginning of accepting some responsibility for what was happening in his life and career, although he was still imagining himself at the whim of the waters, too.

"So let's dig in, shall we? We have three major personnel issues that have come up in our discussions – Nate's handling of Simpson and Simpson, Don's ultimatum, and Christina's request for a raise. Which would you like to tackle first?"

"Well, why not start at the front door: Christina? She's been giving me weird looks all this morning and her work has gotten significantly worse in the past two weeks. What am I going to do with her? If I cut her loose, I might save myself some money, but . . ."

Again, I let Richard know that I understood what he was saying about money and layoffs, and I assured him we would pursue that course if it became necessary. I told him, however, that Christina was an excellent person to work with using the Core Energy Coaching process – and that if he was ready to grab the reins, he could begin to practice one of the skills of a conscious leader.

"Well, okay, chief," he said, "Except today I don't think I could even lead a horse to water, forget about making her drink."

"All right," I told him. "But this experiment could give you some short-term proof of our long-term potential."

At my mention of "proof," Richard inched forward. "Let's give it a go," he said. We both knew he would be more enthused if he believed there was a genuine chance that the system I was proposing might work.

So I asked him about Christina and how he handled the situation when she asked for a raise. He responded that, hoping to buy some time, he simply told her that he would give her an answer as soon as he could. This wasn't surprising to me, as avoidance is a typical behavior of people experiencing Level 1 energy.

Our lunch arrived, and while we ate, he went on to tell me that Christina had been with O'Connell Consulting for 10 years. Even though her official job title was administrative assistant, her potential value to the company was far greater. In fact, she probably knew more about O'Connell Consulting's inner workings than anyone other than Richard himself. As Richard saw it, the information at her command could also pose a problem. He feared that she might know too much and felt pressured to give her the raise. If he chose not to, and particularly if he fired her, because she had "the goods on him," he worried she might reveal them.

That piqued my interest. "What goods?" I asked.

His answer was ambiguous, so I asked some direct questions. It quickly became obvious that Christina had nothing "on" Richard that could make the company vulnerable. His real worry was more down to earth. Because Christina knew so much about his business, Richard fretted that she might rush off to work for one of his competitors. I resisted a smile. Given Christina's current level of energy, might not her working for one of his competitors actually be in Richard's best interest?

I asked if he would be willing to meet with Christina as soon as possible to let her know he was seriously reviewing her salary situation. I also requested that he solicit her help in creating a solution that might make sense for both her and the company. He agreed to both requests without question.

"Considering how much she knows about O'Connell Consulting," I said, "perhaps you could ask her what she thinks the company can afford to give her, and why. How does that sound to you?" This approach would put the ball in her court, buy Richard the time he wanted, and ease the tension between them.

"Interesting approach. Thanks for the idea," he said, asking if I would sit in on the conversation.

"I'll be happy to," I said. I added that it was important for him to know that the meeting had been his idea, not mine. "I just took what you said and put the pieces together. Remember, I'm not in your box."

I wanted Richard to understand that what might have sounded like advice was actually information he himself had provided. His buy-in would be assured if he knew that he, not I, was at the ship's helm. I would have stayed focused for as long as he needed to gain this insight. But he convinced me that he'd made the connection.

"Got it. Why not do it now?"

"Great, Richard. Let's call her in."

Richard turned to his computer and messaged Christina to come to his office. When she arrived, she obviously expected to be asked to clear the lunch trash. But Richard asked her to sit down, because he wanted to talk with her about her salary. When he asked if she'd mind my observing, she agreed without questioning why I was there.

Richard delivered his statement calmly and concisely: "Christina, you've asked me for a raise, and you're due a thoughtful response."

"Uh-huh. Thanks."

As he and Christina began to converse, I watched her, and she furtively watched me. At first she seemed disengaged. As Richard continued, though, something seemed to shift inside her. She began paying less attention to me and more to Richard. When he finished his request that she propose a salary arrangement that would work for both of them, she committed to doing just that.

"How much time should I take?" she asked Richard. I was surprised how much her energy had shifted, and how easily Richard's had shifted in tandem.

"As long as you need," he said, probably thinking, *the longer, the better.*

As Christina stood to leave the room, she said something I myself could not have scripted better. "Thanks again," she said, smiling. "I didn't think you cared."

Richard's smile reflected hers. After she left his office, he told me, "Hey, that felt pretty good!" For a moment or two, he puzzled over what had just happened. While nothing had changed externally between Christina and him, he felt an immediate shift in their relationship.

He looked at me and nodded. "I'm ready to give a real try to this change process," he said earnestly. "I'm ready to repair everything I've damaged."

★ ★ ★

Richard was starting to get on board, and it was time to talk about what was happening. "Right now, you seem to be averaging Level 2 energy. That average is from a combination of some Level 1 victim energy, some Level 2 conflict energy, and some Level 3 responsibility energy. When you operate on an average of Level 2, your world seems in conflict, threatening, and unsafe. Again, this explains why you think the way you do and act the way you do. Even your nonaction, such as not completing your assignments, makes sense. You're normal, Richard. *Relax.* You can stop beating yourself up for everything and just accept where you are now. You have already made progress and are in the perfect place to initiate the kinds of changes you want."

Richard mulled that over. I was in no rush to do anything but allow him to process his feelings. He turned his head from me and raised his hand to his face, perhaps to hide his emotions. When he spoke again, his tone was mellower, and he appeared resolved. "You really think it's normal to feel this way?"

"Normal? Yes. But as I said to you before: Is it necessary? Absolutely not," I emphasized. "And I'm going to ask you to make a very important choice later today. Your decision will determine your fate. I'll tell you right now, though, that I have a lot of faith in you and don't expect that you'll disappoint either one of us."

"Thanks," Richard replied.

"No problem," I said, hoping he'd catch my double meaning.

Richard told me that he needed to get more excited about our work, and that his lack of seeing a clear picture of success was holding him back.

Validating him again, I assured Richard that given his perspective on the previous year's events, his lack of vision made perfect sense. "If we don't believe something can happen," I said, "the picture isn't ready to be taken, much less developed." I paused to consider where we might move next. "Before we go further, Richard, tell me how things would be different for you if you achieved long-term success."

Richard's glance shifted toward the ceiling. "It would be a dream come true."

I sensed some further spadework was needed for Richard to touch what he really might see.

"You've mentioned letting some employees go a couple of times," I reminded him. "Tell me what's driving that idea for you."

Richard hunkered down. He said that his deepest fear was running out of funds. "That would be a nightmare," he said.

Richard had a clear picture of the nightmare, and he was already experiencing some of it. So I decided to keep him focused on the dream: "In our proposed miracle six months from now, what would one successful thing you might achieve look and feel like to you?"

Richard looked blank.

---

## Look Inside

If anyone tells you he or she doesn't know the answer to something, remember that the person actually *does*. People sometimes just don't know how to find the answer within themselves, because it lies in a place they're not used to accessing.

The vast majority of people spend most of their time living in the first circle of awareness, in Level 1 and 2 energy, buffeted between victim-passivity and anger-conflict. Their fear-based energy makes them accustomed to focusing on problems instead of solutions. The solutions are there; they just haven't paid attention to them.

At this point in our coaching relationship, it's up to me to find a way to help Richard see that he already has all the answers he's seeking.

### Energetic Principle #2

**The answers to all questions lie within. Every one of us is greater and wiser than we appear to be.**

---

"Humor me," I requested. "Remember, it's a miracle."

"Okay, let me think," he responded.

He seemed to be struggling, so I tried a different approach. "Imagine you were to leave this office today and the miracle we talked about hadn't taken six months," I said. "Imagine that it hadn't taken six weeks, or even six days. Fantasize that it has occurred overnight, and somehow, magically, all of your challenges have been solved. What would be the first thing you'd notice tomorrow morning when you walked through the office doors?"

Richard's answer came quickly after that. "My staff would respect me again, I'd see people smiling," he said, the faint hint of a grin arising in his own expression. His tone of voice expressed a lightness I'd not heard before, and he seemed to be enjoying this way of thinking.

"Why would they smile?" I pressed.

"Because they'd have confidence in the company."

"That's a fine answer, Richard. What about your walking in would make them smile?"

Richard shrugged good-naturedly. "I guess I would have been the one who helped them see prosperity ahead," he said.

"How do you believe your employees would *feel*," I asked him next, "if they had confidence in the company and if your walking in made them smile?"

"If my staff were to become smiling and confident, I suppose it would be because they'd feel rejuvenated," Richard replied.

Once again, I posed a question. What benefits could arise if his employees felt rejuvenated, instead of on the chopping block?

Richard's whole being became more animated. "Without the added stress, they would relax more and probably focus better . . . they might even be more productive."

---

**Core Energy Technique**

*Empathize*

In the Core Energy Coaching process, empathizing connects one person emotionally with another. It's not sympathizing, which is

*(continued)*

feeling sorry *for* someone else. It's feeling emotions *with* someone else, without judgment.

Getting Richard to step into his employees' shoes allows him to feel empathetic, reconnecting to his emotionally estranged staff. It also helps him see things from their perspective.

With that established, we could move the action forward. Remember that Richard's goal was to find solid evidence that he might actually turn his company around. We now created another "baby step" toward this goal, in a development completely within his control. Once he was able to take this step, his energy would slowly increase to a more positive and productive level.

"A wise assessment," I told him, referring to reduced staff stress. "Who specifically might we put at ease, at least for the moment?"

Richard pondered, then phrased optimistically the news he felt he could give his key personnel: Don, Tonya, Christina, and Nate. "I'm not happy with them," he said, "but the truth is, they've all been with me for a long time. Our current situation isn't really their fault. Still, Don shows up in a sour mood continually talking about problems every day, making threats, and although visibly at his desk, he seems a million miles away. The others aren't much better: Tonya stomps around this place looking angry all the time; Nate barely makes any effort anymore; and Christina . . . well, maybe things will be better since we had our talk, but I would hardly start engraving her employee of the month plaque yet. My 'Fantastic Four,' huh?"

"That's good, Richard. Can I use it?"

"Sure," he offered. "But I was being facetious."

"I know, I know," I acknowledged. "Nothing wrong with a little humor. Irony aside, what's one thing you could say or do to ease their worries and get them back on track to give you the support you want?"

"I could be honest and tell them what's going on," Richard said. "I could let them know that the only way I'd let them go is if we had to close the company down." He paused, then added softly, "I could tell them that I care about them. That seemed important to Christina, and I imagine it could be to the others, as well."

"That's powerful," I said, feeling the impact of his words.

I thought for a moment about a few of his employees, particularly Nate, and wondered if Richard would be able to keep this promise. For now, though, I decided to let this concern go and allow him to continue to roll. "How would you expect them to respond?"

"I think this kind of message might go a long way toward alleviating their fears," he said.

I let him know that he himself had now devised the formula that could result in the proof that he was seeking. I suggested that once he saw what could happen with even a small shift in energy, he would have more faith in the transformational process that was possible. I asked that he communicate his caring to his key staffers as quickly as he could.

"I'll do it within a day or two," Richard said.

He hadn't said "right after you leave." Nor had his answer been definitive or enthusiastic. I made a quick note to address this issue later.

"Things sound good so far," I told him. I paused to collect my thoughts. Then I mentioned another observation I'd made in my visits to his office: his staff looking at me, perhaps wondering who I was. "What have you told them?" I asked.

Richard hesitated. "I didn't tell them anything," he said. Then, after another moment, he voiced what I knew was a deep-seated fear: "I didn't want them all to know we were in real trouble."

"How likely is it that they don't know already?" I asked.

Richard chuckled, realization dawning. "I guess not very."

I reminded him that one of his goals was to be respected again by his employees, and asked what he believed would earn that respect.

"A lot of things," Richard replied. "Honesty, for one."

"Yes," I said, "and that's one of the reasons I respect you. I find you to be remarkably honest. So what's the most honest approach you can take to remove some of the mystery about what's going on here?"

"I guess it wouldn't necessarily be a bad thing if I let everyone know you're working to help me turn things around."

"Besides that," I added, "what might this information accomplish?"

"Well," Richard said, "at least people would know I'm not giving up."

"So it sounds like you're seeing some benefit?" I prodded.

"I am," he replied. "It would be nice if we all lightened up a bit." His eyes met mine directly. "I could get the word out by the time you come in for our next session."

Richard had now agreed to two small steps on the path to saving his company. But he didn't yet seem totally committed. We talked further, even specifying what Richard would say to his entire staff. We couldn't afford for Richard not to complete his next assignment. It was almost time for the ultimatum.

---

### Core Energy Technique

*Get an Energetic Buy-in*

Don Taylor isn't the only employee who seems entirely absent even though he's sitting right there in his office. Year after year, surveys by Gallup[1] and others show that a large proportion of workers are disengaged and dissatisfied with their jobs.

Since job satisfaction is usually an emotional issue, the best way to engage people is through creating an energetic buy-in that allows them to emotionally connect to what they see as a positive future. The "high" created from such a connection can shift energy and

---

[1]https://www.gallup.com/workplace/352949/employee-engagement-holds-steady-first-half-2021.aspx

motivation in dramatic ways. Once people connect emotionally to what they're doing, they're more engaged, focused, and productive.

How much of an energetic buy-in someone has for a specific goal can be a good indication of their "core intention." This core intention, not what they say or agree to, is what is really driving a person.

We usually censor words before we speak. But our core intention – what's really going on for us – is deeply rooted in the thoughts, feelings, and emotions that are actually doing the "speaking."

*Intention is the crux of commitment, and commitment is equal to one's level of engagement.*

What Richard had said was appropriate. But his level of engaged energy, the amount available for him, wasn't strong enough for Richard to actually take the steps we'd discussed. I decided to assess more closely where Richard's energy level actually was. Then I'd know how to proceed.

"On a 1 to 10 scale, with 1 being not at all and 10 being a great deal," I asked, "how much effort are you willing to put into the two assignments you just agreed to, as well as this process in general?"

Richard pondered. "Honestly?" he asked. "I'd guess a 3 or 4."

If he would have said a larger number, I would have let him know that I heard one thing but felt another. Richard's tremendous strength in being honest made working with him a pleasure.

Our challenge, as in our previous session, was that he continued to focus on what he believed was impossible. To move his energy to a place where we actually had the chance to create a shift, we needed to generate engagement through an emotional buy-in.

"Why only a 3 or 4?" I asked, referring to what Richard had just told me.

"Because I still don't really know that we can save this company. When all is said and done, my employees may still wind up out of a job. But as I told you last time, I'm willing to try anything for six months."

I knew he was committed to *trying* something – he made that totally clear. But I wasn't here for Richard only to try. "I haven't asked you to commit to the whole six months with me," I said, "at least not yet. I only want you to do that when you have a clear picture of success."

"What if I don't get that picture?" Richard asked.

I shrugged. "Then this will be our last session. But before you worry about that, let me do what you're paying me for, and we'll see where it goes. Let me help you visualize a snapshot of what's possible."

I reminded him that in our first session we'd discussed how he could raise his level of consciousness. "What do you think the benefits of doing this might be?" I asked.

Richard began working through his answer. He remembered from our previous conversation that consciousness is a process of awareness and an awareness of this process.

His rhythm of response now quickened. "It could be gaining insight into who I am and then being able to authentically 'walk the talk.' I know it's a cliché, but to me that means I don't just say the things an effective leader says, but I back that up with action and with my own beliefs and behavior, too."

"Well put," I responded. Knowing that what he envisioned was only the beginning, I sketched out the other benefits that are possible as you become more aware.

Richard leaned back, listening carefully.

## Tackling Challenges at the Root Cause

The entire Energy Leadership process, I reminded him, was just what the name implied – a process. None of us knows precisely where this pathway will take us. Just as every human being is unique, so is each person's journey in expanding awareness.

"Keep an open mind," I said. "Welcome change in whatever form it appears. This process has no time frame, and it's never-ending. If we work together effectively, however, we could almost immediately see some positive results in your business."

Being conscious at a higher level could provide a perspective and a philosophy of life that carried real advantages for both Richard and O'Connell Consulting, including:

- Higher consciousness enables you to balance all areas of your life.
- You can break through your limiting beliefs, your fears, and any other blocks that prevent you from living a more joyful and purposeful life.
- A conscious leader can help company personnel achieve a higher consciousness/energy as well.

Expanding on all the benefits and how any one of them could change Richard's life, I went on to list some of the more profound things that could happen:

- He could tap into what psychologist Carl Jung referred to as the collective unconscious, linking with the universal energy that permeates and surrounds all living things.
- He could also unlock his innate ability for genius, accessing brilliant ideas and unlimited energy from everyone and everything around him. "It's like tuning a radio to a station that allows you to hear totally clearly."
- He could become an extraordinary leader for his company. In his new ability to lead, he could:
  - Discover how to assess where any of his employees were, energetically, at any given moment, and help them become more engaged.
  - Make fast, accurate decisions.
  - Reduce stress in himself and others.
  - Prompt sustained excitement.
  - Inspire everyone in the company.

I continued: "You'll also come to understand how you and your employees are forms of energy and learn how every thought and emotion has its own energetic vibration and power level." Even more fascinating is this: Negative thoughts and emotions, like fear, worry, and guilt, have a slower energy rate than positive ones. Although Richard was holding on tight to these negative kinds of emotions, he could teach himself how to alter this energy rate. In doing this, he'd alter his life.

Richard said, "That's more on the I Chart, right?"

Exactly.

I asked him to think about what it would be like if he were able to lift his level of energy past anger, worry, fear, self-doubt, hatred, resentment, greed, and victimization. What would it feel like instead to lead a life filled with inner peace and outer success?

Nodding, Richard confirmed his interest. "This sounds like it's worth a ton more money than I'm paying you. Not that I'm negotiating to raise your fees."

"Of course not," I teased.

A smile started tugging at the corners of his mouth. "I don't want to be greedy here, but since we're talking about miracles, what about the other aspects of my life? From what you've said before, it sounds like my marriage and my health could improve, too." He paused again and allowed himself to grin. "And while we're at it, how about boosting my golf game?"

We were quickly approaching the buy-in I was coaxing Richard to make. As soon as he made a genuine commitment, we could begin the real process of forging his success.

"It's not greedy for you to ask these questions, Richard." I explained that at home, just like at work, he would learn to resolve conflict and enhance his relationships by improving his level of communicating. In learning to relax and just be, and to accept people for who they are, he would be better equipped to receive vital information from the people in his life and perceive their greatness.

"If you chose to," I continued, "you could even develop a more intimate relationship with your wife."

"She would certainly appreciate that," Richard said. He added with a grin, "She'd probably ask me to give you a bonus."

"I'm sure she would," I responded, "and you probably would, too. But there's no extra charge for your personal life. Or your health. Or your golf game, for that matter. And yes, they can all be affected by the consciousness/energy-raising process."

I wanted to give him a clear picture that changing energy levels ultimately affects all aspects of an individual's life.

"Let's look closer at some of the effects of changing energy. People who resonate with a higher level of energy feel much better physically and emotionally. Think of it like deep meditation, but without closing your eyes, and you'll even get a lot of the same physical benefits, such as lower blood pressure, increased oxygen circulation, and improved digestion. A higher energy level also enables people to relax more deeply, release stress, improve sleep, reduce physical and emotional pain, lessen how hard their heart works, improve physical vitality, and even lengthen their lives. Most important, their quality and appreciation of life is vastly improved."

"I could sure use some relaxation," Richard said.

"There are social benefits too. I mentioned the relationship with your wife. But you'll change your relationships with others, too. You'll become a beacon for others, and people will want to be around you. One of my clients told me that great people kept coming into her life, out of nowhere, wanting to share her energy and listen to what she had to say.

"You asked me about golf. When it comes to physical activities," I told Richard, "expect an increase in your athletic ability and stamina. You'll develop the capability to create an 'in the moment,' peak experience whenever you want to play at the top of your game – and you'll do so without worrying about the result. Lessening the emphasis on winning and losing, one tennis player I worked with raised his game to an amazing level, enjoying the sport far more than he had in the past."

## Laying Off the Fear

"For a while there, it almost didn't matter any longer what happened to my company," Richard said. "I want that picture that you've drawn. I want everything you've said – the change in work, stress, my relationships – and I'll definitely take you up on that golf game. I feel like that girl in the Willy Wonka factory: 'I want it now!'"

Richard's level of engagement was so high that this was the perfect opportunity to break through his panic-driven idea about starting to cut his staff. "Let me ask you this," I said. "You've told me that long-term success would be your ideal dream, and that your deepest fear – running out of funds for your company – would be a nightmare. Because of your fear, you've concluded that you should start laying people off. I have a challenge, and I need your help."

"Sure," Richard replied. "I'm ready to take it on."

"My job is to help you live your dreams, not your nightmares, so how do you want me to respond to your conclusion that layoffs are part of the solution for O'Connell Consulting?"

For a moment, Richard rested a finger against his lips. "I'm speechless," he said. He was silent a moment more, pondering the choice and question I presented. "I don't know what to say. I guess it makes sense to see what else we can do first, before we pull the fire alarm."

"That does make sense," I responded. "Now it's time to decide. In a moment," I said, "I'm going to ask you to fully commit to this process." Before firming up this commitment, though, I wanted to describe more precisely what I was looking for.

To illustrate what real commitment entails, I talked with Richard about former San Francisco 49ers football star Ronnie Lott. After facing the option of surgery on one of his fingers that would sideline him for the rest of a season, he chose instead to have the tip of it amputated, so he wouldn't miss a game. In fact, he didn't miss a single down. That was absolute commitment.

"The way it sounds, you've already experienced an amputation of sorts," I told Richard. "Your soul's been cut off from your business. I'm inviting you to get back in the game. You take the quarterback position and I'll be the coach. I'm fully committed to teaming up with you. But for this to work you must have an unshakable commitment to doing everything in your power to make our miracle a reality."

"Start the clock for the first quarter," Richard said, looking fully animated. "Let's play."

This time I believed him.

# 5 | All That "Matters" Is Energy

*I say, stamping the words with emphasis, drink from here energy and only energy.*
—Stephen Spender, poet and essayist

"Welcome, everyone."

Richard surveyed the vacant looks and defensive body language of his staff. *Oh, boy.* He thought. *Here goes nothing.* Just as he committed to do, Richard called a meeting not just with the Fantastic Four, but with the rest of the staff as well to discuss the two points we had agreed needed to be relayed to them. He would first address my presence in their offices, and shortly after express to them his genuine concern for their success and well-being.

"I've called this meeting to address questions many of you may have on your minds: 'Just what's happening with O'Connell Consulting . . . and do I need to update my résumé?'"

Richard chortled, hoping others would join in. He assumed that making light of everyone's concerns would lift the mood, or at least prompt some nervous laughter.

Nope. As Richard's smile faded, the silence started to feel oppressive. He reminded himself to breathe.

Inhaling deeply, he remembered that he was committed to being honest and compassionate, not sardonic and depressing. *All right, let's start over.*

"Listen, I know it's been tense around here because things obviously haven't gone our way lately. You may have heard that we recently lost a big account, Simpson and Simpson, and this comes on the heels of several quarters of downturn. I could stand up here and blame the industry, or even people in this room, but the reason I brought you all together is to tell you that I take responsibility for what has happened, and I am committed to doing what's necessary to turn things around."

A few people looked surprised at the news about Simpson and Simpson, but not many. The rumor mill was working efficiently, even if other lines of communication had broken down.

By accepting full responsibility, an act out of character for most everyone in the company, Richard had gotten everyone's attention. Richard felt incredibly exposed and defenseless as he said all this – in his mind, he was publicly airing his personal failures – but the immediate result was positive: it felt as if an invisible hand were at his back, steadying him and urging him to go on.

Richard continued: "I'm sure you've noticed me taking a number of closed-door meetings with someone. I introduced him to most everyone last week, so some of you already know him as Bruce, but I haven't really explained why he's here. Any guesses?"

Despite the slight release of tension in the room, he was met with more silence.

"Christina, Bruce sat in on a meeting with us. Who did you think he was?"

"Well, I don't know. Maybe a banker . . . ?" Christina looked over at Betty Donaldson, the company's Human Resources manager.

Following Christina's lead, Richard asked, "What about you, Betty? Who did you think he was?"

Betty smiled at the other people in the room but avoided Richard. "Good question, right? Is he a number cruncher? Or a *people* cruncher?" Her coworkers exchanged sideways glances.

It was becoming clear to Richard that this, in fact, had been the subject of watercooler conversation and that he actually had escalated the fear by keeping everyone in the dark. People had started imagining all kinds of things. Both Don and Tonya were furiously scratching notes.

"What about you two? Don? Tonya?"

Each started to talk at the same time. *I stepped into that one,* Richard thought. "Sorry about that. Tonya, what were you going to say?"

Don pursed his lips.

"Based on the confidentiality you've been keeping, I thought he was an attorney," she ventured.

Don broke in, "Or someone negotiating to buy the company."

More people started to offer guesses until all the speculations were on the table.

Richard revealed, "He's not any of those things. I realize now I should have been up front with you, because it sounds like you've all been imagining the worst. I'm not selling the company or seeking a loan. I'm not planning on any layoffs right now, either, so don't worry that he's a downsizing consultant.

"Actually, he's someone I hired to help us straighten things out: a coach. He's working with me right now, but it's likely he'll work with each of you in the months to come. I hope you'll welcome him and cooperate to get things back in order and, ultimately, put all of us back on top of our game."

To Richard's surprise, most of the people in the room looked even more relieved. (Nearly everyone laughed when a few people exhaled loudly at the same moment, sounding like a collective "Whew!")

Even more unexpected, Tonya offered, "Richard, let me know if there's anything I can do to help. Certainly, the entire team is at your service, but I want you to be assured that I'm behind you 100%."

★ ★ ★

An hour later, after discussion with his staff about what had been causing the revenue slide and what could be done to reverse it, Richard made
a point of shaking hands with everyone before they left the room. He was
riding high, feeling as if he just made a major breakthrough, and he wanted
to thank his people for their contributions to the company thus far and for
their commitment to a mutually successful future.

When Richard was alone in the room, he found a note he had seen
Nate slip into Christina's hand near the end of their meeting. She must have
dropped it on the floor.

*Rah, rah, rah,* Nate had written. *Whatever.*

★ ★ ★

At our next Friday appointment, Richard reported that the meeting had gone smoothly despite its rocky start. People had become really
engaged when he started asking them for advice instead of trying to act as if
he had all the answers. "It was a great beginning to our rebuilding process,"
Richard announced.

Congratulating him for a job well done, I asked him what he learned
from doing this with his staff. First, he admitted it had been ridiculous to
pretend that people in his office hadn't known O'Connell Consulting was
in trouble. "The best thing I did was honestly state what's really going on
instead of trying to gloss it over or ignore it altogether. That's when the
energy in the room shifted. I could feel it change."

Most revealing, when he asked what they thought the trouble was,
he received all kinds of answers: Our pricing isn't competitive. We have a
weak salesforce. Our internal communication sucks. We aren't doing a good
enough job of marketing. We aren't managing expenses while revenues are
down. We have poor customer service. We don't have clear lines of accountability. Our office makes us look fly-by-night and is uninspiring to the
people who work here, too.

"When I asked them who they thought you were, I wasn't surprised at all to hear a lot of different answers," Richard declared. "But it never dawned on me before that they would have just as many ideas about what was causing the company's slump and what we could do to turn the energy around. And you know what? Just about *all* of them are right. Or maybe I should say all of them are *accurate,* because I'm finally getting your point about no right and wrong when it comes to people's perspectives. But what I'm saying is that these people are a gold mine: they're able to identify a ton of things we can improve here, and all I had to do was ask."

★ ★ ★

Based on Richard's growing understanding of how everyone fit into the big picture at O'Connell Consulting, the time had clearly arrived for him to learn more about who *he* truly was, making today potentially one of the most important days of his entire life. To fully benefit from what I was about to say, I asked again that he open his mind. I proposed that by the time we were through, he would never see himself or the world in the same way as he had before.

"You're on," he said. He seemed to have a renewed fire in his eyes. I found that I genuinely liked this man, who now exuded curiosity, intelligence, and no small measure of determination.

★ ★ ★

Richard put on a studious face as I began to review Isaac Newton's centuries-old physics. "Bear with me," I said. "This starts out as dry science history then veers into some really wonderful and weird territory that, honestly, could change your life."

Richard said he had always enjoyed science, so I should fire away. I started with Sir Isaac Newton, who proposed that the world is made of matter, and *each person is separate from everything else:* every object, other people, the molecules of the air, and so on. His theory also states that *events are caused by relationships between solid objects,* including people. Using the limited scientific instruments and understanding of his time, he studied large, slow-moving objects, such as planets, and he concluded that their composition must be solid.

However, Newton's theory began to show cracks when quantum scientists later discovered that matter is anything but solid. In fact, at the subatomic level, *what initially appears to be solid matter actually vibrates and moves.* At its core, *everything is pure energy.* Most important, *outer forces don't strictly determine the events in our lives; instead, events are influenced — and maybe determined — by the forces within us.*

More than a hundred years ago, Albert Einstein addressed the scientific community, passionately presenting the idea that everything we see, hear, taste, touch, and smell is energy, not matter. Instead, *everything that "matters" is energy.* Einstein proved that we are not what we appear to be. We are not solid and dense (despite whatever Richard may have thought about certain staff members).

"Every single cell in our body is a world of its own," I told him, trying to convey the incredible expanse of each individual's personal universe, complete with subatomic particles of energy.

"And as we've discussed before, everyone's energy vibrates, or resonates, at a different rate. A person's energetic resonating rate is directly related to the individual's level of consciousness. The more conscious a person is, the closer to their potential that person lives, and the more positive energy they have available to use.

"Bottom line: The only way to make real, sustainable changes in your life and your organization is to change the level of energy. You start with yourself. At the same time, a conscious leader will also have the skill of reading other people's energy and helping them raise their levels, too. That's something we can begin to tackle today if it suits you."

"Yes!" Richard exclaimed.

Both of us could feel that we were headed toward something big.

---

**Core Energy Technique**

*Assess Energy*

There are three primary ways to "watch" energy to see what level someone is registering:

1. *Visual*: Observe facial and body expressions to see how much and what type of energy the person is showing.

2. *Auditory*: Listen carefully to the person's tone of voice, volume, word emphasis, and silences. Also listen for intention behind words spoken.

3. *Intuitive*: Use any of your senses to detect clues about energy that aren't readily obvious.

---

"Richard, you said that you realized that the people who work with you are a 'gold mine.' You also said that the details you shared with everyone helped them relax and engage. These are two signposts for what I call an anabolic leader. That's the opposite of a catabolic leader."

## Catabolic Versus Anabolic Leadership

I explained that, at the cellular level, *catabolism* usually refers to a breakdown of complex molecules, while *anabolism* is the opposite. When we're talking about a person's catabolic or anabolic *energy*, however, we're making a broader statement about destructive and constructive forces within that person, who is made up not only of individual cells but also of thoughts, beliefs, and behaviors, which have energetic force, too. So you can have catabolic and anabolic energy in a single cell, a particular organ of the body, a certain system in the body (such as the nervous or digestive systems), or the entire person.

These energetic processes happen in organizations as well as people. What Richard was experiencing the past several months was personal, staff, and company catabolism. By constantly responding to their circumstances with worry, fear, doubt, anger, and guilt, people at O'Connell Consulting were constantly catabolic.

Richard understood my ideas about personal energy, but he questioned the idea that organizations as a whole are energetic as well. "Are you suggesting that my organization is *alive*?"

"Yes! That's exactly what I am suggesting. People who work in a company are part of a whole system – although they may appear physically separated, they profoundly affect one another. In this way, a company is indeed alive, not just an organization but a kind of organism.

"Anything *anyone* feels, *everyone* feels at some level. Thoughts are indeed contagious. When even a few people in an organization have negative feelings, it can spread like a virus. 'Groupthink' sets in, and their thoughts become group 'fact.' Once that occurs, the company can implode energetically in a swirl of gossip and negativity.

"Remember that 'groupthink' begins with 'leader think,'" I said. "At its core, an organization strongly reflects how its leader thinks, feels, and acts. Think of the leader as the heart: If you beat erratically, your people will follow erratically, and if you beat steadily, then your people will follow steadily. Whatever you think, do, and believe gets transmitted to everyone in the company. Of course, that's assuming you're actually the leader, and not just a figurehead. The person with the most influence is the real leader. If you don't take that mantle, then the next most influential person takes over.

"Who's the leader here?" I asked him.

Richard gave my question real consideration. "I think Don and Tonya have been running the show because I've been hiding out in my office."

"You might have something there, Richard. It's also possible that all three of you have been communicating catabolically with everyone here. To put a fine point on it: Perhaps there's been no clear leader because you've bowed out. And it's likely that all three of you have been influencing the energy of the company. Think about what the core catabolic thoughts have been, coming from each of you."

"Until recently, I know I've believed that nothing would save the company," he began. "And as for Don, it's pretty easy to intuit what he's been thinking because he's been so vocal about it, telling everyone, 'You guys are a bunch of screw-ups.'

"Tonya . . . I don't know. She comes off as superior and commanding but incredibly frustrated."

I offered, "Maybe it's something like, 'If they don't start doing it my way, the company will fail.'"

Richard gave me a knowing look. "That sounds like her."

"But, Richard, you have to realize that *all* of this can be transformed by you, because ultimately it emanates from you."

Misunderstanding, Richard fretted, "So it's my fault people have been so negative?" As if I had flipped a switch, the insightful leader had suddenly become the victim once again.

"Can I be blunt?" I asked.

"Be my guest," Richard invited.

"You seem to have an almost total lack of faith in yourself and your staff." As that settled in, I went on to suggest that his business and the people who worked for him were a mirror reflection of his own negative energy and deflated self-image. Further, his negativity was a normal result of what had transpired over the past year in his life and company.

"So, no, it's not your fault that things are the way they are. Everyone collaborates to make reality, that should be clear now. But as the leader, it *is* your responsibility – and an incredible opportunity – to change your part, thus affecting the whole organism of your business."

---

**The Catabolic Leader**

Employees are positive and productive when they feel confident about their leader. They want to believe that their leader is strong, resilient, insightful, and able to take care of both the company and their personal needs.

When a leader resonates with catabolic energy, however, chaos ensues. Employees no longer feel they're walking on a firm foundation. They tread cautiously to make sure they don't fall.

**A catabolic leader is not the result of the challenge. A catabolic leader *is* the challenge.**

---

I made it clear that he would never see people's true potential through the lens he was currently using most of the time. When he takes the blame, I explained, he's wallowing in energy Level 1; when he blames others, he's agitating at energy Level 2; but when he takes responsibility, he's elevated to energy Level 3. Levels 1 and 2 were clearly bogging down the organization already: corporate catabolism in action. But he also just demonstrated how quickly Level 3 could change the dynamics – and that he was ready for change. The exciting thing was that by reshaping his automatic ways of thinking, feeling, and acting, he just might encounter his staff, and himself, for what would seem like the very first time.

"Think about how Tonya reacted to you when you behaved differently in your meeting. You were kind of shocked, right? That's because your own 'stuff' had been getting in the way of her being someone different with you. But once you got out of the way . . . Consider how others might be different with you when you change your own thoughts, your own behaviors, your own emotions," I prodded.

"There's a big difference between a company that succeeds and one that doesn't," I continued. "Your workers, whether they realize it or not, already believe *you* are the difference!"

## The Anabolic Leader

"Also keep in mind, Richard, that catabolic energy can be either *chronic* or *situational*. I suspect that much of the Level 1 and 2 energy here has been situational, brought on by stress and exacerbated by the general atmosphere of chaos. Yet there may be some cases where chronic catabolic energy is present. What I mean is that, for some people, the Level 1 and 2 energy is more deeply rooted.

"We'll be able to help transform the situational negativity far more easily and quickly than its chronic, intrinsically negative cousin. If we find that you're working with employees whose issues are chronic, they may need psychological counseling. You may even need to end their employment, because you could waste a great deal of time leading them nowhere."

Richard was nodding along, perhaps not yet realizing that I was talking specifically about Nate, who showed all the signs of chronic catabolism.

Everyone leads. Anabolic leaders have the ability to motivate and inspire themselves and others to do extraordinary things. "The objective is to transform each person in the organization into an anabolic leader, not just you, Richard. The idea is to get people to understand that they are responsible for the quality of their experience." I showed Richard the following chart listing crucial differences between a catabolic leader and an anabolic one.

## Is Your Leadership Style More Anabolic or Catabolic?

| *Catabolic Leadership* | *Anabolic Leadership* |
| --- | --- |
| • Manages: Controls by pushing and pulling | • Leads: Encourages others to take their own steps |
| • Delegates fully (and then points and blames) | • Project shares (becomes part of the plan) |
| • Gives information without justification or buy-in | • Shares (detailed) information and gets feedback and buy-in |
| • Self-assesses | • Utilizes others' feedback |
| • Works in crisis mode | • Plans and develops, is future focused |
| • Emotionally disconnects | • Utilizes emotional intelligence |
| • Uses left-brain analysis | • Uses whole-brain thinking |
| • Focuses on problems | • Sees only opportunities |
| • Takes advantage of staff | • Sees the true human resource |

Richard studied the chart in silence. An occasional nod told me he comprehended the shifts really possible. He looked up and tilted his head, asking, "How can I shift my energy from catabolic to anabolic?"

"I was hoping you'd ask," I said. To help him make the jump, he needed to make the insights of the I Chart his own. "It will help you see where you are and then create a picture of where you'd like to go," I said. Once he had that picture, he would be able to climb the first step up the ladder of consciousness.

There was no delay in his response. "Let's do it!" Richard boomed.

He was enthusiastic and ready to tackle what was ahead. I was feeling compassion for him though as I knew the very next thing we should address would be Nate, a friend he considered loyal, an employee he had allowed to be unaccountable and untouchable until now. It was time to meet Nate, face-to-face, and address what should no longer be ignored. Would Richard be able to do what the company needed him to do? Or would he sink with Nate to Level 1 and drown there with him?

# 6

# Time for a Corporate Shock Treatment? (Level 1)

*The victim mentality may be the last uncomplicated thing about life . . .*
—Anna Quindlen, writer

Although he experienced the beginnings of an energetic transformation, Richard still harbored a lot of Level 1 energy. That meant the information I gave him next was sure to be hard to swallow.

"Leaders operating with a predominance of Level 1 energy work in crisis mode," I told him. "They're always dealing with problems, because that's what draws their attention most of the time. When people's energy resonates with problems, they attract and are focused on what they *don't* want.

"You have the choice to see anything you wish. You can direct your attention to the beautiful rose or the thorns on the stem beneath. We can say that at Level 1, leaders completely miss the flowers, the solutions. Instead, they perceive only the problems that stem from victim consciousness."

As I reviewed this information, Richard started to look dejected.

"It sounds like you're talking about me," Richard moped.

"It's about *all* leaders demonstrating a lot of Level 1, Richard." Richard had opened the door for me to be direct. "But please do take what I'm saying personally," I clarified.

Looking him straight in the eye, I said, "It's time to cut the crap. You need to start leading and living to your potential."

With my deliberate change in tactics, Richard didn't quite know how to respond. This was the first time I'd gotten in his face. He knew I was right, though. He recognized that this was part of why he'd hired me. He also knew it was now or never. While he was thinking, I decided to shake him up further.

"Now that I'm on the subject, I want to point out that you've lost control of your company. We've talked around this before, about how Don and Tonya's energy has become so influential. Maybe they're in charge, and maybe not. I don't know who runs this company right now, but it's not you.

"As you've already acknowledged, people are fighting, employees are often absent, and victims are laying everywhere. If you're not going to stand up and take the lead, there's no hope for this company.

"I wonder whether you're going to continue to scratch your way to survival or if you're ready to strive for greatness?"

I paused but didn't expect him to answer. "Because *greatness* won't be achieved by tiptoeing around but instead by taking some bold leaps of faith. We're all waiting for your next move to see what kind of leader you really are. I already have a sense about who you are and what you can do. My question is, do you?"

Richard was staring me down, obviously waging some kind of internal argument. In quick succession, his eyes widened with shock and perhaps shame, then narrowed with irritation. Then, more slowly, I could see resolve. Richard was coming to the conclusion now that I was neither arguing with

him nor insulting him, but speaking directly to the part of him that resonated with victim energy. It wasn't long before I could tell he also decided
that this part of him deserved a good talking to and maybe a swift kick in
the backside. When he spoke, it was obvious: he agreed with me that he was
much greater than he'd performed so far.

The hard-line approach worked. "Yes," Richard said. Sitting up straight,
voice pitched low and resolute, he declared, "I'm ready. I get it. I've been acting
like someone I'm not, like someone who shies away from anything that's difficult.
But that's not who I am. I want you to know, right now, that I'm committed to
changing the way I show up as a leader – I want to show up as a man who cares
about this company and will do what's necessary to make the needed changes."

★ ★ ★

I was glad to hear Richard stand up for himself, because that would
help remove some of the Level 1 energy. I described leaders with a lot of
Level 1 as disconnected emotionally, as if they check their souls at the door
or become robots. They wonder why no one respects them, and they feel
completely misunderstood. And of course they are misunderstood! How
can you be understood if you're disconnected not only from other people,
but from your very essence, too? What's left for others to see?

At Level 1, some leaders are numb; others feel emotion but are afraid
to show it. They succumb to the limiting belief that emotions make them
look weak, when the opposite is true. Energetically, employees see and feel
weakness when they don't see emotion.

Without emotion, at Level 1, leaders have no passion or commitment
to the company's mission. Often, they don't even remember it. They have
no real plan for where they're going, because they're almost always reacting
to crises. Their communication skills are poor to nonexistent, as is their ability to truly inspire and motivate others.

Finally, as if that weren't enough, I let him know that at the very lowest
resonating level of energy, leaders blame themselves for anything negative
that has happened in the company previously, continually focus on the past,
and beat themselves up over current setbacks.

"Oh, my God," Richard said, laughing yet seeming genuinely relieved. "I'm glad I said I'd change before you rattled off the rest of it. It's so depressing!" Everything about him remained strong, though, including his posture, volume, tone, and gaze.

"It's time for your second test," I told Richard.

"Wait!" he exclaimed. "I missed the first one."

"Did you?" I asked, smiling. I informed him that he already passed the first test. Functioning at Level 1, he saw himself as a victim, refusing to face reality or take the action necessary to improve himself or his company. I then helped him move to Level 2, the level of conflict, by challenging him. My "attack" was intended to get him to defend himself. By agreeing to take action, he demonstrated Level 2 energy. He sent a message to himself and me that he was worth fighting for.

"I knew I had it in me." Richard was enjoying his newfound focus. "Seriously, I had no idea you were working directly on my energy level. So I guess that when I'm dealing with Level 1 people, my job is to move them to a place where they're willing to fight for themselves."

"You've got it," I said, giving Richard a high five. "Nearly all people need to shift one level at a time. Later, I'm going to offer you an assignment that will help you jump into the higher levels without advancing one level at a time, which I think you'll find intriguing. But when you're helping someone else, it usually needs to be one level at a time.

"One important point I didn't make before. I noticed that you said 'Level 1 people.' If you listen carefully, you'll hear that I talk about people experiencing Level 1 energy or people with a lot of Level 1 energy – I avoid labeling them as 'Level 1 people,' because a label seems permanent, and energy is certainly not permanent. Make sense?"

Richard nodded. "I'll watch out for that."

"Great," I replied. "Now that you have a sense of how Level 1 affects people, plus at least one idea about how to begin to shift from Level 1 to Level 2, how would you feel about putting your new ideas into practice?"

## Time to Get Personnel

Richard told me he was ready for the next step.

Excellent. All that was left was for me to emphasize how important it is to deal directly with employees who resonate around Level 1 and to explain how to do it. I pointed out how troublesome they are: They're unproductive and bring down everyone else's energy. They're like a losing stock in a portfolio. You can have a bunch of winners, but one losing stock will lower the total gain.

For any person experiencing Level 1 energy, the leader must decide whether the individual is in a situational or chronic state, as I described earlier. This means assessing whether the employee's energy level is being prompted by the leader, the company, or another outside factor — or if it's intrinsic and chronic. If it's chronic, letting the person go may be the best idea.

The leader must decide whether to move or remove such individuals, and it has to be one or the other.

Warning signs can be an indicator that someone has a chronic victim mentality. These include a belief that there's no hope, that nothing will ever improve. Phrases like, *I can't* and *I shouldn't* pepper every conversation. When presented with possible solutions to challenges, such people are quick to reply, "Yes, but . . ." They see only problems and impediments.

Tolerating this type of energy can lead to the organization's downfall. Moving anyone's energy from the lethargy of Level 1 even to the anger of Level 2 will prompt action, a step in a more productive direction. Richard now understood that although anger can be detrimental, it's still an increase in energy from depression, and certainly from no feeling at all.

I applied the new concept to O'Connell Consulting: "So who in your organization do you believe might be at Level 1 right now?" We both knew the answer to that question, but I asked anyway.

Richard didn't hesitate. "Well, there's Nate. He's supposed to be our key salesperson, and he actually was better at his job at one time. But now he has a poor attitude. He mopes around, complaining that he can't make a sale. And he's even worse since he lost the Simpson and Simpson account.

"You mentioned that he used to do better. What was his attitude like then?"

"Well," Richard said, considering, "better but still not great, and he never really was what you would call a superstar. I don't know if I've ever seen him 'up.'"

"I see. Maybe we can move him up the chart. Based on all we've talked about so far, what ideas do you have about how to do that?" I asked.

Richard looked at a few pages of his own notes, nodding a couple of times in the process.

"I guess I could challenge him to fight for himself and see how he responds, but I'm not really comfortable doing that."

"How about," I offered, "if I demonstrate how to do this with Nate, then you can try it yourself with someone else?"

"Yes, I'd definitely like to see that," Richard said. "I started making changes with Christina, and she'd be the perfect person. I'll continue to work with her on my own."

★ ★ ★

"Nate, Bruce would like to ask you a few questions, if that's okay with you," Richard began for me.

His hands in his pockets, Nate slouched in the doorway. "Uh-huh. Okay," he said.

I invited him in and offered him a chair. When he sat down with us, I let him know I appreciated him taking the time to speak with me directly and that I was hoping this would be just the first of many positive conversations to help him get what he wanted in this company.

Nate looked at me suspiciously and said, "All right. Whatever."

*This is off to a roaring start,* I thought. *Well, let's get down to business: First I'll acknowledge and validate his feelings.*

"It's obvious that you're unhappy, and I think that's a normal response to what you've been experiencing and your frame of mind. You know, Richard found a note you wrote to a coworker during a staff meeting. It certainly reflects what I imagine you've been thinking and feeling."

I handed him the "Rah, rah, rah" note.

Nate recognized what he'd written, looked embarrassed, and turned to Richard. "Oh. I shouldn't have written that. I never expected you to see it."

Drawing his attention back to me, I said, "That note makes perfect sense based on what's happened and your current level of thinking. But let me be clear: The note isn't the challenge. It's the thinking behind the note that concerns us. Tell me what you were thinking when you wrote that."

Shifting uncomfortably in his seat, he was silent for a minute and then tried to explain. "You know . . . just what it says. I don't know . . . I don't really think all this talk will make much of a difference for me. I feel bad about the Simpson and Simpson account. I don't feel appreciated around here, and I don't know that I'll ever be what Richard really wants me to be for this company. It seems like I can't ever do anything right."

It was as if Nate was reading from Level 1 crib notes. But was his energy situational or chronic? *Let's find out.* "Thanks for sharing how it is for you here in the office. How is it elsewhere?"

"Personally, you mean? Well, things are okay, I guess. I don't have all the yelling and stuff that we have here. I can't say it's all that great, either, but, you know, whatever happens, happens. What are you going to do?"

*It was sounding pervasive.* Based on Richard's comments earlier, it seemed that this was a long-term situation that extended beyond Nate's work: chronic Level 1 energy.

Changing direction and launching my so-called attack in the hopes of getting him to raise a defense, I asked pointedly, "So why do you think you lost the Simpson and Simpson account?"

Without missing a beat, Nate reported, "That was just pure bad luck, there. A competitor stole the account because their rep caught the VP on a good day and talked her into jumping ship. She convinced Simpson himself. Good luck for the other rep; bad luck for me."

I gave him another chance to defend himself by being even more direct: "I'm thinking it's not just luck. You know, it was your account, and I'm wondering how you might have contributed to the loss of it." I was remembering that Richard had said that he'd repeatedly asked Nate to call on the account but that Nate simply hadn't followed through. I'm sure there was more to it than that, and if Nate was going to own up, now would be an obvious time to do it.

Nate took a minute to respond while his face turned red. "I don't know."

"I'm sure that if you had some time to think about it, you'd come up with something."

"Okay, let me think about it," he countered quietly.

"Of course. Why don't you check back with Richard on Monday? Meanwhile, what else would you like to share with either of us?"

"Well, I'm wondering if I'm still going to have a job here."

"Fair enough," I admitted. "I'd like Richard to address that."

Richard responded, "Nate, buddy, at this point, that's completely up to you."

Inside, I was beaming at Richard's firm grasp of the dynamics in this situation. Then I noticed Nate staring off into space, looking despondent. "Nate, what are you thinking about?"

Slowly getting to his feet to leave the room, he said, "I guess I'm screwed."

★ ★ ★

After Nate left, I asked Richard what he thought about his employee's final response.

"I'm not sure what to think," Richard replied.

"What would a Level 2 response sound like?"

"Okay." Richard thought about it. "The guy is fearing for his job. I tell him that it's up to him to decide his fate. So at Level 2, he's going to be *defensive, maybe combative*. How about: 'Everyone around here has been messing up, so why am I the only one on the chopping block?'"

Good answer. "Excellent. How about a Level 3 response?"

"Level 3? Let's see. He's going to be taking responsibility for his actions. Something like, 'The good news is that I'm not fired, and if this is up to me, it's my responsibility to save my own job.' He might even explain what had happened and acknowledge his part in it, right?"

"Right," I assured him. "So then, what would a Level 1 response be?"

"Oh, gotcha. Nate's response exactly: 'I'm screwed.' In other words, 'There's *nothing I can do*.' What if Nate doesn't come around?"

This was the moment for Richard to understand the usefulness and purpose of this exercise. By being aware of behaviors and responses, Richard had a better understanding of the level on which Nate was operating, as well as the level Nate needed to reach before his attitude and outlook on his job and himself would improve. Analyzing responses in relation to where they fall on the Energetic Self-Perception Chart can clarify for the leader (and possibly the employee) what changes are needed.

"Do your best to stay detached from results, Richard. You may master this technique, but that doesn't mean that you'll become some kind of 'change magician.' People will do what they will do, almost always based on their own energy and motivations. The purpose of the technique is to help you move those who will rise to the energy levels you want to create an anabolic organization, or remove those who won't. It gives you the best chance to create empowerment here.

"You've told Nate that his fate rests with him, so allow yourself to rest with that. It's not your job to ensure Nate's future, just to figure out what's best for the future of the company."

Richard was silent, obviously torn between his loyalty to his friend and his commitment to the company.

"Listen, Nate's a tough one," I acknowledged, "and it remains to be seen how he'll respond. I'm sure you remember that when I did this with you, you instantly rose to defending yourself and then taking responsibility for your actions. Nate didn't do that."

★ ★ ★

Switching gears, I requested, "Talk to me about Christina, Richard. How's she doing these days? When I arrive, she's still usually hiding behind that monstrous desk of hers, but she has caught my eye once or twice in the hallway. What's going on there?"

He recapped for me: After Richard asked her for further input on her request for a raise, her response had been positive initially, but he was still keenly aware that her energy level was low at best, and that she rarely smiled. Richard said Christina had once been a very "up" person and that she, like many of the others, had taken an energetic tumble over the past year.

Those were useful insights, and I suggested that the drop in Christina's energy might be rooted in a lack of trust in herself, in the organization, or even in Richard. "Trust is essential to great leadership," I assured him. "Something that creates a more trusting relationship is honesty." Richard's employees might not always like what he had to say, but saying anything honestly would help develop trust.

"Yes, I'll be candid with Christina," Richard said.

"Great. You and Christina got off to a nice restart in that meeting the three of us had a while ago. As you continue to engage her, she could respond in one of three ways: She could either bounce back like you did, come back slowly, or she can just remain in victim mode – which I hope isn't where Nate's headed. Now, let's finish today's discussion on Level 1 energy by looking at the way an organization with this Average Resonating Level (ARL) would cope in the marketplace."

## Organizations with Predominant Level 1 Energy

Organizations with an ARL between 1 and 2 eventually implode; that is, they spiral downward into bankruptcy. Some tumble faster than others, but destruction is inevitable. Richard recognized that this is what had been happening at O'Connell Consulting, and took a deep breath as I continued.

Energetically speaking, organizations are made up of many components. These include the combined ARL of the employees and managers, as well as the mission. Some organizations honor their mission statement. Others don't. Also important is how they function on a day-to-day basis.

Catabolic, or Level 1 and 2 businesses, look a lot different from their anabolic, Level 3 and above, counterparts. Focus is the main difference because organizations at this level attend to basic needs only, such as safety and survival. Everything about these catabolic enterprises is indicative of their focus:

- The expression on people's faces and their general demeanor,
- The quality of interpersonal relationships,
- The attractiveness of physical surroundings, and, in an often dramatic and direct way,
- The level of profits.

"Think of your consulting firm as if it were human," I suggested. "Remember, it's a living, breathing organism.

**Business Biology 101**

The corporate body is not unlike the physical, or corporeal, body. The corporeal body is made up of individual cells. There are brain cells, heart cells, skin cells, and more. The corporate body is much the same. There are many kinds of living cells, or aspects, within a company.

Some of the organizational cells include:

1. Mission, goals, and strategies;

2. Team dynamics;

3. Sales and marketing;

4. Customer service;

5. Recruitment;

6. Retention;

7. Job design, implementation, and work productivity;

8. Succession planning; and

9. Performance appraisals.

The health of each of these kinds of "cells" is vital to the host entity.

"We're going to come back to your organization's ARL but first we must understand the impact of these lower energy levels on the individual. And, as you know, it's most important that we focus on you, so now it's time for the special assignment I mentioned earlier," I now told Richard. The assignment, as I explained it, had to do with developing his overall energy, which, as he understood, was the way to most rapidly boost himself on the energetic chart. Once he developed his energy, everything about him would improve. I explained that I've taught this technique to thousands of people who've since experienced remarkable results. It's something I began many years ago to improve my athletic ability.

"To make a long story short," I explained, "I can't even imagine what my life would be like without it. Everything I know myself to be and everything I've accomplished I owe to the process you're about to learn. It's called *centering*, which is a form of meditation that unlocks the door to a new world."

"Okay, I'm not going to say anything about touchy-feely stuff, because I'm keeping an open mind, here," Richard remarked.

I suggested an analogy: Centering is like clearly tuning in to your favorite radio station. When you zero in on your channel, what you experience is like energy at Levels 6 and 7. When you add some of that energy to your current level, your entire average rises.

---

*The benefits of centering are wide-ranging. In fact, with regard to the psychological benefits, science is just now beginning to understand concepts such as psychoneuroimmunology, or the mind-body connection. In addition, there is the phenomenon of neuroplasticity, which shows that brains form new neural connections throughout life. This discovery is in dramatic contrast with the antiquated notion that the brain stops learning after childhood.*

---

"I can talk about centering all day long," I told Richard. Instead, however, I suggested he just dive in and see the results for himself. "Brace yourself, though. You'll open a door you'll never want to close again."

I paused, "What do you think?"

"It certainly sounds promising enough to try," Richard said. "If you're this excited about it, count me in."

"Glad to hear it," I said. "Here's something more that will get you started." I handed him some information on the Basic Centering Technique. I asked that he make the effort each day to try this exercise for as little as 10 seconds and as much as 15 minutes, preferably up to three times a day. "Do at least a morning session after you wake up."

---

**Basic Centering**

The idea with this technique is that it helps you get to a deep level of relaxation and a sense of oneness with everything around you. This is something you can do just about anywhere, anytime, because it's a breathing exercise, and you don't need any equipment.

When you have practiced this enough times, you will feel yourself entering into that centered state, and you'll be able to center yourself "on demand." (See Appendix B.)

---

"Let me see if I have this right," Richard reviewed. "I'm going to meditate a minimum of once a day, preferably first thing in the morning, for however long I want, every day?"

"Exactly."

"That's a deal," Richard said.

★ ★ ★

I left Richard with a recap of his assignments: Most important, follow up with Nate on Monday and spend more time with Christina, both of whom we acknowledged had been working at Level 1. He was to be honest and see if either of them would be able to move to Level 2. With Christina he would use the same tactic I had used with Richard and demonstrated again with Nate. (Meanwhile, he was also to communicate with Don, giving him an update and letting him know that he wasn't ignoring Don's request for a change.)

But first, he was to imagine the way a leader would react to each individual at each level of energy. If he was experiencing Level 1, how would he respond to Christina's dreary performance and request for a raise? What if he was at Level 2 (conflict)? What about Level 3 (responsibility)? Likewise, how would he react at each of the three levels to Nate's nose dive and Don's ultimatum?

To prompt Richard to roll up his sleeves an inch or two further, I also asked that he pick one or two projects he could work on to raise his own energy level according to the I Chart.

Richard seemed already to have a mental inventory of tasks he wanted to tackle. He told me that he was getting some good benefit from doing his previous assignment to journal his judgments, and he wanted to continue that. Then, he said he wanted to craft a new, clear mission statement for his company. Next, he said he had a corny idea, but one that he really liked: "What if I got a flat rock and painted a P on one side for *problem* and an S on the other side for *solution*? Throughout the day, whenever I encounter a problem, I can look at the rock and remember that the solution is always on the other side."

Chuckling, I told him I loved the idea. "And if you want to make it even cornier, try this: put your stone on a stand with a sign that says, SOLUTIONS ROCK!"

Richard groaned as we laughed together. "Ooooh, that's bad," he said. "I'll do it."

★ ★ ★

## Richard's Assignments

- Start redesigning his business by creating a clear mission statement, along with initial goals and strategies to match.
- Continue his judgment journal. Richard had been sporadic in making notes at first, but then he'd recently gotten into it, grabbing his journal the minute he realized he was passing judgment.
- Create a "Solutions Rock."
- Speak with Nate and Christina to see if either has the potential to shift their energy, and update Don; think about his upcoming conversations from the scenarios we discussed.
- And finally: Begin centering daily.

I cautioned, "Be sure the number of assignments you take on is reasonable. You're welcome to add to or reduce the load as you choose."

Richard had shaken his head assuredly. "This is fine. What can I look forward to on your next visit?"

I told him that in our next session we'd explore Level 2 energy, which predominates in the corporate world. We also planned to discuss how to resolve conflict — something that would come in handy dealing with Don and Tonya — as well as how to overcome the "Big Four" energy blocks, and see how far we could move his company out of the hole.

Richard seemed ready to begin some power lifting.

★ ★ ★

As soon as I left the office, Richard scheduled time to meet with both Nate and Christina and made a note to himself to write Don an email, which he sent the next day. Then he turned his attentions to the first part of his assignment and imagined his response at the different energy levels to each of these people. I explained to him that the purpose of this was to help him acknowledge where his energy level had been (Level 1) and where he was now (Level 2), and then conceive of where he'd like to be (Level 3). Here's what he came up with:

*Scenario 1:* Christina has asked for a raise, and I can't afford it. I've asked her to review the information and come up with a proposal, but I haven't heard back from her yet.

> *My Level 1 reaction:* "How can you ask for a raise now? Doesn't anyone care how bad things are for me? I'm relieved that you haven't gotten back to me because I don't want to deal with you right now."

> *My Level 2 reaction:* "It doesn't matter what you propose, because you already cost me a fortune, and I'm not getting what I want from you. Why would I even entertain a raise?"

> *My Level 3 reaction* (this took a little more time for Richard to imagine): "To put it behind us, I want to deal with this issue once and for all. Just know that however we end up, I respect your request."

*Scenario 2:* Nate's performance has deteriorated to unacceptable levels, and his lack of account servicing lost us our biggest client. (Seeing this in black and white, written in his own hand, helped Richard come to grips with how serious Nate's situation was.)

*My Level 1 reaction:* Do nothing, or commiserate with him. (Oh, boy, this is mostly what I've been doing so far.)

*My Level 2 reaction:* "We can't keep you on if you remain unproductive. Perhaps you should think about getting a new job."

*My Level 3 reaction* (again, Richard struggled for a while, but came up with this response): "The company is suffering because of the drop in sales and the loss of the Simpson and Simpson account. I'd like to arrange for some one-on-one coaching for you, just like I'm getting for me, to help you deal with your challenges."

*Scenario 3:* Don has a personality conflict with Tonya, and he's given me an ultimatum to get rid of her or he will leave.

*My Level 1 reaction:* "It's up to you two to work this out. I'm too overwhelmed to deal with everyone else's issues. I've got my own problems."

*My Level 2 reaction:* "Fine. I can't run this company without Don's marketing expertise, so Tonya, you're out. Don, don't ever pull something like this again, or I will fire your ass, too. Believe me, I'm going to start looking for marketing backup right away, as soon as I fill Tonya's position, so you better watch yourself."

*My Level 3 reaction* (now that Richard was in the swing, he arrived at this relatively quickly): "Even though your ultimatum is upsetting, I am the boss, and it's up to me to solve this challenge so this doesn't come up again. Let me work to come up with a solution and I'll let you know by the end of the day."

★ ★ ★

Christina sat at her desk, surreptitiously thumbing through a catalog she'd received. She was supposed to meet with Richard in just five minutes, but she had completed her proposal a week ago and had been sitting on it, waiting for the right time to bring it up. She was relieved when Richard initiated this second meeting, since she had expected him to do his standard, vague, "follow-up" conversation with her: he would invite her in, seat her across the desk from him, and then start their lame dialogue.

"How are things going?"

"Fine."

"What about that thing I asked you to do? Last week? You were going to have it to me sometime?"

"It's done."

"Okay, please leave it on my desk and I'll read it."

Then he would never get back to her. Or he would ask her for it again in another week. That's just how it worked. But she really wanted him to respond this time, and he said that he cared about her when he asked for the damn thing, so she planned to ask that he read it in front of her right then. No, she was going to insist on it. Demand it. Not leave till he did it.

*All right, 10 o'clock. Let's do this.* She stood, straightened her sweater around her hips, and then practically marched into Richard's office.

★ ★ ★

Who was this? Christina stood at Richard's door, glaring at him, daring him to ask her in. *I don't think she's looked directly at me in months,* he thought to himself. *It doesn't even look like her, and I think I like this feisty person better than the wilting flower.* "Come on in," he said, smiling broadly. "Have a seat next to me."

As Christina settled into a chair next to him at his work table, he realized exactly what the difference was in her: On her own, she had shifted her energy from Level 1 to Level 2. She wasn't shrinking from him, hiding, but instead she was here, ready to fight. *I didn't plan for this one,* Richard thought. *She's moved herself to Level 2 on her own. Maybe I can move her from Level 2 to Level 3? Okay, we're at conflict and need to get to responsibility. What do I need to say? What was my Level 3 response . . . ?*

But before he had a chance to figure out what to say, Christina abruptly said, "It's done." She slapped her proposal on the table in front of Richard.

Startled, he picked it up and looked at the cover page, then flipped quickly through the five pages she'd prepared: professional, crisp, direct, clear, just like he remembered Christina from her first days at O'Connell. "This is a really strong presentation," he began.

"I want you to read it while I'm here," Christina said. "I don't want it to get lost in the, uh . . . I'd just like you to read it. Before I go. Now."

## How Not to Get a Buy-In

Christina was at Level 2 and her demand was catabolic. Richard's level was higher, and so a confrontation could be avoided. Catabolic forces equally oppose each other, but if just one of two people in a relationship can respond anabolically, it defuses the conflict. Lucky for both Christina and Richard, her catabolic demand was met with an anabolic response.

If Richard had still been at Level 2, Christina's forceful attempt to create action would certainly have led to a confrontation, and probably to a reaction by Richard that she definitely wouldn't have wanted. But through our work together, he was starting to learn how to respond instead of react.

What happened next was a real testimony to that.

Richard hadn't prepared for this, but it was obviously important to her, and he took his time before answering. He quickly went through his choices and remembered his Level 3 response. "I'm happy to read it now, Christina. I'd like to deal with this issue once and for all. And however it goes between us, I respect your request. I'm also going to need some time to think about what you've written, and I'll probably have some questions or points to discuss with you later."

Christina's energy seemed to flag, so Richard continued, going back to the approach that had made a difference to her before. "Look, I know it's been difficult for you to deal with me for a while. That must have been frustrating. Right now, I want you to know that I asked for this proposal because I care about you and I want us to come up with something that works for both of us. I'm not going to make a unilateral decision. Of course, defining your position and pay are ultimately my responsibility, but this will be a collaborative effort. Can I ask you to trust me on that?"

Her eyes widened, and he continued, "It was a long time ago, but we used to have some fun together, and I think we liked each other back then, too. Are you willing to be patient with me while I reconnect with my original vision for this company – the one that got you excited to work here in the first place?"

Christina was astonished. There was a hint of the old Richard in all this, plus something new that she couldn't pinpoint. Whatever it was, it made her want to support him, to do what he asked and be patient. She actually believed him when he said that he would collaborate with her on a decision.

"You know what?" she responded. "You don't need to read it right now, as long as we set an appointment soon for a discussion. Is that something we could do?"

"Absolutely," Richard told her. "I'll read it and we'll get back together on it no later than tomorrow afternoon."

"That would be . . . really great, Richard." Christina, completely floored by this change in her boss, was staring at her hands in front of her on the table.

He leaned forward and said, "Hey, you wanna bring the key lime pie, or should I?"

# 7 | Without Fear, What Could You Do? (Level 2)

*The greatest menace to our civilization today is the conflict between giant organized systems of self-righteousness — each system only too delighted to find that the other is wicked — each only too glad that the sins give it the pretext for still deeper hatred and animosity.*

—Herbert Butterfield, historian and philosopher

It was already our fourth meeting and Richard still hadn't dealt with the issues between Don and Tonya. But Don's message made Richard think he might be able to put things off for a while yet.

| From: | don@oconnellcon-sulting.com | To: | richard@oconnellcon-sulting.com |
| Subject: | Re: haven't forgotten | cc: | |

OK. I'm in the middle of trying to untangle something, too, and have other things on my mind for the moment.

Don

-----Original Message-----

**From:** Richard O'Connell [mailto: Richard@OConnellConsulting.com]
**Sent:** Friday, August 26, 2006 9:19 AM
**To:** Don Taylor
**Subject:** haven't forgotten
Don,

Just wanted to let you know that I'm giving your concerns the time and attention they're due before reacting. I want to give you a more considered response so that we can come up with some solutions that make sense for the whole company. Please be patient for just a while longer as I work this one out.
Richard

When Richard showed me their exchange, I thought we should pursue the issues with Don and Tonya that day. We were ready to tackle Level 2 energy anyway, and certainly Don and Tonya would keep us right on schedule.

Because I had spent some time with both of them, and the rest of the staff, I was alert to Don's concerns and the overall tenor of the office. My main objective with everyone was to learn their feelings about the company, about their relationship with Richard, and about me being involved. Nearly all of them said they believed that O'Connell Consulting was a good company to work for and could be turned around with a strong effort, and everyone genuinely liked Richard but said he was "hard to know." Most said my presence in the company was needed and welcome.

As I told Richard about this, I also revealed that the overall energy of the personnel was higher than I'd expected. Was it because of Richard's influence over the last few weeks? Quite possibly, he said. He had been on task, more enthusiastic than usual, and had completed all his assignments.

Giving Richard a thumbs-up, and of course after getting their permission to do so, I divulged some details on my interactions with the Fantastic Four. Christina's energy was most intriguing, I reported. She initiated our conversation by talking about how she and Richard had spent some time together reviewing her raise request and proposal, and that they were definitely on a good track. She confided that she and Richard had talked about upgrading the appearance at the front desk, and that she had just started an exercise program she hoped would get her back into some of her more tailored office attire: "I just have a few pounds to drop, and then I can really start to 'work it.'"

I had to comment to Richard on her emerging personality. "She had this amazing combination of lightheartedness and professionalism. You know what I'm talking about?"

Richard nodded yes with a knowing smile.

I told him her eyes had twinkled as she talked about making her whole environment and herself more appealing to those who came through the doors at O'Connell Consulting. This would be her first contribution to getting revenues moving forward. "The impression we make on our clients, and ourselves, is so important! We're getting this new, beautiful desk for me. Since we agreed that would be a pivotal improvement, plus we're going to make some other upgrades around the office, I'm going to wait a few months to see how we're doing before pursuing the full raise. But things are looking up, and if – excuse me, when we pull out of this slump, everyone's going to benefit."

Christina was a new woman. She was enjoyable, positive, sparkling, and I let her know it. For the first time since we met, she smiled – and not just with her teeth, but with her whole face, which told me she appreciated the positive reinforcement and the time I spent with her.

Nate was a different story. Trying to be as objective and nonjudgmental as possible, I still found it uncomfortable to speak with him, I told Richard. His answers had come at a slow and frustrating pace, and his voice had been its usual monotone. He said he was glad I was there to help but had no energy behind his words.

"Tonya has some work to do," I continued. While talking to her, I had the feeling I was being interviewed. She wanted to make sure I knew she was "in charge" of the business. Of all the people I spoke with, Tonya expressed the most negative perspective on my presence, about the company's chances for success, and about Richard. I was taken aback when she said he was a nice guy but that he needed a lot of help from her to turn the company around. She, of course, needed no help at all.

"If we can inspire her to raise her energy," I imagined aloud, "I have a hunch that Tonya's extreme confidence and incredibly incisive mind will prove to be huge assets – big opportunity makers. It's just a matter of seeing if she's up for moving into the anabolic zone."

As I watched Richard's eyebrows knit together, it made me think about the brain creating new folds whenever learning occurs. Viewing Tonya as a source of opportunity was clearly a new one for Richard.

"Okay, how did it go with Don?" he asked me.

Don's meeting was more a venting session than a brainstorming meeting. He complained about everyone, saying the staff was lazy. When I asked him what he thought he could do to improve others' productivity levels, he said he was supposed to keep "his" people in line, and the "rest of them" were not his responsibility.

"I just keep the monkeys in monkey chow," he joked, though I hadn't found it particularly funny.

"So that's what I've gathered from the troops. What's new with you, General?"

"I feel pretty good," he said, nodding once for emphasis. "I'm ready to take our next steps together."

"All right, then. Let's get down to business: tell me what you feel has changed since our last session."

Richard now shook his head in momentary disbelief. He shared that he had started coming into the office earlier and not dreading it as much. "In fact, I actually look forward to it from time to time."

Searching for the gift in what he was sharing, I asked, "When do you most look forward to it?"

"I am remembering how much I enjoy teamwork, so I usually enjoy the days when we have team meetings. We've started scheduling these meetings every Wednesday, and we've had two meetings since you and I last met," Richard informed me, looking pleased just in mentioning that he instituted this new schedule.

"You said you *usually* enjoy your Wednesdays," I noted. "Why not always?"

Richard said that there was plenty of ego parading and bickering, although he liked it that everyone was at least in the same room once a week, and people often had good input. Yet Don and Tonya still wouldn't speak directly to each other, and Nate wouldn't say much at all. Christina seemed to have made a complete 180, though. "The truth is," he said, "that I get a lot of satisfaction just knowing I'm no longer alone in working to turn our company around."

"Got it," I said, then added: "You're halfway there. You're creating a support team, and that takes a lot of the pressure off you to get it all done. On the other hand, since the team isn't quite functioning as a complete unit, you still experience some frustration."

"You bet," he said. "But that's not the whole of it. My support team has divided into two camps. Guess who are the captains? Tonya and Don. Each side wants to win."

"I understand how these things can happen," I said. "Where are you in this process?"

Richard slumped a bit, and he said that he didn't want to show favoritism to either side. His strategy was to let them fight it out, as Don no longer seemed determined to have him fire Tonya.

It was important to help Richard discover how he could break through his habit of avoiding anything unpleasant. But first, he needed to know that

I understood his position. "If I'm hearing this right," I said, "you're feeling that you've made great strides in creating these meetings. You've taken a major step toward rebuilding rapport between you and your executive staff. Now you don't want to ruin this progress by taking sides."

"Yes," Richard replied emphatically. "That's exactly how I feel."

*"So what would it look like if you didn't take sides but instead took charge?"* I asked.

Richard pondered my question. He said he needed help to get to a point where he could make that happen, and I was once again impressed with his honesty.

We put that on the agenda for the day. "I'm sure you'll come up with some ideas for leading them both to a solution that works for the whole company, just like you said in your email," I encouraged.

"I hope so," Richard said, his tone of voice trusting but tentative.

---

### Core Energy Technique: Plant the Unconscious Seed

What kind of seed? In Richard's case, it was an expectation that he would be the one to come up with the ideas necessary to resolve things with Don and Tonya and effectively run his team meetings. Because I expressed my confidence in his ability to do that, the thought will linger in his mind. Whether he consciously thinks about it or not, a part of him will be working on a solution.

I love this technique and use it often. Saying things like, "I'll ask you again later because I have complete faith that you'll have come up with something," puts positive pressure on the psyche and, more often than not, results in creative solutions.

This is a wonderful way to empower the people around you to come up with their own solutions instead of waiting for you to "fix it" for them.

When I asked Richard to give me some details about how he fared on last week's assignments ("How does it feel to get them all done?" I asked. Beaming, he said, "I feel incredible."), he let me know that most of them had gone extremely well. He struggled, though, with the mission statement exercise and wasn't sure why.

I stretched out a hand. "Let me see what you have," I requested.

Richard showed me:

**Mission:** O'Connell Consulting is an organization that meets the marketing needs of small- to middle-income businesses. We strive to offer creative answers to even the most pressing marketing challenges, while keeping a close eye on budgetary concerns. This enables smaller businesses to compete well with larger competitors to ensure success.

**Goals and Strategies:** Create a new list of target clients from database and secure three new clients within the next month. Use an email campaign and consider creating a social media channel.

"Okay, what do you think about what you've written?" I asked.

Richard slowly shook his head. "Something's off," he said. "Somehow, it just doesn't feel right. It's not very exciting."

"What if I told you," I said, "that the very fact that it doesn't feel right is evidence that we're making serious progress?"

"You're kidding, right?" Richard looked perplexed. Then he added, "How?"

To answer that question, I directed him to the first part of the statement: *O'Connell Consulting is an organization that meets the marketing needs of small- to middle-income businesses.* I asked him to keep the I Chart in mind and tell me at what level he thought this statement resonated and why.

Richard considered for a moment. "I guess it would reflect thinking in the first circle of awareness, because it is about needs, not wants," he said.

Once again, Richard was proving to be an inspiring client. He was a quick study and eager to use what he'd learned. "That's a keen observation,"

I told him, and added that, usually, fear and anxiety are associated with need. Shifting the message from the realm of *need* to *want* would certainly raise its energy level. Also, making this shift would attract people he would enjoy working with more, because they would resonate with anabolic instead of catabolic energy.

"That makes sense," Richard said with increasing conviction. He looked down at his own copy of the document. "What about the rest of it?"

"Let's see: *We strive to offer creative answers to even the most pressing marketing challenges, while keeping a close eye on budgetary concerns. This enables smaller businesses to compete well with larger competitors to ensure success.*

"Tell me about the energy level of this part," I suggested.

Richard leaned back in his chair. He realized that the focus was on problems instead of solutions – dealing with challenges, not having enough money, and not being able to compete with the big guns.

He shook his head and began to laugh. "It's the same thing!" he said. "Levels 1 and 2 energy."

"That's it, Richard," I responded. "The goals and strategies you wrote match the energy level of the mission statement. So now I have some more good news for you."

"Good news is always welcome," he said and smiled.

The news was that the energy level in his statement, compared to how he felt about it, told us he was no longer resonating at an average level of 1 or 2. If he was still there, the Level 2 message would feel accurate and familiar. "In other words, if I hated myself and wrote a personal description of me, it would not be very flattering. That doesn't mean I would like what I wrote. It only means it would feel familiar to me; it would be comfortable."

Richard's expression told me he was following my thought process.

"Your new level of awareness is causing dissonance for you: You're aware of the discrepancy between what you really feel and believe and what you've written here. The mission statement you wrote was from the 'old' Richard, based on old circumstances. Your new level of thinking and energy is resonating higher than that."

For a moment, Richard's eyes danced.

"Yes, I can see that," he said. "I've definitely changed my thinking. I feel like I've made some major shifts."

This was a good time for Richard to pat himself on the back, I told him. He'd already made a great leap in consciousness.

"I agree," Richard responded, and credited his use of the centering practice I showed him on our last session together. He had kept to our agreement and performed the exercise every day. He said it was challenging to keep focused, but that he believed meditating already had a positive effect on him. "I'm more relaxed and more focused at work. My wife even said that I'm smiling more than I used to."

"That's wonderful. How would you feel about keeping these enjoyable experiences going?"

"Of course I'll do that," Richard responded. "Will this help me with improving the mission statement?"

I assured him it would and that he should start thinking about how operating with Level 3 energy might influence the statement. We wouldn't be exploring Level 3 in detail until our next session (Level 2 would keep us plenty busy today), but that didn't mean he couldn't start applying what he already understood, which was that Level 3 is all about cooperation, forgiveness, and responsibility.

Speaking of responsibility and forgiveness, Richard said, the judgment journal exercise had definitely caused him to pay much more attention to what he said and thought about himself and others. "I'm getting pretty finely attuned to my habit of perceiving people right or wrong, good or bad. I think I can stop making entries into my journal and just keep noticing when this happens. Oh, and I got this done, too."

He handed me a large, smooth black stone with a P on one side and an S on the other. "Here's my Solutions Rock," he said, obviously pleased with himself. "It's not as kitschy as I originally planned . . . I kind of went with a Zen theme."

"I'm glad you're more aware of the judgments you make," I said, taking the rock and enjoying its cool weight in my hand. "We can put the journal aside, since that's what you'd like to do."

I couldn't help but run my thumb over the rock's surface and repeatedly turn it in my hand. "Your rock looks and feels great," I commented. "How has it helped you?"

Richard explained that when he held the rock and looked at it, it would remind him of the success that's possible. So whenever he got stuck, he would turn the rock over to the problem side, stare at it for a few minutes, and then flip it to the solutions side. "Twice when I've done that," he said, "I've come up with something useful."

"It sounds like you've found an effective way to remind yourself about where your answers come from," I said. "Well done."

## The Frequency of Success

Each person has his or her own "success frequency." In Richard's case, the rock represented a psychological/energetic "anchor," or internal point of reference.

Once the pattern had been established – that he could discover answers by the process he'd described – each time he looked at the rock, he was able to tune into that same frequency for success.

★ ★ ★

As we got up to head out for some lunch, I asked Richard if we could return to our conversation about Don and Tonya, and start covering some Level 2 territory. Still feeling good about having completed all his assignments, Richard was up for it, eager to hear what I had to say.

We walked down the busy sidewalk, and I explained that energy at Level 2 is based on thoughts of conflict, as well as emotions and feelings of fear, anger, and anxiety. This results in resentment, retribution, and defiance. Level 2 is all about control – or, more specifically, attempting to control others.

People resonating at Level 2 are usually acting from either fear or pride. They usually think in black and white and see life with tunnel vision.

If they feel they are wronged, they hold grudges and never release resentment. No matter how much evidence might prove otherwise, their egos tell them they are right.

"Being 'right' works out okay driving in traffic," I said, pointing at the cars whizzing by on the street, "where there are laws everyone knows about how you're supposed to drive. But suppose everyone had their own ideas about who should go first after a stop, whether it's really necessary to drive between the lines on the road, how fast or how slow you should be going – you get the picture. You're asking for major damage. That's not so different from how it is when Level 2 permeates an organization. You've got a bunch of people assuming they know best and crashing into each other."

With this "reality," people at Level 2 are understandably quick to see the people and circumstances in their lives as dangerous, usually because they're afraid they won't survive the next crash. ("Not surviving" can mean any kind of loss: tangibles such as a job, money, or friends, as well as intangibles such as love, respect, or status.) Their listening skills tend to be poor: instead of hearing what others say, they're thinking only about what their own response will be.

"To live in the shoes of Tonya or Don," I said, "would be to walk from one collision into another. In a self-fulfilling prophecy, such people look for, and therefore find, all the problems they are usually accustomed to seeing."

Individuals at Level 2 have a negative impression of the world, I continued. They believe that in order for them to win, someone else must lose. Eventually, when people with this perspective have dosed themselves enough with this kind of energy, they experience some kind of breakdown.

I then pointed out to Richard something that may not have been so obvious about Level 2. Energy is not based on good or bad and right and wrong. All levels of energy have advantages and disadvantages. Realize that people who are experienced using Level 2 energy know how to get what they want. They know how to play the "game" according to most other people's rules. They know how to win. However, the price they pay for that is unhappiness, because a short-term catabolic gain usually leads to long-term catabolic effects, such as loneliness, lack of fulfillment, and even depression. And all this doesn't even begin to talk about the catabolic effects on those who "lose."

## Advantages and Disadvantages at Each Level

### LEVEL 1

*Advantages*: You don't have to lift a finger. You spend little effort and energy.

*Disadvantages*: There's a lack of engagement in roles and tasks, plus the lack of ability to lead yourself or others.

### LEVEL 2

*Advantages:* Your aggressive behavior leads to getting a lot done by yourself; you can also motivate others.

*Disadvantages*: Others' motivation is from anger or fear, thus results will not be satisfactory nor, most likely, will those results sustain themselves; you can't inspire others and your forcefulness will cause them to be dissatisfied, unproductive, to quit, or worse, give up and not quit.

### LEVEL 3

*Advantages*: You don't allow other people to stand in the way of what you want; you have the ability to avoid, block, and/or release the negativity of others; you're able to engage.

*Disadvantages*: You could be manipulative and self-concerned; hopes and promises are not given from the heart, but from the head; you're not concerned if things don't work out because you "did your best."

## LEVEL 4

*Advantages*: You take little personally; you truly care for and help everyone to do their job the best they can.

*Disadvantages*: You can get caught up in people's stories and become overly sympathetic; you may lack boundaries; you want others to be happy, so you may choose to put off taking unpopular actions.

## LEVEL 5

*Advantages*: You find opportunities in all challenges and take little to nothing personally. You are curious, open-minded, and optimistic.

*Disadvantages*: You can experience paralysis by analysis and be disengaged from emotions.

## LEVEL 6

*Advantages*: You're empathetic: you have the ability to feel and connect without judgment. You're also able to access intuition.

*Disadvantages*: You might not be grounded and could be out of touch with others and viewed as aloof. You may be a high risk taker.

## LEVEL 7

*Advantages*: At this level, you can create anything you choose, whenever you choose to – as quickly as you believe possible. You are connected to an intelligence of the highest order

*Disadvantages*: If any, there is less emotional drama as nothing is seen as real (which is why there are six other levels).

## Leaders with Predominant Level 2 Energy

"So let's say that Don and Tonya's Level 2 energy has been leading this company," I conjectured. "Then that might help explain why some of the staff have been, until recently, pretty dissatisfied."

Richard and I arrived at our lunch spot, an upscale pizza and pasta place. As we sat down and perused our menus, I mentioned, "When we had our first session several weeks ago, you talked about how often people were quitting. That's typical of an organization with leaders who have a lot of Level 2 energy."

They believe they can do anything better than any employee and, as a result, they constantly judge others. This creates tremendous damage energetically. It reinforces most employees' deepest fear – most anyone's deepest fear – that they aren't good enough.

When they are resonating at Level 2, leaders put their needs before others and don't give credit to anyone else. They believe that when employees work for them, they "own" the employees and all of their accomplishments. To stay in full control, they micromanage. This type of leader is often bossy and condescending, ignores others' responses, and sometimes actually gets pleasure from being unkind to others.

"Who do you know that might bear a resemblance to this description?" I asked Richard.

"This sounds like two someones I know," Richard said. His eyes narrowed.

★ ★ ★

"Be careful about getting sucked into that energy," I cautioned Richard. "That's no way to deal with it. Let's go back to that method you used successfully before. What would be the Level 1, 2, and 3 responses to Don and Tonya?"

"I identified those as part of my homework: Level 1 is to let them duke it out while I ignore it – oh, boy, that's the same as not choosing sides, isn't it? Okay, I guess we're not following *that* plan," Richard made fun of himself. "Level 2 is to pick a side and fire someone, and Level 3 is to seek resolution between these two people. Wait a minute. I have a question: Am I still at Level 1 or 2 if I don't act like it? In other words, is it my actions that demonstrate my level of energy?"

We placed our lunch order then returned to our conversation. I explained that even if someone's behavior reflects a certain level, that doesn't mean they're at that level. People can repress feelings as well as express them. Either way, it's the same energy. It's not what's said or done that matters; it's the intention of the person who says it. *The true measure of your energy is based on your core beliefs.* So what matters most is the focus of your thinking.

"So if I'm angry and resonating at Level 2 in that moment, which if I'm honest is pretty much where I feel like I'm going with Don and Tonya right now, whether I actually strike out at them has more to do with self-control than my energy level?" Richard asked.

"Exactly," I said.

Richard had certainly raised his "average" energy from the first circle of awareness. However, as he acknowledged, he still had some Level 2 energy, which I would help him release. Last time, to help move him from an average of Level 1 to Level 2, I had surprised him with an indirect approach. This time, I let him know in advance exactly what I was going to do, which was to help him release more catabolic energy by removing some of his anger and resentment.

I explained that some of the resentment he was feeling toward his personnel was normal, but it was also holding him back from reaching even higher levels of energy. I asked what he thought he could do to let it go.

His reply: "I think talking to Christina helped already, so I'll do that with Don and Tonya, as well. Also, I'm going to put myself in their shoes and figure out why they do what they do, to normalize their behaviors, so I can let go of the resentment."

"Perfect!" I exclaimed. "When you do both of those things, you'll be connecting with Don and Tonya, and you'll be able to *understand* their behavior more easily. That will certainly help *release some of the catabolic energy* you hold."

What's more, I told him, he should watch out for an amazing possibility: a simple conversation, or even his new way of thinking, could have a positive effect energetically on Don and Tonya.

To help him further, I asked him to identify the strengths Don and Tonya possessed that he could put to work. "Why do you believe Don and Tonya argue so much?"

"They argue about who runs the office," he responded.

"Nice insight, but it doesn't answer my question. You told me what they fight about, and I asked *why* they fight." I was again testing him to put his awareness into action. "What might be at the core of their thinking?"

---

### The Fight for Success

The purpose of this part of my conversation with Richard was twofold.

First, by putting himself in the shoes of Don and Tonya, he was clearly able to see why they'd acted as they had. By doing so, he was able to move away from his judgment and core belief that they were just trouble, and instead, release his catabolic energy through understanding.

Next, by acknowledging and validating Don and Tonya, he would be able to help them further their cause in a positive way, thereby taking responsibility for their future instead of battling one another to "win."

In both cases, all parties begin their shift from Level 2 to Level 3 energy.

Richard considered this most powerful question. "Maybe they want to be important and feel valued. Maybe they want to make a difference," he said.

"Could very well be," I said, thrilled about his insight. I asked where those thoughts came from and Richard said, without hesitation, Level 2, and from need.

"And there you explain the anger," I said. "They're fighting for what matters to them most – their self-worth. You can use their desire to be valued as a gift and instead of fighting with them, get them to fight for success, and you'll help them move to Level 3. Get it so far?"

"Sure do," Richard said.

★ ★ ★

About halfway through our lunch, I pointed at my half-drunk glass of water and resurrected the old adage that some people look at a glass as half-empty, while others see it as half-full. "But I suspect there's another group of people who outnumber the other two combined. This third group looks at the glass and asks, 'Who stole my drink?'"

Richard hid his snicker behind his napkin. He knew what I meant right away. Then he told me that he thought many employees believe they're entitled – to perks, to raises, to parties, and on it goes – and the company ought to provide it all and ask nothing in return. "It's as if they think O'Connell Consulting works for them," he observed.

A sense of entitlement stems from Level 2 energy, I explained, and it sees leadership through contemptuous eyes. To show Richard how this might be affecting him, I also reminded him of something he said several weeks ago: that he felt he "owed" Nate something because Nate had been there from the outset. If Nate felt that way, too, it would double the pressure on Richard and could be one of the reasons he was so reluctant to confront him.

Personnel resonating at Level 2 often argue, I pointed out. They frequently display negative body language and verbal dissatisfaction with others. Because this is the level of conflict, at Level 2, staff members are in a competition with everyone. They try to make themselves look better by making others look worse.

> *The result is employee burnout. The stress caused by Level 2 competition and emotions leads staff members to become disengaged from their jobs. A 2020 Gallup poll found that, globally, only 20% of employees are engaged in what they do. In the US, 15% are defiantly and actively trying to sabotage their organizations.*[1]

"That's a truly frightening statistic," Richard broke in. "How can I make sure my group works as a team?"

"What do you think of starting by bringing Don into your office with us for some of what I call 'Breakthrough Laser Coaching'?"

"Great idea," Richard agreed. "I think it's time we face this situation head-on."

"I'm glad to hear you say so. Let's do it."

Richard quickly called Don and asked him to meet us in the office in half an hour. Richard hung up and told me we were on as soon as we got back.

"Excellent. Please keep in mind that what I do with Don today I'll teach you to do as soon as you're ready."

Richard was intrigued but willing to wait, he said. "Should I take notes?"

"Never a bad idea, but it's more important that you stay engaged in the conversation. Even if you're not saying anything, it would be great if you keep your energy with us."

★ ★ ★

In addition to having our meeting with Don, I requested that Richard tell everyone that he was working on a new company mission and invite them to contribute their own ideas. I also requested that he ask them about their personal mission and their goals for their job. "What do you think about engaging your personnel in this manner?"

---

[1] https://www.gallup.com/workplace/352949/employee-engagement-holds-steady-first-half-2021.aspx

"I think it makes sense. I'll do it," Richard replied.

Richard also needed to see the potential benefits from his initiative. "What would you hope to gain from doing what I've proposed?" I asked.

He said this approach would generate more of a buy-in from each employee regarding the mission statement, getting them more engaged, and maybe even getting some good ideas to boot. He said he might also learn how connected or disconnected his company's mission was from each person's individual one. "If I can get this information," he said, "we'll be able to bridge the gap later."

## Organizations with Predominant Level 2 Energy

We finished up our meal then headed back to the office. As we walked out the door, Richard asked how you could tell if an organization was at Level 2. I told him that they're usually shortsighted and exhibiting fight-or-flight survival tendencies. Because they're so concerned about finances, they take advantage of workers and consumers, reaping as much financial gain as they can, sometimes at any cost.

Most such organizations say their staff members are their most important asset. Yet at the core, they don't believe it.

Organizations at Level 2 require staff to work longer hours and to take on much more work than they can handle. It's no wonder their employees are stressed and feel taken advantage of. While economic factors may indeed require expanded job responsibilities, these organizations neither share any reasons for their actions nor get a buy-in from staff. Company philosophy: it's our way or the highway.

## Customer, Serve Us

I told Richard about a recent experience I had when I tried to get some help from a cell phone provider, and the representative I spoke with had cited two sections from her "procedures" manual to prove to me why

I couldn't get what I wanted. Floored, I asked if I was really speaking with the customer service department.

She assured me I was, and what she was reading to me, the representative had said, were the "rules" that constituted company policy. They weren't flexible, so the representative felt she couldn't be, either.

Lucky for me, I felt flexible enough to switch providers.

When companies misunderstand what it means to serve their market, they lose customers. "In these kinds of situations, customer service is replaced with 'customer, serve us,'" I said. I shared my shock in how some organizations treat the very people they rely on to maintain their existence. Level 2 thinking is all about winning and losing. In many companies, this kind of thinking leads to policies that are black and white, which turns people away.

Richard said with a sigh, "I'm not sure how we react to customer challenges here." He said that he had people in charge of customer service, but gave them the message that it's their job to deal with challenges. He promised to think more about that.

"What other comments or questions do you have about Level 2 energy?"

"Many organizations control a great deal, and they seem to make a tidy profit in the process," Richard noted. "But it sounds like you're saying that using a lot of control doesn't really lead to success."

"Again, as I mentioned earlier, it depends on what you mean by success," I replied as I opened the front door to O'Connell Consulting. "Profits can be forced, but at what cost? Even if there is some success, it's usually temporary. At this level, something or someone eventually breaks down."

## Breaking Through with Don

When we got to Richard's office for our meeting with Don, Don arrived looking a little distracted but willing to talk. "What's up?" he asked.

We asked Don to sit at the table with us, and then I opened the floodgates saying, "Don, you're obviously frustrated, and Richard has given me his perspective about what's been happening with you and Tonya. I hope you'll feel comfortable to share your thoughts and feelings with both of us. Please feel free to be honest; you don't need to pull punches with Richard or me." Richard nodded his head in agreement.

Don didn't need to be asked twice. Don vented. Don cleared the air. Don talked for about 20 minutes without stopping. But when he did pause, he took a deep breath and said that it felt good to get all of that off his chest.

Richard and I both thanked Don for being so candid. Then Don asked, "Is that all? Is that what you wanted to know?"

"Well, yes, that's part of why we asked you here." I told him. "And there's more that you can help us understand. You've mentioned that you feel as if you have to 'watch these people like a hawk,' and that otherwise it's like 'pigs at a trough.' And I seem to remember that you referred to them as 'monkeys' when I talked with you a couple of weeks ago."

Don's face flushed. "That's a lot of animals," he observed awkwardly.

"Indeed." I smiled at him. "But it's really all about how you and the other employees here are not always on the same side. I'm wondering how you think your attitude here has affected the company?"

Don got on a roll again. With his Level 2 energy in high gear, he began to defend himself. He told us that it was up to him to keep the marketing team productive, and if he didn't do it, no one else would "ride them" to keep them hustling. What's more, he offered, one of the company's chief problems was that it was stagnating, and his agitations stirred things up.

Don finished, "Plus someone's got to keep Tonya in line or she would try to stage a coup, or a take-over, or whatever it is that cutthroat attorneys do to topple a defenseless business. We'd be belly up in under a month."

Looking as if he was daring Richard to contradict him, he folded his arms in front of his chest and was tapping the fingers of his right hand on his left bicep.

"Okay, that's helpful to know," I said. "Thank you again for being honest with me. Now I'm going to ask you to be honest with yourself: how effective have these attitudes and actions really been in fostering the success of this business?"

At first, Don just sucked in his breath and held it. When he let it out, it was slow and barely audible. It took him a while to speak up.

"I suppose it hasn't exactly skyrocketed us to the top," he admitted.

"What potential negative results can you imagine are directly related to these beliefs?"

Don's answer came a little more quickly this time: "People might feel pitted against one another, overworked, unsupported by management. If I'm going to carry the animal thing all the way out, they might feel like they're in a cage working for scraps, stressed out by having people's eyes on them all the time, and wishing for a time when they were able to run wild with the wind in their hair."

Don realized he was getting carried away with his metaphor, and he started to smile as he hummed to the old tune, "Born Free." Richard broke in with the lyrics, and they both started laughing.

"Seriously, though, I think it would dampen creativity, make people feel undervalued and as if they work only for a paycheck," Don continued. "That's how it would make me feel."

Don's insight was encouraging and inspiring, so I asked him to dig deeper: "What other old thoughts might you have been carrying around about the company and the people who work here?"

"I guess I was thinking that the people are down, morale is shot, the company's not run properly, and pretty much everyone but a few of us are slackers," Don revealed. "Sometimes I think I'm the only one actually working around here."

"How does it feel to think that?" I probed.

Don said simply, "It's not a great feeling. This is a downer."

"This may help: what new thoughts could you adopt that would lead to much different results?"

Here's what Don came up with:

- These people are my partners.
- I don't have to do it alone.

- I don't have to push anyone.
- The people here are not a drag on the business; they're our greatest hope for success in the future.

And he couldn't resist one last one for fun:

- In this circus, I am not a zookeeper. We're all under the big top together.

Richard and I both congratulated Don, and I asked him, "With this new perspective, and the positive feelings that the perspective would bring, what would be your new actions?"

Don floored us with his response: "The first thing I'm going to do is talk to Tonya and see if we can work something out together. I'm sure we can put our differences aside and start moving forward in a new way. I can see that a lot of what's been going on between us has been directly related to what I've told you today, and that's reasonably easy for me to change. It's about time I stop cracking the whip and start getting to know my colleagues better."

★ ★ ★

Richard turned to me after Don left and expressed his amazement. "I don't know how Tonya will react to Don like this, but it already feels as if there's less Level 2 in my life."

"There's plenty of historical evidence and research showing that team conflict is inevitable and cannot be avoided. You've said yourself that squabbles and turf wars are par for the course. What's your sense of this now, Richard?" I asked.

Richard mimicked me: "That may be *true*, but is it the *truth*?"

We both laughed. It does seem normal to live in conflict. But I suggested that's only because most people are so used to conflict energy. Conflict occurs when energy matches, not when it doesn't. "It takes two people to create conflict," I said. "But here's something paradoxical: all conflict is self-conflict."

I pointed out that Richard could remove much of his conflict with others if he had no conflict within himself. When conflict arises, it was usually occurring between his head, which is clouded with judgments, impressions, fears, and doubts, and his heart, which knows the truth. "If no dissonance exists between the two, nothing you ever hear will bring you conflict."

"So if I'm clear in body, mind, and spirit," Richard asked, almost as if thinking aloud, "I would feel no conflict within me, and so, I wouldn't argue as much with others?"

"Yes, but it's a bit tricky," I said and explained further. For Richard to fully understand, every aspect of him must agree. Even if he completely believed something was true, he would still feel dissonance, and so a conflict would arise, if what he believed wasn't the truth. I added: "This is because, *at your core, you are connected to Universal Truth, whether or not you are consciously aware of it.* In other words, you can't just fake your way through life and be successful."

He became quiet, thinking about what I just said. "I'm going to chew on that for a few days."

Richard continued with, "Hey, here's another question. Do you think all conflict is bad? I mean, doesn't it move people into action, spark growth and creative thinking, that sort of thing?"

"Nothing I'm talking about is good or bad," I again clarified. "I'm only talking about energy." I relayed that while conflict can be a motivating force, we really didn't have to "force" anything. Because there is simply more energy at Level 3 than at Level 2, cooperation will lead to dramatically more success than conflict.

Expanding further, I explained that there are two types of conflicts. The first is interpersonal. It arises from our personality and is ego-based. The second is task-focused, which is created simply by a difference of opinion about how something should be done. From what I've seen, task-focused conflict is not that debilitating, unless it's mixed with catabolic emotion.

"Who said that everyone has to agree with everyone else?" I asked. "Pardon the cliché, but we can at least begin by agreeing to disagree. When we consciously disagree without having catabolic emotional reactions, disagreements are negotiated to agreements."

"That answers my question," Richard said. "So what can I do with my team?"

"I asked you before what it would mean for you to take charge instead of taking sides. What is your thinking about that now?"

"I was thinking that if I could just be a mediator and get a buy-in on that, then I could still remain neutral and we'd make progress."

"I knew you'd come up with something. Congratulations," I said. "I like your increasingly creative ideas. I'd also like to challenge you regarding one more thing."

"That's fine," Richard said, more aware each session of how our game plan was unfolding.

"Let's recap here. What resonating level of energy do you believe is involved in remaining neutral?" I asked.

Richard took his time before answering. "I'm just worried and fearful about not being liked," he confessed. "I'm avoiding confrontation and the real issue. I guess this sounds like victim thinking. I suppose it's Level 1."

"Okay," I said. "Then what would a Level 2 and then 3 response look like?"

"At Level 2," Richard replied, "I would control the meeting and not let the egos dominate. At Level 3, I think I would try to get everyone to cooperate?"

"Great," I said. "We'll cover Level 3 in more detail next session. For now, how would you like to respond to your teaming challenge?"

Richard's tone was now emphatic. "I want everyone to cooperate and I don't want to avoid the issues."

I shared an approach that he might find valuable. It helps when parameters of relationships and a clear understanding of everyone's roles, including his own, are established. Doing so can create a buy-in, as well as let his group know how challenges will be handled in the future. In this approach to teaming, any current challenges that are brought up are dealt with immediately. Once everyone agrees to the plan, he will have done a great deal to shift the energy of the group.

"This sounds a little like a group contract," Richard commented.

"You could say that," I agreed. "I'm somewhat hesitant to use the word contract, though, because it seems a bit too 'legal.' I prefer agreement. So, if you like this strategy, what's one way to convey your goal to the team and get the buy-in you want?"

"Perhaps I can tell everyone what I've been experiencing and ask them for their impressions?"

"That's a start. What next?"

He thought carefully and then said to get buy-in, he could ask each person in the group to offer ideas about team roles, goals, and strategies, and brainstorm those ideas into ones to which they could all agree. He could also ask what role they believed he should play. That way he could get permission from them to lead in the way they all agreed. "Then I wouldn't be the bad guy, I'd just be doing my job." He said.

"You're on to something useful here," I said. "How would you feel about adding the actions you've just mentioned to the list of your assignments?"

Richard responded more slowly, yet deliberately. "There's a fair amount of work involved here," he said. "I'd like two weeks to complete all my assignments."

I agreed and asked him to confirm what they were.

Richard consulted several pages of notes. He first said he would continue with his centering exercises. He would also meet with each of his staff and get to know them better, and to ask for and listen for their gifts. He would tell them he was revising the mission statement, get their viewpoints, and ask them to talk about their personal mission and their own goals. Then he would rework the mission statement and create objectives from there. He'd try to create a vision of how he could use each person's gifts so that everyone won. He'd also try to coach Nate out of Level 1, and Don and

Tonya out of Level 2. For his team, he would discuss in his next team meeting what should be their roles and objectives.

"That works for me," I said. "Before you have that meeting with your team, I'd like you to consider something that may come up within yourself and the other members of your group." It was time to address conflict from where it originated, which is from the Big Four energy blocks that exist within each of us. To do so, I decided to make perhaps the most unusual request that I had ever made of a client.

# 8 | The Big Four Energy Blocks

*There is nothing either good or bad, but thinking makes it so.*
—William Shakespeare, *Hamlet*

"Something you've never asked anyone to do before? It won't be like one of those crazy reality show stunts, right?" he chided. "Just so you know, I'm not eating anything disgusting or doing any fire walking."

"No, no, nothing like that," I assured him, chuckling. "It's only that my gut tells me we should try something unusual. If it's okay with you, I'll wait to make my request until after I've told you the purpose of what we'll be examining next."

"Sure, why not?" Richard had been laughing before, but now he looked genuinely relieved that I wasn't going to present him with a bowlful of crickets or something worse.

★ ★ ★

I had mentioned the Big Four energy blocks to Richard in an earlier conversation, and now it was time to explain them in detail. When I asked if he was ready to remodel himself and his business by recognizing and removing these energy blocks from his organization, Richard told me he was more than ready — he had already begun the process. In our work together, Richard had come to realize that many of the obstacles he was facing were based on inaccurate thinking.

Richard clarified, "Before, I was chained to an identity I thought I'd be dragging around with me for the rest of my life. Now I feel liberated to choose who I'll become, and that includes being a true leader."

---

**What You Believe Makes You Who You Are**

Today's version of you is the result of everything you've ever experienced. From your birth right up to the meal you ate last night — every thought, feeling, and emotion you've ever had, and every action you've ever taken shapes who you are today.

Yet today's version of you is a work in progress, as if it were created in clay and not set in stone. The past doesn't determine your future. Instead, by carefully examining the sculpture that's you today, you can choose to remold yourself and increasingly become more of who you truly want to be.

**Energetic Principle #3**

**Each moment describes who you are and gives you the opportunity to decide if that's who you want to be.**

---

Now, by understanding and identifying the Big Four energy blocks, Richard would have the opportunity to unchain himself further by learning what was holding him back. "A block is anything that restricts you, whether that's external (like money or time) or internal (your beliefs and attitudes about yourself and the world around you). Usually, though, the external reflects the internal, so we could say that 95% of the time, it's internal factors that hold you back. The four blocks are:

- The limiting beliefs you hold
- The false assumptions from the past that you bring to today
- The false interpretations you make
- The fear that you are not good enough, or what is sometimes called a "gremlin"

I offered, "It will be incredibly useful for you and your staff to understand each of these. Once you know what's getting in your way, you've taken the first step toward removing those blocks and reshaping your world. This part of the training is important for everyone in the company to take part in. Please gather all your employees in the conference room so I can provide real examples and explanations of energy blocks to the entire office.

"And now for my unusual request: I'd like to use you as our example."

Richard knew that if he did this, he might get embarrassed, but he was now a man on fire with courage and conviction for his company, willing to do what was necessary. Plus he trusted me. He said as much when he agreed to be what he jokingly called my "spokesmodel."

★ ★ ★

Richard walked from desk to desk, double-checking to be sure that each of his staff members had received and opened the email he sent to announce the meeting that would start promptly at three that afternoon. While he did that, I made the conference room a quiet enclave, taking the time to center myself and carefully craft my thoughts.

★ ★ ★

## Tonya

So now Richard wants a "team meeting" and he's finally insisting that everyone attend. Okay. I'm game. Better late than never. I guess we'll see if he really has the guts to follow through. Like I said, I'm behind him 100%, but I'm just waiting to see if we're actually going anywhere with this new enthusiasm of his.

It's been so frustrating watching this company sink while Richard stands by acting as if nothing's going on. He's been in such denial about the problems around here that he has gotten less and less willing to take my advice – I think my attempts to fix things just remind him of how bad things have become – and now is the time when he needs my help the most.

I suppose that's why my arguments with Don got so loud, too. It's as if we both thought that if we could stand in the hallway and make a commotion, then Richard would finally have to do something. Not that we were playacting: Don and I definitely have different ideas about how this company should be run. And he can be such a horse's ass.

But Don's not really the problem. I worked with plenty of jerks in corporate law and we got things done okay. People ask me why I left that practice – all the time, they ask me. They say I seem like I would thrive there. But there just wasn't enough heart in it.

Shocking, right? Old Tonya needs to feel the love? Well, it's true. I didn't feel as if I was making any kind of difference for anyone. Not for my colleagues, nor for my clients, although we were certainly all lining our pockets.

When I went to law school, I had these idealistic notions of how being an attorney would change the world – no, I'm serious – I really thought that, and I didn't even know it was a cliché. Then I got sucked into business law because everyone who was being "smart" about it went that direction and the coursework and case studies interested me. But when I got out in the real world, I grew to hate how impersonal it was. I missed how it felt when I thought I could change the world.

So O'Connell Consulting comes along, Richard and I decide to work together, and I can see how I'll apply what I know in a small business with people instead of giant companies. Maybe I wouldn't change the world, but I would definitely make it a better place for the people who work here and for our clients. And it was that way for a while. We were doing really well, and I had a hand in that. Then everything went to hell in a handbasket and Richard seems to have forgotten what I did to help him get on top in the first place.

Whatever we're doing in this meeting, I'll be damned if I'll sit quietly and let anyone run us all into the ground.

★ ★ ★

When the meeting time arrived, I was thrilled to be standing in front of the staff. About 25 people altogether, the group seemed happy that Richard had gathered them all and made clear how important it was to him that every single person attend. I was glad, too, that I had had the opportunity previously to meet each one of them, learn more about who they were, and let them get to know me. This way, we could get right to the business at hand.

I thanked everyone for attending on such short notice and reiterated that I'd been working with Richard to help turn things around, and then I let them in on the purpose of our meeting.

"We're going to focus on a subject that can benefit everyone here, not only on the job, but in every area of life," I began.

First I described what energy blocks are, just as I had with Richard. Then I explained that they'd be learning about the blocks from a real-life example: Richard had graciously agreed to serve as our case study. Diving right in, I posed a question to the entire assembly: "What do you believe is your major block to success at O'Connell Consulting, or anywhere else?"

As is usually the case when you ask a group of people an intimate question like this, the room went silent, and you could almost feel people holding their breath. This gave Richard the perfect chance to lead. It was a risk to ask him to respond off the cuff, but I had as much faith in him as he had in me.

"I can understand why people might be hesitant to speak first. That's normal. So, to get the ball rolling, I'll ask Richard what he might have to say."

When I turned to Richard, I noticed he was holding his Solutions Rock inconspicuously in his right hand. After fiddling with it briefly, he answered, "One major block to success here is that everyone feels overwhelmed and burned out. We're each doing the work of more than one person. So I'd say stress can prevent ultimate success."

A few people nodded their heads in agreement. With a quick show of hands, the group indicated they thought Richard was right.

"Feeling stressed at work can certainly slow progress," I observed. "What do you believe causes stress? Let's hear from someone else."

Don was the first to jump in: "Isn't it the amount of work? Isn't that what Richard meant when he said we're all doing the work of more than one person?" Don seemed surprised by my question, as if the answer was obvious.

"Thanks, Don. That depends on the person," I said.

I pointed out that stress isn't something that happens *to* someone. It's something someone *feels* about what's happening. Your capacity to deal with any outer situation is based on your inner perspective.

"Let's say you're an athlete competing in a triathlon. Pretty grueling, right? But why wouldn't you just quit on one of those intense uphill climbs?" I asked. "Because if you're a triathlete, you don't see the 'workload' as a negative; it's a vehicle that gets you where you want to go: the finish line."

Christina chimed in, "So it's how we see things that determines our level of stress?"

She was on the right track. "Yes, thank you, Christina. To put a fine point on it, **how we see *ourselves* determines everything**."

Your current self and world views are based on your life experiences and how they have affected you, and the Big Four energy blocks are the four greatest barriers to seeing yourself the way you'd really like, I explained. "When these blocks exist within you, they shape how you view yourself and the world in which you live."

We were ready to examine each of the blocks: limiting beliefs, false assumptions, interpretations, and gremlins.

## Energy Block #1: Limiting Beliefs

"How do your beliefs hinder or help you?" I asked.

We began our discussion of limiting beliefs by defining what those are: **Limiting beliefs hold you back from success.** If you don't believe something is possible, you're not likely to attempt it. Even if you do, you won't devote much energy to achieving that goal.

> *More often than not, you accept a limiting belief as true because you've learned it from someone else, often your parents, another authority figure, the media, a book, a movie, or through any direct or indirect experience.*

Here's a classic example of a limiting belief: Up until 1954, it was commonly held that running a mile in under four minutes was impossible. Moreover, physiologists believed it was extremely dangerous even to attempt it. Yet on May 6 of that year, Roger Bannister crossed the finish line in 3 minutes and 59.4 seconds, thereby disproving the myth forever.

Of course, it's remarkable that Bannister accomplished his feat: It required that he completely ignore the prevailing, limiting belief and construct an entirely different belief system for himself. What others saw as a limitation, he perceived as opportunity. And once he disproved the presumed limits of the human body, less than two months later, another runner, John Landy, broke Bannister's record with a mile dash of 3 minutes and 57.9 seconds. What's more, within a short period of time, dozens of runners were leaving the four-minute mark in the dust.

As I told Richard's group about this legendary break, I made sure they understood that this phenomenon held true for all four of the energy blocks: *Once you overcome them, they can no longer hold you, and very possibly those around you, back.*

When I asked the group for another example of how limiting beliefs can be broken, Sheila Williamson, Don's assistant, spoke up. "You know our Post-it Notes? This scientist at 3M, Spencer Silver, came up with them while he was supposed to be working on a super-strong glue. But all he could make was a super-weak one. Instead of just throwing his invention away, he realized that his 'failure' could actually be turned into a major success."

"That's a great example, Sheila," I said. "What was the limiting belief that Dr. Silver broke away from?"

"Well, I suppose he ignored the idea that glue that sticks forever is the only one worth having. Glue that doesn't stick turns out to be just as useful."

"Exactly. The rest made business history."

At that point I asked Richard to rise. "I'd like to share an example from your beloved founder, Mr. Richard O'Connell. Let's all give him a hand!" I teased. With a wide smile, I led the applause.

I revealed to the group that during my first meeting with Richard, he said he couldn't get past how he felt about what was going on within the company. His emotions were hindering his ability to deal with things the way an effective leader should.

"I also heard him saying that he believed emotions, especially those of a leader, don't belong in the workplace. So even though he felt them, he never showed them." I turned to Richard for his response, putting him in a position where he needed to be open and honest. "Please say more about that, Richard."

Richard sensed where I was going with my line of questioning and responded, saying that in the past he honestly believed that he would be seen as weak if he showed emotion on the job. He always thought that a good leader was unfailingly strong and didn't let his feelings get in the way of success.

"However," he went on, having far more to say, "I'm reconsidering this belief – perhaps a limiting belief – in a new way. And I'd like some honest feedback from you all about it. I'm thinking that it isn't wise to try to separate yourself from your emotions. In fact, people might understand me better and see me as more accessible if I let them know what and how I feel about our business."

Richard took a deep breath and forged ahead.

"Perhaps it would be beneficial for everyone if I expressed how much I genuinely care about you all." He paused again, allowing the emotion to fill his heart and enrich his voice. "I know I have not been forthcoming about how much I appreciate you, but when I allow myself to reflect on what a gift it is to have you here, when I stop and think how much of your lives you pour into this business, of the time and talent you choose to give to this company – and that you could choose to devote somewhere else . . . For a long time, I was so wrapped up in my own stuff that I couldn't even see the amazing team we have assembled here. I feel so fortunate to have you in my life and the life of this company." Richard's eyes started to tear up and his voice got softer. "You need to know that I think of all of you as part of my family."

Silence filled the air, and each person's eyes were fixed on Richard's. Many had the soft, radiant look that true affection brings to a person's face. Some had tears in their eyes, too.

That was moving, but what happened next was shocking.

From opposite sides of the room, and nearly simultaneously, Don and Tonya rose to their feet and began to applaud Richard. This time, it was not in jest. When the rest of the group stood and joined them, Richard was overwhelmed. Pulling out a handkerchief to wipe his eyes, he said "Thank you" to the group, then turned to me and said it again.

★ ★ ★

After the applause had run its course, people took their seats, and I asked Richard, "What do you think now about your belief that emotions are best left out of business?"

"I guess . . . do I need to rethink all of my old ideas and figure out where they've come from?"

"Actually, just reassessing your beliefs today and choosing what you would like to believe going forward will work just fine."

"Okay," Richard responded, "I'll keep that in mind." Richard was showing how invested he was, not only by serving as my example but also by doing the inner work necessary for his personal and professional breakthrough.

"What other beliefs that you've heard me mention do you think might be worth addressing here?" There were a number of Richard's other beliefs I could have brought up, but I chose this one first: "It's up to you to separate fact from fiction here, but I found it interesting that you stated, as if it were a fact, that people in your type of business are looking to make a quick hit then get out – that they're not in it for the long haul. Tell us about why you believe that's true."

"Caught me." Richard smiled and turned to face his staff. He told them that even though he said that to me, he hadn't wanted to believe it. "I was probably trying to rationalize what I thought would be the end of all our hard work – that despite your work with me we wouldn't be able to stay afloat. In retrospect, I think I didn't want to blame myself (although, internally, I did), and I was looking for scapegoats."

What he was saying made good sense. And it also lay another stepping stone for boosting the energy of the group. "So what do you really believe?" I asked.

"That we can sustain this business for as long as we want," Richard answered quickly. "That we can achieve this goal through determination, creativity, and the flexibility needed to meet market challenges."

"Sounds like you're also saying this industry may not be so bad after all."

Richard nodded, relaxed but energized. "It's neither good nor bad; it simply is what it is," he said. "If we want to prosper, we need to roll with the punches."

At this point, the meeting had taken the tenor of a rally, and the group once again applauded Richard. I congratulated him, too, saying that he was clearly challenging his old beliefs and creating new ones that worked for instead of against him and the company. "How do your new beliefs affect your actions?"

"My new beliefs keep me focused in the right direction," he replied. "For example, since I now believe that we can be in this for the long term, our plans will address that goal."

I zeroed in on another old belief. "In one of our early conversations, I remember you telling me that life was hard, that few people were trustworthy and that fewer were truly happy. You also said that most people are afraid of something. Please tell me more about how those ideas may have held you back."

Richard nodded, his conviction deepening. "I see what you're getting at," he replied. "Well, I do believe life can be hard. But I guess that's just a perception, and if I continue to believe that, then some of what we'd like to accomplish in this company may appear too daunting to attempt. Perhaps it's better just to say that life is what it is, and while many people see it as hard, we can see it in any way that we choose."

Now we were picking up speed. "Ahhh," I said, celebrating the links we were making. "If that were true, what would be different for you?"

Richard's eyes fired with new light. "There would be the possibility I could emulate Roger Bannister. I could change at least my own ideas of what is possible. That way, I'd always be able to choose how I feel about anything." Richard was now operating using Level 3 energy. He was more consciously choosing how he felt about each situation in his life.

"So, while you might not run a four-minute mile, you might indeed run a successful business?"

Richard shook his head and smiled. "You never miss an opportunity for a pun, do you?"

"Got me," I acknowledged, smiling.

★ ★ ★

Testing the group's grasp of how dramatically our limiting beliefs can hem us in, I asked them, "What might be a more productive conviction to adopt than Richard's earlier conclusion that people are untrustworthy and unhappy?"

Joan Hendricks, Richard's bookkeeper, quickly met the challenge.

"People are just people. For Richard and me, and for everyone else in this room, it's really up to us how we see anyone," she said, her eyes comfortably looking into mine.

"Great thought, Joan," I said. "Even if someone seems untrustworthy to us, this doesn't mean that's what they are. In the same vein, if we view someone as a trustworthy person, this may not be true, either. Joan was right on. People are just people. The labels you give them are the ones you choose. We would all be able to accept and relate to others better if we just avoided using labels and judgments," I concluded.

Several people nodded their agreement, and everyone seemed in agreement with what I was proposing. Focusing my attention back on Richard, I said that I wanted to illustrate one more belief that could keep him from improving himself and his business.

"You said that most people were afraid of something. Whether that's true or not isn't the issue. What's important is this: what's true for you?"

"My perspective on that has changed as well. I'm not most people," Richard said with a natural smile. "I'm me. Generalities have nothing to do with me. I can think, feel, and act any way I choose."

"And how does that relate to O'Connell Consulting?" I prodded.

"My new belief tells me that just because taking a risk, or trying something new might be scary, it doesn't have to stop us from doing it. The people in this room are not most people, either, and we're not just another company. From now on, no one, including the doubting Thomases within each of us, will tell us what isn't possible for this organization."

Everyone was riveted by Richard's words, and many were smiling and nodding in agreement. The feelings of camaraderie flooded the room with powerful, positive energy.

During these moments of solidarity, you could feel how everyone was bonding. Before my eyes, Richard was becoming a transformed leader, inspiring everyone at the meeting, including me.

---

**Core Energy Technique**

*Challenge Limiting Beliefs*

There are many ways to challenge limiting beliefs. Among these, we can:

- Provide evidence to the contrary
- Explore what effect the belief has had on the person's life
- Ask the person who stated the belief for proof of its truth

In addition, simply examining the belief with questions like "How true do you believe that is?" and the rhetorical "Where did you get that idea?" can also work remarkably well.

---

## Energy Block #2: Assumptions

"Let's move on to the next of the Big Four energy blocks," I said. "This one crops up from our false assumptions."

For our purposes here, I told the group, we would define an *assumption* as a belief that, because something happened in the past, it's going to happen again. For example, I ask someone out on a date, but get turned down. As a result, I assume that when I next ask someone on a date, I will meet with the same rejection. Because this has happened once, I conclude that it will always be the case. This assumption, in turn, prevents me from asking anyone out ever again.

"False assumptions are especially debilitating to businesses like yours," I told Richard's employees. "When you believe you already 'know' something won't work because of a past experience, you might not even consider it as a possibility in the future. Further, if you do try it, you might either subconsciously sabotage your own efforts, or move in a counterproductive direction. To see how this works, let's look at something that Richard said previously."

I wanted everyone to pay close attention to my example, so I asked Richard if I could divulge information about an assumption he made about a few of his staffers. He agreed, and after I assured the group I wouldn't embarrass anyone, they gave me their go-ahead, too.

When Richard and I first met, I told them, he said that some of his key personnel didn't communicate effectively. (A few heads surreptitiously swiveled to see how Don and Tonya were reacting to this line, but both of them kept their faces unreadable.) He believed that nothing could change this. At the time, that assumption led to a disturbing conclusion. Richard believed that he either had to live with the way things were, or find a new team.

"I'm telling you this because history doesn't predict the future," I said, "and I'm urging you to avoid making decisions based on assumptions. Just think about what might have happened if I had not questioned Richard about this." I explained that Richard and I had talked about whether his assuming that key staffers could never communicate effectively was accurate.

Richard stood without my prompting him. "You know, the fact that you're all here now speaks to the fact that I no longer believe that our communication can't be improved. The people I have on my team are all truly talented. I have no doubt that soon we'll be communicating far more effectively than before. And today's meeting is the first step toward making this happen."

Applause sounded again, now becoming a register of each energy change in the group. It seemed a good time to get more personal, so I shifted gears. "To continue, in one of our first sessions, Richard told me he hadn't been able to rev people up about their jobs. He was convinced he could never be a leader who inspires. But once we challenged Richard's assumption about his potential, the issue was no longer if Richard would become a great leader, but when."

I paused for emphasis.

"As most of you know, Richard has worked overtime to point O'Connell Consulting in a new direction. From what we've heard so far today, I think we can all say something with complete conviction: the man before us today is not the same one who uttered that ridiculous statement about his own limitations."

When the ovation ended, we stopped for a 15-minute break. Three things were notable. First, Nate remained in the back of the room while everyone else scurried about. Second, a group gathered around Richard to shake his hand and to chat. And third, Don and Tonya walked into the hallway together, talking in muted tones. *Well, that's a huge difference right there, just turning the volume down*, I thought.

---

**Core Energy Technique**

*Challenge Assumptions*

The main question to ask when challenging an assumption is simply "Just because that happened in the past, why must it happen again?"

Challenging assumptions can sometimes be more involved than challenging limiting beliefs. This is because limiting beliefs are usually created from what you've been told, while assumptions are primarily based on personal experience.

As a consequence, assumptions are usually more internalized and emotional than limiting beliefs. The result is that, after an initial challenge, resistance is natural. You may have to delve a bit deeper to remove the emotion of the past experience before you can move forward. Validating the perspective (acknowledging that it's "normal" or "what you'd expect") will usually lessen the emotional attachment to the assumption.

---

★ ★ ★

"I was going to talk with you about the same thing," Tonya said.

"I'm glad we're clearing the air," Don told her. "This has gone on long enough. If we stop fighting each other, we can put more energy into reenergizing this company. And if we're going after someone, then let it be the competition. And let's do it together. They won't stand a chance."

Tonya was glad that Don had approached her, but she wasn't totally surprised. He had called her a little earlier that day, before they were notified that the meeting was scheduled, and asked if she had some time to speak with him. When she pressed him to find out what he wanted, he finally said, "Look, Tonya, it's about time we sit down and come up with better ways for us to work together. I realize that I've been carrying around some heavy weight, and that you probably have been, too. How about we stop trying to drop it on each other's heads?"

And then he laughed, which she found completely confusing, because they just didn't laugh together. But she'd joined him anyway, awkward and trying to figure out what he was up to.

So here he was in front of her now, owning up to a number of *assumptions* and *limiting beliefs* he'd had about her and the company.

"You're really taking this meeting to heart," she observed.

"Hey, I saw you standing up and clapping with me earlier," he teased her. "Don't try to play it so cool."

"Mea culpa." This time Tonya laughed easily. "Okay, so you and I obviously both love this man and this company. I think we can set aside our differences and get through this. We'll just have to agree to disagree on certain things, but our different opinions may work to the company's advantage, you know? Checks and balances, and all that."

As Don and Tonya talked, they discovered that once they stopped bickering and really listened to one another, they actually agreed on a number of key points. One of them was what to do about Nate.

As people began shuffling back into the conference room, Don motioned to Tonya, "Hey, we have to get back in there, but maybe later you and I can go see Richard together about getting rid of the dead wood around here."

Tonya and Don shook hands and walked back into the meeting, a few minutes late but light years ahead.

★ ★ ★

When we reconvened, Don and Tonya sat next to each other. I wondered if Richard noticed.

## Energy Block #3: Interpretations

We were ready to move on to the next of the Big Four energy blocks: the barrier built by interpretations. I explained that when you interpret something, you create an opinion about an event, situation, or experience in life. What's the result?

> *Most people believe their interpretations are the only possible explanation for an event, when actually an interpretation often represents only one viewpoint among the many that are possible.*

My earlier example of dating came in handy again. This time, I explained that I had interpreted the woman's "no" as meaning I hadn't dressed nicely enough. While that could have been the actual reason, when you make interpretations, you decide that your viewpoint is the *only* one that's true. That leads to certain actions, which in this case might have meant spending a lot of money on new clothes.

Tonya was listening closely. I asked her what the repercussions of this behavior in the workplace would look like. When she spoke, I supposed that she was speaking to Don first, and the rest of us next.

"What you're saying is easy enough to see," she said. "My viewpoint of a particular situation is what I believe is the only explanation. If I'm not aware of another point of view, I might waste a lot of time marching off in the wrong direction."

"Exactly," I said, emphasizing that the "wrong direction" could also cost the company a truckload of money. I also made a mental note: *Tonya is starting to acknowledge that things may not always be so black and white. She's definitely moving into anabolic territory.*

Offering another instance, I mentioned an interpretation that Richard had made several months back. He'd told me that his staff was laughing at his leadership ability. "If anyone in Richard's position felt that to be true," I said, "just imagine how emotionally devastating it would be to them. They might not even want to come to work.

"Why don't you tell us, Richard, what led to that interpretation?"

Richard was candid, although it was a little uncomfortable for him. "Well, I was seeing myself as a lousy leader already when I was walking past the kitchen area one day. Christina, Joan, and Ruth were together, taking a break. As they saw me pass, they stopped talking. When I continued on, I could hear them laughing."

"So you decided they were laughing at how much you'd failed to lead?"

Richard shrugged. "I wasn't sure, but the thought certainly crossed my mind," he admitted.

"What do you think today?"

"I'm still not certain, but I know now my initial interpretation probably wasn't the only possible one," he replied.

I told the group that we can't always find out what other people are thinking and feeling. "The point is, however, that it's usually not in our best interest to believe that our interpretation is 'reality.' How much sense does this make?"

Christina decided to answer my somewhat rhetorical question: "You know, it really does make a lot of sense," she said. "But can I take a moment to talk about the day that Richard's mentioned? I do remember it." I nodded, and she focused on Richard. "Ruth was telling us a joke. Not exactly in good taste. It was actually pretty funny, but when I saw you walk by, I remembered one of the company memos saying we needed to gossip less. I thought you might be upset because we were fooling around. I did all I could to hold my laughter until you passed!" Joan and Ruth both said, "True!"

"There you have it!" I announced. Not only did Richard falsely interpret the event, but also his three employees also generated an assumption: although Richard counseled his staff against participating in office gossip in the past, Christina, Joan, and Ruth interpreted that to mean he would always react negatively if he saw his staff talking and having a good time.

"I could even delve deeper and ask how you interpreted his initial memo, and then invite him to clarify it, and so on," I said to Christina.

"That's why it's so important to break through these blocks, because they build on one another and eventually tumble, or at least continue to impede us until we let them go."

Pressing on with another example of an interpretation that could really hit home, I mentioned the brainstorming session they had completed together in a previous meeting. "Richard told me that when he asked you what you thought was causing the decline in revenues, there were dozens of answers, all of which were perfectly valid. Before Richard asked you this, he had assumed that his own answer was the only one. But by entertaining other possibilities, look at how it's created opportunities for correction and creation."

"Let me repeat this, just so it's crystal clear," I said. "*If you stick with your first and only interpretation, you have little chance of focusing on any other possibility. It means that all of your focus, and therefore your energy, would be displaced.* As with any of the Big Four energy blocks, if you feel you have little control over what may happen tomorrow, your level of engagement will also be low."

The body language of several staffers suggested they were seeing with different eyes. Richard's comment expressed the continuing transformation. "I can see more and more of the picture you're painting," he said, then addressed the entire group. "Are you all getting the same thing?"

They responded with a chorus of agreement.

"That's great," I replied, feeling my own energy continuing to build. "How possible is it that your previously bleak interpretation of your company's future affected the rest of your thinking, and your actions as well?"

"I get your drift," Richard replied. "If I believed at the time that we were going down, and I interpret the reasons why as being outside our control, then I may unconsciously have already given up. That would *definitely* have affected my decisions."

I nodded an emphatic yes. "For all of you, going forward, pay attention to the interpretations you make because they lead to emotional reactions and decisions that match."

## Core Energy Technique

*Challenge Interpretations*

Interpretations can be directly challenged with a single question: "What's another way to look at that?"

It's also helpful to ask what another person might say happened. This is particularly useful for resolving conflict when someone is upset about something that someone else has done. Asking the person to imagine what the other individual's perspective might be can lead to a more objective point of view.

One way to prompt this understanding is to ask, "If so-and-so told us why she'd become so upset with you, what might she say?"

## Energy Block #4: Gremlins

It was now time to tackle the last, but certainly not the least, of the Big Four energy blocks. This barrier is the gremlin within every one of us: the part of us that makes us hold back and stay safe and small. Unlike the inner critic, which judges and criticizes what we've already done, the gremlin tries to scare us to prevent us from doing something in the future.

*Your gremlin tells you not to try, never to take a risk, always to take the safe road, and to compromise your life by playing small. The message from your gremlin's warnings is that you're just not good enough to reach the summit of success or maintain success if you even got there.*

"Regardless of any evidence to the contrary, the gremlin's annoying voice continues to whisper: 'It ain't gonna happen.' This debilitating message bubbles up in many forms: 'I'm not smart enough, experienced enough, or attractive enough.' It all comes back to a simple and quite vicious block: 'I'm just not good enough to cut it.'"

I took a second to look at Nate, someone I imagined was regularly in the grips of his personal gremlin. He was hunkered down in the corner, and I couldn't tell if he was taking notes (an encouraging idea!) or if he was napping. Either way, I couldn't see his eyes, and I couldn't gauge whether he was connecting with what I was saying. No matter; I addressed my comments to all the people in the room, many of whom were scribbling furiously but looking up regularly to make sure they caught everything.

"Each gremlin is highly personal," I went on. "It's rooted deeply inside us and carries the most intense emotional charge of any of the blocks we've explored. Your gremlin thrives on fear. When you hear its whispers, your motivation to try withers. You dread failing, feeling pain, and being embarrassed. You can even be scared of succeeding if the gremlin convinces you that you'll fail eventually.

"The most effective way to corral your gremlin is to expose it to the daylight." I said.

Richard had made several statements during our sessions that had clearly been mouthed by his gremlin. In bringing them before the group, I hoped he would recognize a few of the messages these statements were sending. That way, when he heard the statements again, he would know that they came from a part of him that always tugs at him to play it safe.

"Richard, you told me before that you failed as a leader, that you let everyone down, and that you blamed yourself for your company's hard times. These are all variations on the same theme: 'I'm not good enough.' But that wasn't you talking. It was your gremlin in the shadows."

"How can you know that for sure?" he asked, seeming to speak for everyone.

"Think about those statements for a moment," I prompted him. "How did they make you feel?"

"Well, certainly not good," Richard said. "In fact, they felt like a pit in my stomach."

I nodded, since we've all trudged down this road. "That's dissonance you feel," I replied. "The dissonance surfaces from the gremlin's battle with the part of you that knows the truth."

"So while part of me is a gnarly gremlin, another part of me has a far more accurate message – if only I'm willing to listen?" queried Richard.

"Exactly," I said, pleased at Richard's bull's-eye. "You can designate this positive part of who you are with whatever label you want. In business, I'm inclined to call it something like your inner genius. In other contexts, people call it the higher self or the soul."

I switched my focus to the group at large. "Remember," I said, "we can always choose which voice to heed. The good news is that if you pit your genius against your gremlin, your genius will trump the gremlin every time. Not just sometimes, but every single time."

---

### Core Energy Technique

*Dispatch Gremlins*

The easiest way to banish a gremlin is to reveal its face. Once revealed, actually giving the gremlin a name helps to separate it from you. (When naming the gremlin, do not choose the name of someone you know, as that makes it harder to distinguish the gremlin from that person.)

In iPEC's training programs, I often ask that people create a gremlin – a puppet, an action figure, a paper doll, whatever – and bring it to the training. By learning how this mini-monster looks outside of them, they can come to see it in objective terms. Then they can lessen its power.

Remember that the gremlin is only a small part of who you are, not the whole identity. By talking about gremlins, and perhaps even by giving them names, you can sap some of their strength. Then, by getting reconnected with your true self, you'll easily quiet the yapping of the gremlin.

I thanked everyone for their time and participation. The meeting was over, but the catharsis had just begun. Everyone chatted in relaxed conversation before leaving the conference room. Everyone, that is, except Nate. He snuck out as soon as he could.

# 9 | Removing Obstacles to Success (Level 3)

*Everything can be taken from a man but one thing: the last of human freedoms –*
*to choose one's attitude in any given set of circumstances – to choose one's own way.*
—Viktor Frankl, neurologist, psychiatrist,
and Holocaust survivor

The day before our next scheduled appointment, Richard called to tell me some "good and perhaps disturbing" news. Since our team meeting, he was no longer avoiding Don, and instead, the two of them had been talking regularly – and when they talked, Don no longer focused the conversations on getting rid of Tonya. He seemed to have dropped that line of thinking altogether.

"In the last couple of weeks," Richard said, "Don has been much more engaged, and I haven't heard one shouting match between him and Tonya."

The good news continued. Even though Don's title was marketing director, he had started taking some of the sales work on himself and had even secured a few new accounts. This meant that not only was he making Richard's life easier, but he was also bringing in some welcome income.

"But here's the part that has me a little rattled. I'm wondering if this is just the quiet before the storm, because Tonya has asked to speak with me immediately. What she has to say won't wait, she tells me. So I'm scheduled to see her first thing tomorrow morning. Do you think that my spending so much time with Don has sent her over the edge?"

I cautioned Richard about the traps of assumptions and interpretations and reminded him that if he didn't fret in advance, his energy wouldn't be unnecessarily zapped. He'd find out what was really going on soon enough.

Richard said he'd prefer it if we didn't delay my arrival the next day. Could I stop by for the meeting with Tonya? He already asked her about that, and she said it would be fine.

Sure, I told him, but I was wondering if a part of him had slipped back into Level 1 and wanted me there as a crutch. So I wouldn't have to speculate, I mentioned my concern.

"Oh, no," he replied. "You misunderstood me. I don't need you there. I want you there so we can both see how well I can handle myself in this challenging situation."

Music to my ears. Now I was looking forward to the next day.

★ ★ ★

When I arrived, Christina greeted me warmly. *That's a new one,* I thought. *I like it.* She said she loved the team meeting and she was feeling optimistic, both because of the meeting and the other changes underway at the company. She thanked me for my help. This was a new woman, indeed. Her desk was organized; the boxes were gone. In a word, the reception area, and especially Christina, looked *fresh.*

Expressing my appreciation for her, I saw that Richard was already on his way to the front door before she could alert him to my arrival. Even though we might be on our way to facing Tonya's wrath, Richard seemed calm and confident.

"Hi there, Christina. And good morning, Bruce. Good to see you both," he said cheerfully. "Excuse us, Christina, Tonya's waiting for us in her office. Unless you need anything before we start . . . ?" He raised his eyebrows at Christina, who shook her head in response.

"Okay, Bruce, let's get to it."

*Great! No waffling, no buying time, no avoidance. And he's treating Christina like someone who's important to him! Let's get to it, indeed.*

Tonya's office looked different from the last time I visited, too. She had redecorated, added plants, put some pictures on the wall, and made one addition that startled both Richard and me.

Don Taylor stood beside her desk.

He invited us in and closed the door behind us like a father lion protecting Tonya's sacred den. Before anyone even spoke, they had provided some significant details. First, since Richard was unaware of Don's presence in Tonya's office, I figured that Don and Tonya must have been working since early morning, before Richard arrived. *Was this the beginning of a partnership?* Second, the two of them were interacting comfortably, arranging things for us and putting us at ease. This was obviously a well-choreographed meeting. Third, the mere fact that Don had closed the door showed a newfound conscientiousness about privacy. I couldn't wait to hear what they had to say.

"Richard, Bruce," Tonya began, "Don and I have been discussing a few things that happened recently. One was the meeting about a month or so ago where Richard said he'd stick with us until the end, if it came. It was clear, then, how truly dedicated to the company you are," she said, nodding at Richard while she spoke.

"Next, the group meeting you ran, Bruce, was an eye-opener for us both. We realized how our actions have affected Richard. And how our perceptions have been skewed. We apologize for that." This time, Don was nodding.

"Here's where we are now: We want to help. And we've decided that instead of counting on everyone else, it's up to us to take matters into our own hands. We've spent a great deal of time drawing up the beginnings of a new marketing plan."

"It's excellent," Don added, "if we do say so ourselves!" He chuckled and patted Tonya on the shoulder.

Richard was stunned. Relieved yet still skeptical, he couldn't help but wonder, *When does the boom get lowered?*

But there was no boom, except for the booming silence from Richard. Emotionally overwhelmed, all he could manage was a quiet "Thank you" as he took the plan. Then, starting to snap out of it, he promised to study it carefully and talk with them soon about implementation.

It appeared that two of the Fantastic Four had just become the Dynamic Duo.

"Listen, Richard," Don said. "We've got something important to ask you. We've been reviewing some budget and personnel issues and considering where we can make some improvements. We need to ask you do something difficult. Honestly, it's not that difficult for us – for Tonya and me, I mean – because we're not close to him, but . . . it's Nate. You know the numbers, Richard. The guy's dragging all of us down. We want you to consider letting him go."

Unfazed by this potentially negative turn in the conversation, Richard said, "Don, you're right that this is an important issue to address. Let me assure you that I'm on it."

Don regarded Richard like a parent humoring a child.

Tonya crossed her arms in front of her chest, looking unsatisfied with Richard's nonanswer. "Look, if you decide you want one of us to give him the boot, you just say the word. We can take care of this for you."

"Thanks, Tonya. I'll let you know what I want to do. I'll see you both later. And I mean it, you guys: *thanks.*"

With that, Richard and I left Don and Tonya in her office.

★ ★ ★

I nudged Richard. "That was a nice surprise, wasn't it?" I asked.

"You know it," Richard affirmed, still beaming. "Hey, what did you think about Tonya saying that instead of counting on everyone else, they decided to take things in their own hands? Doesn't that sound like a shift to Level 3? Taking responsibility?"

"Great insight, Richard. Why Level 3 and not Level 4?"

He thought for a moment and then asked for a hint.

"What message did they give you about the others in the company?" I prodded.

"Ah! I get it," he exclaimed. "They still judge the others as inadequate. They released blame and anger toward everyone else and shifted the focus onto themselves, which is definitely Level 3. At Level 4, there would have been no blame and maybe they would also seek to help the others do their jobs better. Or seek their advice on how to make other improvements.

"Really, Bruce, this is getting exciting, not only experiencing these levels for myself, but also seeing the people around me changing, too. It makes me feel more like a leader, knowing that I had a hand in it. But more than that, I can see how the success of the company hinges on all of this, and I'm very encouraged."

We were at his office door now, and I looked at "my" new chair with undisguised delight. This lovely piece of furniture was only one of several upgrades Richard had made as part of O'Connell Consulting's facelift. Apparently, they were going for a look of casual luxury, as it was obvious the chair and the accessories they selected cost the company no small amount, but they were unpretentious and inviting.

"Hey, Richard," I teased, assessing the posh new environment, "what's going on here?"

"You mean, 'What's a guy doing spending money on top-grade leather and new carpet when the ship's sinking?' I have a little secret to share with you. I haven't emailed you about it because I wanted to tell you in person.

"Remember I've been having team meetings with several groups in the company, including sales? Well, that's started to pay off. Couple it with the fact that Don has been attracting a few new clients, and O'Connell Consulting is making a major financial shift. We're not sinking. We're not living off of our cushion anymore, and we're not throwing money away, either. I mean, this is a big deal! Profits are up. *Up*, Bruce!"

"That's the best news I could hear today," I said.

As I let my eyes wander around the room, taking in its rich brown tones, my eyes fell on new photographs of Richard with his wife and children.

The feeling in his office was cozy, elegant, accomplished. He looked happy in both the pictures and in real life.

I pressed my back into the contoured leather. "I've got to say, Richard, this is the most comfortable chair I've ever sat in," I said.

"Thought you'd like it," he replied.

★ ★ ★

Things were looking up at O'Connell Consulting, no doubt about it. Tonya and Don had not only reached a détente, but they were working together for the benefit of everyone. Christina had made a complete turnaround, and Richard was in a different frame of mind – one where he was clearing away the clutter, both internally and externally, and building something entirely new.

When I asked about Nate's progress, Richard told me that he'd met with Nate three times since our last meeting, and each time had been left drained. Nate had agreed to assignments and not done them. He didn't seem willing to fight for himself.

"I consistently sense victim thinking," Richard reported. "I'd like to continue to try to get a buy-in and some action from him, but I don't know what else to do. Any ideas?"

"How effective was Nate when he was at his best?" I asked, changing the subject slightly.

"Honestly, his best was never very good. He's been with me a long time. When I began this company, I couldn't afford high salaries, and Nate agreed to work for a lower wage. I'm sure that's part of why I've felt that I 'owe' him something."

"Why do you think he agreed to work at a lower wage?" I probed.

"At the time, I thought he was excited about my vision for the company and wanted to get in on the ground floor. But now, I think it's likely that he felt he was worth only that amount."

"So this question of 'owing' him something . . . Where do you think you got that idea?"

Richard admitted that this was probably just a limiting belief, or even his gremlin, so I asked him, "What's the truth in this situation?"

"If anything, he owes it to himself to get some help."

Eureka! Richard was starting to see something new in all this. So I asked, "Then what's next? You've been working to help him turn it around, but he hasn't come through, and you also realize your hesitation in letting him go has its roots in one of the Big Four energy blocks. So what's your next move?"

Richard seemed to shrink. "I think I'd like a little more time with him. I know Don and Tonya want him gone, but do you think we have to do this now?"

*Ah, Level 1 rears its head.* To help Richard see other options, we talked about what the various levels of response could be.

*Level 1*: "More time," as Richard called it, was just code for not dealing with Nate's poor performance. Avoid conflict with Don and Tonya; avoid conflict with Nate.

*Level 2*: Decide to dismiss Nate and "punish" him for not succeeding: take Nate a box, ask him to clear his desk, and instruct him to get out.

*Level 3*: Go ahead and fire Nate, but have Betty do it for him because there's no need to involve himself. End the "problem" and move on.

*Level 4*: Figure out a way to help Nate as Richard lets him go. Richard could assist Nate in getting the professional and personal coaching he needs to come out ahead.

As Richard came up with each of the responses to the levels, he became more and more aware of how he could choose to indulge an impulse (Levels 1 or 2), do what he called the "right" thing (Level 3), or even go beyond that to do the "best" thing (Level 4 and above). In the end, Richard decided it was time to fire Nate, and that he would do it himself. He asked Christina to move a few things around for the rest of the morning, and then he called Nate.

## Want an Easy Way to Remember the Levels?

Here are two illustrations of dominating thoughts at each level:

FEELINGS . . .

- Level 1: "I hate myself."
- Level 2: "I hate you."
- Level 3: "I forgive you."
- Level 4: "I feel for you."
- Level 5: "I understand you."
- Level 6: "I am you."
- Level 7: "I Am."

WINNING AND LOSING . . .

- Level 1: "I lose."
- Level 2: "You lose."
- Level 3: "I win, and if you win too, great."
- Level 4: "You win, and if I win too, great."
- Level 5: "We both win."
- Level 6: "Everyone always wins."
- Level 7: "Winning and losing are illusory concepts created by the ego."

Richard's conversation with his long-time and long-suffering employee had its ups and downs. Going into the meeting, Richard was ready to help his old friend. He was also more than willing to face his own fears and stop delaying the inevitable. But when Nate started his shamefaced routine, it definitely blurred Richard's focus.

As I sat in the room with them, watching the conversation unfold, I was fascinated by the way Richard moved through the levels, running up and down the chart like someone practicing the piano. He was compassionate and strong, guiding Nate to accept his offer of a month's severance pay, plus career coaching, and even a few months of personal counseling with the therapist of Nate's choice. But Nate wasn't having it and was stuck in a mood of desolation, constantly asking Richard, "How can you do this to me?" So Richard vacillated. When his Level 4 resolve wavered, he dipped into trying to appease Nate's hurt feelings and convince him everything was for the best of the company (Level 3), getting angry with Nate for being so stubborn (Level 2), and staring silently out the window, wishing for a way to escape (Level 1).

The whole thing took about 45 minutes, ending with Richard patting Nate on the back, telling him that he was willing to do whatever he could to ease Nate's transition, and asking Nate to gather his things and leave within the next hour. Nate, utterly crushed and refusing any help, said he'd be gone in 10 minutes.

★ ★ ★

Later, after I'd shared my observations with Richard, we talked about a Level 5 perspective and specifically what opportunities were opened up to O'Connell Consulting as a result of letting Nate go.

"In a way, it's like cleaning up my office," Richard said at one point. "Now there's room for me to bring in an upgrade: a new employee who will really contribute to our success."

"Now you're talking – and continuing to focus on Level 5, Richard," I encouraged him. "What kind of person would you like to bring on board?"

"Before we get into that," Richard suggested, "I'd like to ask Betty, the human resources manager, to join us. She would probably have some great input here."

"Of course. And while we're talking about this, it would be great for you to pay attention to her reactions. My impression is that she's one of your employees with an anabolic resonating level. I'm thinking she's a prime example of Level 3, mainly because of my prior conversations with her, where she's talked about wanting to put the past behind you, focus on the future, let bygones be bygones ..."

"Yes, I know that's Betty's take. She's pulled me aside before to let me know that she doesn't hold my absentee leadership in the past against me and she's looking forward to great things in the company. I like that about her," added Richard.

"Interesting. How did you feel when she said that?" I prompted.

"I felt that she truly meant she'd like to, as you said, put the past behind us. She's eager to do her part. There was a bit of an undertone of 'you poor thing,' but that's just Betty."

"That's just Level 3," I confirmed. "While not the highest level of functioning," I emphasized, "it's more proactive than reactive, so it can enable a person – specifically a leader – to create more positive changes, rather than just put out fires."

## Looking Forward

Level 3 is the first anabolic energy level. It's positive and productive, living in the world of solutions instead of problems. Those who average a Level 3 still judge others, but they don't focus on blame. At this level, forgiveness isn't about letting someone get away with anything; it's about releasing the negative energy you would otherwise hold.

Relaxed and mellow, Level 3 energy breeds acceptance of the way others are, which usually leads to more cooperation between teams and all the members of a staff. People at this level begin to consider that they are one of many spokes on a wheel. They recognize that to turn the wheel, each spoke does its job.

Instead of focusing on "what's wrong," people at this level are more interested in making a difference. They want to make a contribution in what they do, and they take pride in their achievements.

Level 3 resonating leaders, I pointed out, handle people and situations much differently than their catabolic colleagues would. Instead of being caught up in reacting to emotions, these leaders know how to work with emotions to manage them within themselves and others, responding with logic rather than reacting with emotion.

*One key characteristic of people with Level 3 energy is that they tend to think one thing and say another.* While they intend to make a difference, they can be caught up in ensuring that they appear to be doing well, too. At the same time, they may be greatly concerned with "efficiency" (in other words, not wasting their own time) and ensuring that they come out on top.

★ ★ ★

When Betty arrived, Richard returned to the question of the type of person he'd like to replace Nate. "You know, there's this guy, Kyle Pennington, who works for one of our SEO consultants.

"He's so energetic, yet it's not that freaked-out, sell-sell-sell energy that some salespeople have. He's a friendly guy – you like him instantly – and you just want to figure out a way to do business with him. And then he delivers. He's all over customer service, making sure we get exactly what we expect and then some. I'd love to have someone like that fill the position."

As she took notes on what Richard was saying, Betty looked happy to have been included in the meeting.

*Thank God,* she was thinking. *Took him long enough! He's been saying for a couple months now that he wants to rebuild the business. I'm surprised he hasn't called me in sooner to work this out. But at least he's finally arrived at the obvious conclusion: We need someone else in Nate's position. I bet Don and Tonya had something to do with this . . . At least now those two are ready to put the BS behind them and try to get along for the good of the company. Poor Nate, though. Got caught in the crossfire. But it's time to move on. And there's definitely a way for me to do something great here that will put myself in position for a raise, too.*

"Richard," Betty said, "What if I could get you Kyle – not just someone like him – but Kyle himself?"

# 10

## Putting Your Heart into Your Job (Level 4)

*Nothing contributes so much to tranquilize the mind as a steady purpose —
a point on which the soul may fix its intellectual eye.*

—Mary Wollstonecraft Shelley, writer

After our meeting, Betty immediately went to work contacting Kyle and setting up an appointment for his interview. Richard and I said good-bye until our regular coaching appointment the next day, and I hopped on the train to go home while Richard spent the rest of the afternoon with Don and Tonya, reviewing the marketing plan with them instead of on his own. He also updated them on Nate's termination and the possibilities for a strong replacement.

Both Don and Tonya were supportive (and a little self-congratulatory) about Richard firing Nate. Plus they both knew Kyle and agreed he would light a fire under their sales department, but they were also doubtful that he would leave his current position with the SEO company.

"You know, Richard, we might want to consider taking on someone who is a little less experienced, but who we can train," Don offered, "since budget is still an important concern."

"I appreciate that, but no, I'm through hiring people who aren't up to the job, just to save money," Richard responded.

Tonya seemed encouraged, but Don looked down at the papers in front of him and hunched forward. His body language was protective.

When he spoke again, he sounded territorial. "Well, Kyle may be a hot shot, but he's also young and needs to put in his time in the trenches before he's ready to handle the bigger accounts. We don't want a Nate nightmare all over again, Richard. I'm not losing any of my new clients."

*"I"? "My"? Is this some Level 2 competitiveness coming up?* Richard wondered. *Is he actually threatened by the possibility of us getting another rainmaker on board?* Richard decided that acknowledging Don's contributions to the company and reminding him of his real objectives was the best approach. Also, Don's ego offered Richard a great opportunity to get a buy-in.

---

### Playing the Level Field

Please review the chart on pages 108 and 109. Once you are familiar with the various levels of energy, you can begin to choose the most appropriate level to use in any given situation.

In Richard's situation, he masterfully used the manipulative power of Level 3 energy to encourage Don's buy-in. Remember, at Level 3, Richard's main goal was to win. But unlike Level 2, where winning would come at the cost of someone else's loss, the goal at Level 3 is to try to get the other person to win as well.

Keep in mind that this is not the same as a Level 5 win-win, because at that level, the agenda would be for both people to win, and no less. In this case, Richard didn't feel it was an option for him not to win, but if he could convince Don to buy in, it would be to everyone's advantage. Either way it went, Richard was going to get what he wanted. So for Richard, Level 3 was the best way to address this situation.

"Don, you've obviously made a huge impact on revenues recently, which is one of the reasons I think we can hold out for quality. I believe Kyle is the quality employee we are all looking for," began Richard.

"Of course, any new employee will need your guidance in the beginning, and I know you'll do your best to bring him into the fold. Just imagine what it would be like to have someone as skilled as Kyle as your *partner* in landing more big fish!"

Don looked Richard in the eye again. "I suppose you're right," he admitted, only somewhat reluctant. "If he's willing to collaborate, we can really make some things happen."

*All right,* Richard thought. *That's good enough for now.*

Tonya cautioned, "All of this is exciting, but I don't want to get ahead of ourselves. We haven't hired anyone yet, much less Kyle, and there are still all of these other aspects of the plan to attend to. Gentlemen, can we get back to what's on the docket today?"

"Yes, counsel," Richard teased. "Let's do that. Where were we . . . ?"

## IN HIS OWN WORDS

### Don

You wouldn't believe the changes that have happened around here. It's like working in a completely different company – only you don't have to go through all the hassle of leaving the old one.

That's something I know about, for sure. When the dot-com bubble burst, I was right there in the slippery mess. It was pretty bad: People who'd thought they'd be set for retirement by age 30 found themselves out of a job and begging for work. Lucky for me, I'd never really bought into all the hype. Well, at least I'd never bought into it enough to stop developing my network outside the industry, or to let it keep me from cashing in some of my stock each year. I guess I came out of it okay. My nest egg didn't get boiled nearly as hard as a lot of other people's.

But it definitely toughened my attitudes about the people who work for me. Until recently, it felt right to keep them at arm's length and treat them like they were lower on the food chain. That way, if anything happened to blow up this business, they couldn't blame me for getting their hopes up unrealistically.

Now I can see that I've paid a price for that, and it's cost the business, too. Not that I'm perfect now, or so enlightened that I don't still struggle with that gremlin Richard and Bruce are always talking about. I could feel that my gremlin showed up the minute they brought up this Kyle kid. What if he comes in here and just by sheer persistence and hyperactivity generates some cash? What if Richard makes him his golden boy, and I'm pushed out?

Okay, I realize I'm overreacting. And this kind of worrying isn't going to get me anywhere. It puts me right back where I was: at odds with my colleagues instead of in league with them. It's important that I just focus on creating the kind of partnership I would like to have with someone. We could use the infusion of new blood, that's for sure. And if this old dog can teach the new pup some of my best tricks, we'll all be better off.

★ ★ ★

Christina was positively radiant. When I walked through the doors the next morning, she called, "Bruce, look! The new desk has arrived. Isn't it gorgeous?"

"Gorgeous, yes! The rest of the office looks great, too. I know you had a lot to do with that."

"Why, thank you very much, Bruce," Christina replied, shining with self-confidence.

"You seem so lively this morning. Anything special going on besides the desk?"

Her smile faded, and she looked embarrassed. "Is it too much?" she asked.

"No, no, that's not what I meant. I like it. It's just such a change from when I first met you."

"Oh." Now she really looked sheepish. "I'm sorry about that. We were all going through a rough patch back then. It's been, what? Four months or so? Feels like four years ago. Well, I don't feel as if I've 'changed' so much as become more of myself again."

"I understand, and there's no need to apologize. If you don't mind a second or two of my philosophizing, I believe that the greatest improvement we can ever make is becoming more of who we truly are."

Her smile came back as she nodded slowly and kept her eyes on mine.

With that, Richard arrived at her desk, obviously enjoying it as he ran his hand along the curve of the mahogany.

"Hi, Christina. Hey, thanks for leaving your report for me. I read it last night and have just a couple of questions, but it looks great. Let's plan to talk about that tomorrow, okay?"

"You got it. Does 11:00 work for you?"

Observing the two of them in this conversation, I enjoyed watching them have a completely animated exchange about a mundane subject. They were obviously in sync, and it was fun to see.

"Is that okay, Bruce?" asked Christina.

"What?" I had been caught up in my own thoughts and missed their question.

Christina brought me up to speed. "Does it work for you if Richard and I have lunch today to discuss this report? We can't do it tomorrow and Richard doesn't want to put it off. Do you have something you can do on your own?"

"Oh, sure, we can go our separate ways at lunch. Let's just pick a time to reconvene."

Wrapping up our discussion with Christina, Richard invited me back to his office.

When we arrived, I was impressed all over again with the comfortable elegance of Richard's work space. It hadn't been a hovel before, but now it was beautiful, refined yet friendly and dynamic, a clear expression of Richard's personality. The Solutions Rock had a subtle presence on his desk.

"So, Richard, how are things going?"

"Pret-tay, pret-tay, pret-tay good!" Richard said, laughing at his impersonation of comedian Larry David.

Richard reviewed his recent accomplishments. "Deal with Nate: check. Continue working with Don and Tonya to solidify their move from Level 2 to Level 3: check. Meet with staff and get to know them better, plus listen for their gifts: check – but this will be long term, plus I'm in conversations with Don and Tonya about this. Talk with everyone about the company mission statement as well as personal missions and goals: okay, that one's ongoing, too. So is the centering. But everything's on track."

"Excellent! If you don't mind, where are you with the company mission statement?" I asked.

Richard pulled out his current version. "I think we've got something that works. And our new marketing plan incorporates strategies that match this. It's been great working with everyone on it."

"At what level do you think the company is resonating now?" I asked him as he handed me the piece of paper.

"Hmmm . . . I'd say the aggregate energy is probably at least at Level 3, but there's still a lot of fear and doubt, people experiencing Level 1 and Level 2 enough of the time to hold the anabolic trend just at Level 3. But here's the mission statement, along with goals and strategies."

*Mission:* O'Connell Consulting strives to be a leader in marketing for small- to middle-income businesses. We treat all of our clients as if they are a part of our own company, and we offer them an honest and complete effort to ensure success.

We pride ourselves in creating possibilities that produce unique, authentic, and powerful marketing messages and strategies. The result is additional business income for our clients.

*Goals and Strategies:* Capture 20% more of market share, increase our level of customer satisfaction to 90%. These goals will be accomplished by increasing sales efforts, developing new marketing messages, and creating and implementing a new client satisfaction survey.

Nice! I smiled as I told Richard, "It sounds like you've got something that will work, and Don's effort to create some new marketing strategies couldn't have come at a better time."

"Right, and one of the things we came up with yesterday is to listen to each client with an attitude that says right up front: 'We win only if you do.' That's customer service at Level 3, Bruce."

"Great job," I said. "But actually that's Level 5 . . . do you see why?"

"Oh, yeah. Because Level 3 is 'I win, and if you win too, great' but Level 5 is 'we both win,' " answered Richard.

"Right," I assured him. "What's next?"

Without hesitation, Richard told me, "As you and I have discussed before, I see my staff members as having many potential strengths, and Don, Tonya, Betty, and I have been reviewing that together to see if anyone should be moved around within the company. Next I need to talk with the staff again and get any ideas they have about that. I guess you could say we're redesigning more than just our offices.

"We already know Jamal from the art department is moving into sales, since he and I talked about that more than a week ago. So we'll be asking Lisa, another designer, to move from part- to full-time to pick up his work. She's been wanting more hours anyway, so that should be perfect. And I'm strongly considering having Don oversee sales as well as marketing. With Nate gone and hopefully with Kyle coming aboard, I think this makes sense. I think it will give Don a boost in energy and it will be good for Kyle to have someone mentor him."

Because Richard was planning substantial changes in his organization, I thought it would be important that he keep in mind some basic behavioral principles. Specifically, people can feel as if they're stripped of choice when change comes, so it's natural to resist at first. Yet it can be helpful to remember that although no one can completely predict or control change, everyone always has a choice about how they feel about it. And if you're a leader presenting change to people in an organization, you're wise to remind them of this as well as position the change as a request rather than a command.

I talked with Richard about how Don used to bark out orders and how resistant people were to this approach. The result was a continuous battle between Don and those he managed. Don saw his people as defiant, while they saw him as controlling.

Yet resistance isn't defiance. It's simply defense. So it isn't perceptive or effective for leaders to confront resistance with force. This just entrenches Level 2 energy.

Resistance continues only when leaders don't know how to handle people who are experiencing change. *Resistance is the leader's challenge, not the employees' challenge.*

"How clear is what I'm saying to you?" I asked.

"Totally. I'd have guessed that Don probably looked at those who were resistant as resisting him, not change."

Richard had identified a common misperception. Most managers interpret resistance by staff as a personal affront. I told Richard that leaders who adopt this more limited psychology might still get the job done, but their effectiveness is nowhere near what it could be when they don't take things personally.

"It's this other, more objective kind of attitude that lies at the core of Level 4 energy," I pointed out.

---

## Join the Resistance

When I was in graduate school, I interned as a therapist with teens who had abused drugs and were in court-mandated counseling. Talk about resistance! One by one, they'd enter my office, sit, fold their arms, and lower their heads. It was like watching dozens of auditions for the same part. Each time, I played my role exactly the same and got consistent results.

When I would ask these kids what they were doing in my office, they'd say with great conviction that they "had" to be there. *They believed they had no choice.* When I'd point out that there weren't any chains holding them, their reply would usually be the same:

"Well, if I didn't come here, I'd be in jail."

*(continued)*

"So," I'd ask, "if I'm hearing you correctly, the choice is for you either to be here or go to jail, and you'd rather be here?"

The answer was always yes. And what I said next never failed to shift the energy: "Good choice."

That's the point when the teens began to relax and I continued: "Now that you've made what we both believe is a smart choice, what would you like to choose to get out of this?"

Now we were on our way, with at least a partial buy-in, ready to start the process of change.

People experience a completely different energy when they believe they have the freedom to choose rather than be forced to do something.

### Energetic Principle #4

**The greatest freedom is freedom of choice.**

## Life with Level 4

"Remember, Richard, Level 4 energy feels like concern. It involves caring about another person — perhaps your customer — so much that you consider their welfare before your own. At this level, you experience deep compassion for others and feel a genuine connection to them. Your objective is to serve others in the very best way you can, offering them your help without a moment's hesitation."

As I explained more about Level 4, I pointed out that it is closely associated with life purpose. It has to do with making a difference in the world by serving others. And, as I just mentioned, at Level 4, you no longer take anything personally.

- At Level 1: If someone was angry at you, you would feel that you did something wrong and might get upset.
- At Level 2: You would feel undeservedly attacked and get angry, too.
- At Level 3: You might think that the other person just doesn't know any better, so you would forgive the ignorance.
- At Level 4: Your concern becomes helping the other person feel better. The situation is no longer about you, so you have nothing to react to or forgive.

This is a high level of energy where catabolic emotions are no longer internalized. Not taking things personally allows you to deal with challenges more objectively and with greater efficiency.

"Wow," Richard interjected. "It sounds like there are no negatives at Level 4."

"If you mean 'negative' as 'bad,' then I agree: There aren't any negatives. However, each level of energy up to Level 7 does have its drawbacks. People who function at Level 4 tend to have lots of sympathy and a pronounced need to 'fix' other people. As a result, you tend to believe that others are 'broken' and need your help. At this level, you can feel frustrated and drained if you're unable to help someone get 'better.' Obviously, you're also still engaging in a lot of judgment, since you're seeing other people as having 'problems.' You may want other people to be happy and thus avoid taking unpopular actions. And, you might not enforce your own personal boundaries – for example, working late at night in order to help someone else get their work done.

"That said, if you or your company were resonating at Level 4 on the chart, you would undoubtedly reap tremendous personal and professional benefits, including even greater profits."

"Of course I'm interested in profits, but what other benefits are you talking about?" Richard asked.

Interesting: Richard's focus had clearly shifted from making enough money for his company to survive to a keen interest in creating opportunities for other kinds of growth.

Regarding him with growing admiration, I watched him eagerly take in what I had to say next: Managers who function at Level 4 form deep connections with employees. Staff members respect them and see them as trustworthy. They are also markedly loyal. In fact, they'll go to bat for those who work with them as if their employees were family.

I could feel that Richard was resonating with this level in that moment.

Level 4 is where you connect to your heart. So, while leaders at Level 3 mostly engage logic to make decisions, at Level 4, they include and exude emotional intelligence. They're concerned about how their decisions and actions will affect not only their business, but also their employees on a personal level.

Level 4 embraces a "softer" approach to leading, incorporating a more nurturing method of communicating. For example, while the traditional hard-line approach to someone we believe is mistaken might be to say, "You're wrong," the soft approach might be to ask a question instead, such as, "What do you believe the monthly reports say about your perspective?" Since the second approach doesn't aggressively challenge the other person, the individual is less likely to respond defensively.

Acknowledging these differences, it's important not to accept the limiting belief that gentleness is weak and rigidity strong. *Leaders are most effective when they don't abuse their authority and when they consider people's feelings before they act.*

"I saw both Don and Tonya jump into Level 4 several times yesterday," Richard mentioned. "They seem to hang out at Level 3 most of the time now, but things start to get exciting when they're at Level 4."

"It's a lot different from the old, combative Level 2, isn't it?" I asked him. "And when you address the wider world from Level 4, the need to compete with other businesses lessens as everyone in the company starts to understand what true abundance involves, and as everyone comes to see your products and services as unique."

"I know that for myself and many of the people I work with, we now are able to shift our perspectives so that we see our industry – and the whole economy – as set up to allow us to do business in a way that genuinely enhances the destiny of the people who work here."

Somewhat surprised by Richard's point of view, I remarked, "That's a far cry from what you told me the first day we talked. And it's definitely Level 4 thinking."

★ ★ ★

After our break for lunch, I waited for Richard in his reception area. He and Christina were a few minutes late, I noticed. *Must be talking about something important,* I thought. *Or having a really good time.* I smiled, knowing how key their renewed friendship was to Richard's transformation and to the future of his company.

Almost 40 minutes later, Richard, Christina, Betty, and Tonya walked up to meet me, all with sour looks on their faces.

"I'm sorry we're late," Richard apologized. "I got a call from Nate while Christina and I were at lunch, and when we got back, we had to talk to Betty and Tonya right away. Can you all come into my office?"

Once inside, Richard told me about the new drama unfolding. Enraged, Nate had called Richard to yell at him, labeling him a traitor and ingrate and accusing him of breaking several promises – "verbal contracts," he called them. Then he threatened to sue and told Richard he was ready to "take down the whole company down with him."

Richard had reacted in kind, unfortunately. Instead of working to change Nate's energy level, he had taken Nate's threat to heart and roared up like a wounded lion, yelling at him that he had already jeopardized the company with his laziness, incompetence, and insolence. "I told him off, and I have to admit it felt good," Richard reported. He crossed his arms in front of his chest.

"You see what's going on here, right?" I asked him.

"What's going on is that he is being a complete idiot," Tonya responded. "He has absolutely no grounds, and if he tries to sue this company, we will bury him," she said, barely containing her fury.

On the other side of Richard's door, Don knocked then quickly opened it. "They said you wanted to see me immediately. Bury who? What's going on? Tonya, I could hear you halfway down the hall."

Tonya whipped around to Don. "It's Nate, the idiot. He's threatened to sue the company over wrongful termination, saying that he was fired out of the blue for no good reason and with no just cause. Idiot! I'm telling you, he has no case. Richard, didn't you tell me that you met with him repeatedly before you fired him? You documented those meetings, right? There's no way he'll get away with this."

Despite Tonya's gathering storm, Richard was regaining his composure. "Bruce, you were going to say something before Don got here. What was it?"

Taking a deep breath, I said, "Obviously, everyone's upset, and I can understand why. All of you care deeply about this company, and Nate has effectively engaged you with Level 2 energy because his behavior feels threatening to what you are building. The parts of you that still resonate at that level and below have risen up and entrained with Nate.

"What do you think about what I'm saying?" I asked.

Richard spoke first. "I think that's insightful." Then he impressed me with his next question: "Granted we're all mad, but how do we rise above this and resolve it quickly?"

"Don't you be stupid, too, Richard," Tonya jumped in. "I'm telling you: *He has no case.* We will win this thing. You do *not* have to roll over, Richard."

"I'm not talking about rolling over," Richard said evenly. "And I'm not talking about winning. I'm talking about making this work for everyone concerned. Now that I've had a few moments to calm down, I'm trying not to take any of this personally. Can you all try to do that with me? I think we'll arrive at a better solution for everyone."

★ ★ ★

Tonya left the meeting, saying that she would work on this problem on her own. The others remained, and it took some poise and collaboration, but within an hour, Richard and I had rallied his team into a new position, ready to respond to Nate rather than react to him.

After they all left, Richard thanked me for my help, especially with grounding him early on. Then he asked me, "How do you do that? How do you stand in the middle of a group of people basically freaking out and come up with the real dynamics at play? How did you know what was really going on?"

"You told me," I replied. "As you all stood there, I could feel the energy. I clearly heard your past speaking loudly. Your voices were different; your body language was different. It's the same thing I do any time we're talking about your energy level. It's basically observation, perception, knowledge, and logic: All of these are part of what I call holographic thinking. It's also much of what you're learning to do, just by educating yourself and immersing yourself in the coaching we've been doing together."

Richard looked bemused.

"Don't worry," I said. "We'll be working on this more. But for now, let's turn our focus back to the task at hand."

★ ★ ★

For the rest of the day, we focused on what other change strategies he could employ in the organization. We started with some basic groundwork, acknowledging that you can create strategies to shift people in three areas:

1. Actions
2. Emotions
3. Thoughts

## Changing Behavior

First, we talked about what's known as "behavior modification," or the ways you can change a person's actions. It's as simple as just trying something new so you can experience something different, also known as "fake it till you make it." The least effective route to prompting a true energy shift, behavior modification is limited because it doesn't address the underlying cause of the actions. It's like changing the tire when your car's alignment is the real reason the tread's worn out. That said, shifting actions is better than nothing.

"Fair enough," Richard allowed. "But when would you use this approach instead of working with core thoughts and feelings?"

"It's ideal when someone is impressionable and open-minded. With younger children, this method can be effective, especially since thoughts and feelings are difficult to address in the early years, and behavior is still highly malleable.

"In the workplace, it can also be useful when nothing else seems to work. Modifying behaviors can sometimes be a helpful last resort. Sometimes, actions really do speak louder than words. Seeing can be believing."

## Changing Emotions

Second, we dove into the choppy waters of emotion. It can be a controversial subject in corporate settings because of a deeply entrenched notion that emotions have no place in the office. More than a hundred years ago, management theorists were convinced that successful organizations always eliminate emotion[1] from the workplace. When I first met him, Richard had believed this to be true, and even as we were talking about it, he had to admit that he still held onto this belief somewhat. Many of his employees were hesitant to tell him how they felt about things, and he realized that this was mainly because he still felt uncomfortable hearing it.

"It just seems weird," he told me. "It seems way too personal when we start talking about our feelings, even when it's related to a work issue. I realize how important it is to be able to talk about feelings in my private life – my wife has helped me learn that – but is it really all that significant at work?"

"Interpersonal effectiveness is one of the most important aspects of your business," I continued. "Based on the lack of it, which you've experienced in sales and customer service in the past, I'm guessing you'll agree."

---

[1]Stephen Fineman, *Emotion in Organizations* (Thousand Oaks, CA: Thousand Oaks Press, 2000); Benjamin Palmer, Lisa Gardner, and Con Stough, First International Conference on Contemporary Management: Emotional Intelligence in Organisations (2003).

It was clear that he was beginning to buy in. "I can see how understanding and working with emotions might lead to a more effective company. But what, specifically, do I need to do?"

*Time for a mini-course on emotional intelligence*, I thought.

Emotional intelligence is a contributing factor to consciousness-raising. Catabolic energy exists when people have or display low levels of emotional intelligence (usually Levels 1 and 2). Anabolic energy increases with higher levels or displays of emotional intelligence (focusing around Level 4 energy). Like the other characteristics of higher energy, high emotional intelligence helps people frame their point of view to the positive and allows them to choose how they respond to various situations. The result is a creative, caring, and supporting environment where everyone thrives.

There are three key aspects of emotional intelligence: *awareness, expression,* and *managing or controlling emotions.*

Emotional awareness offers people the possibility of recognizing that their emotions are not inevitable – that they indeed come from their *interpretation* of an event. This kind of awareness requires that you take a step back and observe what is going on to generate your emotional responses.

The second main aspect of emotional intelligence is the appropriate expression of emotions. A lack of emotional expression is often cited as a major challenge in leaders. Yet all of us are emotional beings, so the issue isn't so much a lack of emotion as it is one of bottling those emotions up. Not allowing emotions to be expressed creates catabolic energy in oneself, as well as in others.

Remember, though, *emotional intelligence is not about just expressing emotions, it's about expressing emotions appropriately.*

Managing and controlling your and others' emotions is the last of the third key factors in high emotional intelligence and is a significant key to success. Whether working in an organization or dealing with situations in your personal life, having the ability to manage emotions (such as managing your moods and helping to positively shift others' moods), as well as having self-control during stressful or otherwise challenging situations that may evoke strong emotions, is an art. It is also a quality of highly conscious leaders.

Remember that although we may not think so at the time, we create our emotions, and we can re-create them any time we choose. A high awareness of emotional intelligence helps us "use" emotions rather than be at the effect of them.

Although we could have spent months discussing the ins and outs of emotional intelligence, I wanted to answer Richard's question directly and show him how to shift others' emotions most effectively.

Shifting emotions is much more effective than shifting behaviors, because people will feel an energetic buy-in when they emotionally connect with a person or a situation. As a result, *the best way to shift others is to manage your own emotions and mood first, and then help others to remain positive in the face of challenges and crises.*

> *Here are the objectives: Calm employees down when they're "worked up" and, in general, help them feel consistently excited and enthusiastic about their jobs.*

Many strategies can help you reach these goals. To manage your own moods and emotions at work, you must first identify what these moods and emotions are and why you have them. With this information, you can choose to act rather than react to yourself and to people and events around you.

"Richard, you might consider starting a new journal," I suggested. "You can make entries throughout the workday, particularly if you feel angry or down. You just write your current mood and what you believe has caused it. By doing this, you will improve your ability to identify 'triggers' that seem to set off specific moods. Once you know what they are, you'll be more equipped to recognize them as impersonal events – you won't take them so personally – so you can respond thoughtfully rather than go into automatic reaction."

This is how you begin to rethink, or re-create, your interpretation of who people are and what they do. Anyone who pushes your buttons prompts you to come to a real understanding of why you have those buttons to begin with.

"Remember that those buttons are your challenge, not anyone else's," I emphasized.

Once you recognize that, you can create positive rituals to get you back on track, such as quick centering, reading an inspirational letter or message, or looking at a beautiful picture of nature. These steps can help restore objectivity.

"This all sounds like more Level 4 energy," Richard observed.

He was absolutely right. It's all about concern, compassion, and service to others. Most people who resonate in the high range of Level 4 don't take things personally, and even when someone has supposedly wronged them, their motto is "How can I help you?" They do what they can to protect and heal those who are less fortunate than they are.

"When you want to manage the moods and emotions of your employees, it's important first to realize the influence you have over them," I told Richard. Workers often reflect their leader's moods. When working with someone who is "down," you can start by acknowledging and validating the person's current state – the first two steps of the Core Energy Process I'd been using and teaching Richard throughout all our coaching sessions. Empathy also works in the same capacity. When you see things from someone else's perspective, you can help them alter what's probably an interpretation they've made about someone or something.

Richard looked excited. "I don't mean to brag, but this is exactly what I've been doing with Don and Tonya," he said.

"It's okay if you want to brag to me," I told Richard. "Your successes show me how hard you've been working and how far you've come."

## Changing Thoughts

Shifting how you think goes directly to the root causes of emotions and actions. In terms of knowledge and skill, this is the most challenging method for making shifts, but it can also be the most effective.

When you change your core thoughts, it leads you directly to a new paradigm, generating a new perception of yourself and the world around you. This leads to a leap in consciousness, to a change in status on the Energetic Self-Perception Chart, and to increased energy and power.

Any time the organization or its individual members move up, it leads to greater employee efficiency and effectiveness, fewer sick days, less turnover, less stress, more productivity, increased job satisfaction, and more profits for the company.

"Okay, but you said this one requires some finesse. How do I go about developing more of the ability to shift others?" Richard asked.

"Do you remember that most people are held back by one or more of the Big Four energy blocks?"

"Right." Richard nodded.

"If you can become aware of what blocks are stopping someone else, and work with them as we've been discussing, then you can create shifts in others' thought patterns," I explained.

"Next time we get together, I'll show you the Breakthrough Laser Coaching technique, which if you remember, was a technique I used with Don a few weeks ago. It incorporates all that you've been learning and will help you get that 'finesse' you're talking about."

"Still teasing me with what's next? You know I'd be looking forward to seeing you even without guessing what was coming next, don't you?" intoned Richard.

"Never hurts to prime the pump, my friend." I smiled at him. "It's my pleasure to work with you, Richard. Congratulations on everything that's happening for you."

# 11 | The CEO of the Future (Level 5)

*Much of the success of life depends upon keeping one's mind open to opportunity and seizing it when it comes.*
— Alice Foote MacDougall, entrepreneur

Richard asked Don if he wouldn't mind joining him for Kyle's interview. Don seemed a bit perplexed, but agreed without question. They then walked next door to the conference room, where Betty and Kyle were seated. Richard began the interview by welcoming Kyle and introducing him to Don. "This is Don Taylor, who, besides his role as marketing director, is the new head of sales, as well, and you'll be his first sales team position interview."

Don had a big smile on his face and Betty nodded, looking very pleased with the new development.

"Really?" asked Don.

"Without any doubt by me or anyone else," was Richard's response.

It took a few minutes for Don to settle down a bit and it was a fun few minutes, indeed. Don then kicked into the role: "Well, Kyle, nice to meet you. As you can probably figure out, I do these interviews all the time." They all laughed, and Don continued: "So, if we all decide that it's a good fit for you to come to work here, you'll be reporting to me."

Kyle smiled as Don firmly shook his hand. "It's a pleasure to meet you, sir," he said.

Don patted him on the shoulder and chided him, "Now, let's not get off on the wrong foot, son. You're making me feel like an old man. Just call me Don."

Laughing, Kyle told Don that he would be honored to do so.

Although he was eager to put Kyle at ease, it was also clear that Don appreciated the younger man's deference. Kyle was likable and at ease and exuded both confidence and a desire to serve.

As they talked, it was obvious to Richard that Kyle was steadily operating at Level 4, which he found appealing. He liked what he saw as Kyle interacted with Betty and Don; both of them seemed buoyed by Kyle's upbeat and generous spirit. Nowadays, Richard was constantly thinking about how to bring up the aggregate "energy score" in his organization. He was also aware that whenever he was around people with anabolic energy, he found it natural to operate at that level, too. Having Kyle walk through the doors functioning at Level 4 made Richard think that he might not only get to see some Level 4 and higher behaviors in the sales department as it developed, but that it would also carry over to other departments.

Richard didn't really need Don to conduct the rest of the interview to make a decision, but he could see that it would serve a purpose for Don and Betty to continue on: They would both have a greater investment in Kyle's success with the company. And when Richard started thinking about what it would be like to have a salesperson with the support of the rest of the staff, a salesperson who already had the chops to represent his company in a way that Nate never had been able to do, he actually felt his arms and the top of his head start to tingle.

Despite this growing feeling of elation, Richard took a deep breath and centered himself so he could remain focused and calm. During a brief lull in the interview, Richard excused himself. "You're in good hands, Kyle," he said, leaving the room without offering his opinion.

★ ★ ★

When Richard recounted the interview process to me and its inevitable outcome – Kyle was joining O'Connell Consulting in just over two weeks' time – he was still beaming. "I can't wait for you to meet him, Bruce."

"Looking forward to it."

"Kyle's open and honest, willing to listen and learn, and has an undeniable desire to make this company a success. He's the kind of person who makes me want to be a better leader, who makes me feel like I *can be* one, and maybe I already am."

"Congratulations on building the kind of team you really want," I said. "You've made some amazing strides with the people closest to you, and now you've added someone new who sounds like he'll work really well with everyone else. Maybe now when you talk about the Fantastic Four, you can take your tongue out of your cheek."

Richard laughed. "You want to know what else is going on?"

"Of course."

"Well, here's something interesting. I met someone last week – this amazing woman: smart, sexy, soulful, just my type." Richard looked mischievous.

"All right, I'll bite," I told him. "Who'd you meet?"

"My wife, Jodi," Richard said quietly.

"Aah, that's wonderful. More congratulations are in order."

"Yes, thank you. She and I have been talking for a couple hours almost every night lately, and our conversations have been more and more revealing. We've been talking about our relationship and even the business. For a long time, she just didn't want to hear it, because sometimes it felt like my work was what was causing problems in our marriage, but now it's clear that it wasn't the business. It was me. Well, it was her, too, but I think what's important is that each of us is acknowledging our own part and trying not to blame the other.

"That's been at the heart of a lot of our talks, to tell the truth. We've been comparing notes on what each of us thinks it means to be 'fully conscious.' She's been into that kind of thing for years, actually.

"She's been very encouraging about the work you and I have been doing together as well, and she enjoyed learning about the I Chart. Right off, she did her best to identify where she is on the chart, and I told her where I am most of the time. Then we discussed the people here in the office, and she has had some great insights and ideas for how to relate to them better. In sharing all of this, I've learned that Jodi and I have a lot more in common than I thought. And I *like* talking with her about these things: these lofty, big-picture, human nature things.

"We've been married for 22 years, but I feel like I'm getting to know her all over again."

Richard's look suggested that he couldn't quite believe his new fortune. "It's pretty amazing," he said.

"It is," I agreed. "It's great that you're seeing that leadership is not limited to the office."

"I certainly am," Richard said. "What I'm learning has helped me improve not only my business, but *myself*. I can't imagine going back to being my old self."

After allowing him a moment to reflect on what he'd just said, I asked, "So how's your new self's golf game? Since we're talking about personal things."

"Actually, I haven't been on the course as much lately, mainly because I'm focusing on other priorities right now. But I do still get out at least once a week, and I can tell you that when I play now, somehow, it's not the same game I used to play."

Richard splayed his hands on his desktop and looked down at them. "Maybe I'm taking this Energy Leadership stuff too seriously, but I have to tell you something: Before I arrive at the course, I decide which energy level will show up. I stick with Level 4, focusing on the emotional aspects of the game, and helping my golf buddies really enjoy the day, and Level 5, seeing every shot as an opportunity for success.

Looking straight at me, Richard explained. "Keeping that focus, before I take each shot, I take a deep breath and visualize the ball in the hole, and then, it's kind of like autopilot. Amazing. And my scores are better than ever. You know, it's a lot like things here in the office. Before, I tried too hard not to make mistakes and all I did was make them. Now I focus on success with every ounce of my energy, and, well, it's almost effortless."

Richard took a deep breath. "Here's something that's not feeling so effortless." With a quizzical look, he handed me a piece of paper. It appeared that while Richard was focusing on sinking more putts on the golf course, Tonya was still focusing on sinking Nate.

Richard, I suggest we send a letter like this to Nate to rein him in immediately.
—Tonya


D-R-A-F-T

Dear Mr. Allen,

This letter is being sent as a formal demand that you immediately discontinue any actions, including verbal and/or written communication, that in any way defames or is otherwise detrimental to the reputation and image of this company. We consider your threats of litigation to be frivolous and evidence of harassment, and we are prepared to fully support the cause of your termination in any appropriate legal proceedings.

In consideration of your past ties to this organization and to its principal, we have not issued a formal Cease and Desist Order. However, be advised that we are prepared to do so if there is any further action by you which we deem as continued harassment, and any violation of such order may have civil and/or criminal implications.

Sincerely,

As I read the letter Richard had handed me, I glanced at him from time to time and saw him watching me with his eyebrows raised. When I was done, he said, "Okay, obviously that's not the tone I want to take. It has Level 2 written all over it. But I cannot, for the life of me, come up with a better way of addressing Nate's threats and his aggressive stance with me.

"I was hoping we could work on redrafting this letter together," he finished.

"Hmm. Before we work on the letter, how about we dive into Level 5? We can marinate in that for a little bit, then come back to the letter with that in mind. How does that work for you?"

"Makes sense to me," Richard agreed.

## The Level 5 Opportunity

This level of energy, I began, differs from those below it in a number of ways. Most significant, with Level 5, you release much of the judgment you'd normally attach to situations. This helps you come to terms with duality, going beyond the idea that everything contains both "good" and "bad," and reaching a new understanding that those labels are only that: labels. Situations are just . . . situations. Everything else you might think about them is subjective. You still make judgments about things – that's human nature – but you're completely clear that they don't actually mean anything, except to point to elements of your own consciousness. You're able to observe your judgments and see them for what they really are: just reflections of your own mind and, most important to remember, *reflections of your past*.

The driving force behind Level 5 energy is opportunity. No matter what happens, people resonating at Level 5 energy look for opportunities in everything. This leads to feelings of control over their experiences and a deep sense of curiosity. As a consequence, they experience a sense of inner peace and an understanding about how life works.

People at Level 5 tell themselves that there must be a purpose for anything that happens, and so, instead of living in the guilt and pain of the past, they look to the future by learning from the past.

Level 5 energy is highly positive and invigorating. People with an abundance of this type of energy feel powerful, confident, courageous, and connected to others.

"I want to understand something," Richard broke in. "It seems that who you're describing are people who find the silver lining in everything. Isn't that just positive thinking?"

"No," I said, "It's positive people, and those who take action based on their beliefs. They can still see things in practical terms — let's say they see the whole cloud instead of just the silver lining. Instead of bemoaning the weather, they welcome the rain, realizing that it presents opportunities for growth. What do you think about that?"

Richard said that it made some sense but asked me if I could give him a real-life example. So I told him about a client of mine who was almost blind. Each week he would go to the beach and try to see a sunset. Sometimes he could vaguely make it out, and other times, he would see nothing. He continued going every week, though, because he knew there was a possibility of experiencing, and appreciating, something more beautiful than anything else in his world.

My client said that he considered his condition a wonderful gift, because most people take sunsets for granted. He discovered how to experience God in those few moments. In this brief experience, he came to understand and appreciate why he was alive.

Richard looked almost transfixed. "I can't imagine . . ." he trailed off. "I wish that I were strong enough to bounce back like that."

"What would you do differently if you could?" I asked.

"For one thing," Richard said, "I wouldn't beat myself up over my mistakes."

"Here's an idea: You might take another crack at your judgment journal. With each phone call, customer complaint, or new customer, instead of focusing on judging any of those situations as good or bad, you could just ask yourself, with a sense of curiosity, 'What opportunity am I being presented with here?' By consistently answering that question, you can develop a habit of looking for opportunities and start shifting your energy higher. And remember something else, too. I'm not talking about making something good out of something bad, which would be a Level 3 thought. I'm talking about seeing neither good nor bad, only opportunity."

"That helps a lot," Richard said. "I guess asking myself that question would be like training myself to think differently."

"That's what we're doing," I said. "I'm offering you choices and tools. You can choose and adopt the ones that make sense to you."

Leaders operating at Level 5 are powerful, inspiring, and skilled at capitalizing on whatever opportunities present themselves, I continued. With such a high level of resonance, their presence alone allows these leaders to command greatness from others. They also expect greatness from others and receive it. At Level 5, leaders see employees as gifted and full of potential.

- Leaders at this level expect positive attitudes, autonomy as well as teamwork, and high performance. They demonstrate what they believe in by telling staff members exactly what is expected of them. This creates a positive self-fulfilling prophecy[1] in which employees are motivated by knowing that someone believes in them and will hold them accountable to greatness.
- At Level 5, leaders look for opportunities in partnerships and alliances. They're always thinking about synergy and ways to succeed through their many interactions.
- Leaders at this level operate with less fear than the levels below, and thus have the willingness to enact radical change when warranted.

If that's the leader at Level 5, what are employees at Level 5 like? They crave the opportunity to express themselves by using their gifts and talents at work. The result is that they become self-rewarding.

They want to make a difference in the world. They see their contribution to the organization as being equally important to any other, at any level in the organization.

When they aren't afforded the chance to challenge themselves, expand their talents, and contribute a full effort, they become disenchanted and

---

[1]"Leadership and Expectations: Pygmalion Effects and Other Self-Fulfilling Prophecies in Organizations," *Leadership Quarterly* (Winter 1992).

consider leaving the company. That's why it's important for leaders not only to lift people up to this level, but to realize that effort is required to sustain this energy level. This is not a challenge in organizations that are truly productive, because, with the proper mindset, leaders can always find ways to help grow people and profits.

As you might imagine, I told Richard, organizations with an average of Level 5 energy are pretty rare. They're also usually extremely profitable. People have a lot of fun working in this kind of environment. Policies reward desirable behaviors, and staff often have the chance to become vested in company growth with stock options or profit sharing.

Richard looked resolved. Nodding, he said, "This sounds like the direction we're headed. What can we do to move ourselves closer?"

I told Richard that he could start adopting some of the behaviors of organizations with dominant Level 5, if that's what he really wanted. Perhaps most important, this would mean investing in employees in all departments and all positions. In an organization resonating at Level 5, leaders are aware of the costs of replacing quality people, so they do all they can to achieve high retention. Enterprises achieve this goal in a number of ways, including training, creating an intriguing work environment, and encouraging interpersonal relationships and developing effective and efficient communication systems.

Pursuing this approach creates high potential, not only for evolving the best chief executives and managers at all levels, but for major growth in sales, marketing, and all other areas of the organization.

## Breakthrough Laser Coaching

Now that Richard understood the characteristics of Level 5 and was filled with anticipation about becoming a leader and organization at that energy level, it was time to return to his current dilemma: responding to Nate.

"First," I said, "let's look at this diagram for reference." (See Figure 11.1.) "The top of the chart indicates the *Current* situation. Your challenge is that you believe you want to work this situation out so that the result is beneficial

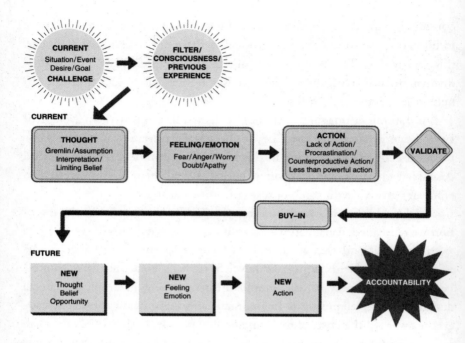

**Figure 11.1   Breakthrough Laser Coaching**
Modified from iPEC Coaching

to everyone, but you have a block preventing you from doing this. If you look to the right of the current situation, you'll see a box called *Filter/Consciousness/Previous Experience*. This shows that all current blocks have their roots in the past. This box is only a reminder; we actually begin working through this process in the box below it, called *Thought*.

"In the *Thought* box you see the Big Four blocks listed, because your thoughts about how to respond to Nate originate from one of the Big Four blocks. For this tool to be helpful, it doesn't matter which of the Big Four is blocking you. What we need to uncover is the core thought process – the underlying, possibly unconscious recorded message in your head – that determines how you see this situation. For example, if you had a gremlin controlling you, we would only need to know what message the gremlin is giving you about Nate. That message would be your core thought. Make sense so far?" I asked.

"Let me see if I am following you," Richard replied. "Even though we know my block is from one of the Big Four, we'll only work with the message I hear, not with the Big Four directly?"

"That's right," I said. "For this tool to be successful, we need to concern ourselves only with the core thought. To find it, I'll ask you this: When you think about Nate walking into your office right now and you responding to his threats of a lawsuit, what comes up for you?"

"I'm still feeling angry that he would even consider trying to compromise this company," Richard said, grimacing. "He's been such a drag on the business for so long, and I've been so loyal, that I can't believe he would now threaten to cut the legs right out from underneath us. Not that I think he's got a chance of being awarded any reparations, but defending ourselves could break the bank. At the same time, I remember how dedicated to me and the company he's been in the past, and how he's been with me since the beginning. I'm grateful that he helped me get this business off the ground. So I feel both that he's being incredibly disloyal and, if I'm really honest, I'm still feeling as if I do owe him something or as if I've been disloyal or let *him* down in some way . . . which makes me angry at both him and me. I can't believe I'm still working on this same stuff."

"It can be complicated, Richard, and people don't always experience change – especially changes in their core beliefs – in a straight line. Sometimes you have to zigzag your way to a new future, you know? No wonder you're challenged with this one.

"So now let's challenge the reality of your thoughts," I said, "Starting with the thought that you still owe Nate your loyalty. We're going to focus on that because it's a thought about *yourself*, which means it's closer to the core, or heart of the matter. Where do you think you got the notion that you let Nate down by letting him go?"

"Well, I'm not sure," Richard responded, becoming curious about the answer. "I mean . . . I feel like, by letting him go, I've given him the message that I don't appreciate all he's done. I suppose this goes back to my old 'nice guy' image. I don't ever want to do anything that upsets the apple cart."

"So you believe that letting Nate go means that you're really not a nice guy."

"Umm, yeah," Richard replied, some uncertainty at first coming through in his tone. Then he added, his voice more certain, "I guess that's it. And here's what's crazy: My reluctance to come up with a Level 5 answer to this is that right now, I don't want to be a nice guy. I feel like Nate should be punished for his disloyalty to me. How confusing is that?"

Richard and I chuckled together. "Don't worry," I said, "we'll untangle this yet. And know that having a Level 2 reaction, such as revenge, is not only normal, but perhaps expected. However, since you are not at Level 2, luckily, we can acknowledge and validate those thoughts, but we have more choices. Make sense?"

"Yes. And at least now I don't feel like I've slipped backwards. Thanks."

"Right," I said." You'll still have a variety of thoughts for all situations, and those thoughts may come from various levels of energy. What we're concerned with is the core thought. We've now identified at least one current core thought," I said. "You think that you should be a nice guy, and letting him go isn't what a nice guy would have done."

"Right!" Richard exclaimed. "I guess I'm replaying my 'bad guy' recording."

"Okay, let's get to the emotion. The next box in the model is *Feeling*. I want to know what feelings you experience when you think you're not being a nice guy."

"It feels like crap," he said without a moment's hesitation. "I feel a pit in my stomach. It definitely has to do with guilt."

"Good," I said, "We're continuing to make some progress. If you look to the end of the first row of boxes, you'll see the words *Action* and *Validate*. To continue to demonstrate how this model works, I'll take what you've said and validate that you're 'blocked' because of your thoughts and feelings about doing this.

"Here's what I want to tell you. Given your idea that since you let Nate go you aren't a nice guy, and the feelings of guilt you harbor, combined with your feelings of being hurt by Nate's actions, it's no wonder that you are finding it a huge challenge to come up with a new solution."

"Thanks," Richard said, a bit relieved. "I guess it does make sense that I'm blocked about it."

I reminded him, "This is what I want you to recognize at the moment regarding your current situation: once I validate your feelings and, in turn, your nonaction, you can become more open to making a change."

"Yes, I can see that," Richard said. "I feel like you understand what I'm going through."

"That's one of the purposes of Breakthrough Laser Coaching," I said. "Another is to let *you* understand what you're going through."

I also asked what his initial thoughts might be on the potential value of this process, and his response was very positive, which was enough buy-in for me to continue. First however, I explained to Richard how important it was to get an energetic buy-in when he was working with others.

I then invited Richard to move to the bottom of the chart. "Now look at the second line, which starts with *Future*. To make new action possible, we need to create a *New Thought* and *New Feelings* from that new thought."

I offered Richard an invitation. "What thought would you like to have instead of the one that makes you a bad guy – or, for that matter, Nate being a bad guy?"

Richard went silent for a moment, but then said resolutely, "I'd like to believe I'm doing the best thing for Nate by ending his stay with us, and that his response to this situation is neither good nor bad. It simply is what it is. His actions are understandable, and it's my choice right now to offer to help make his transition beneficial for everyone."

"That works. How can you justify that thought for yourself?"

"Logically," Richard acknowledged, "it makes sense. I'm not doing him any good here, and I can do an enormous amount of good – if he'll work with me – in moving him on. And if he chooses not to work with me, I can be okay with that, too."

"In thinking it's truly in Nate's best interest that you've let him go, how do you feel?"

"Actually," Richard said, "that thought gives me peace." For a moment, he was silent again. Then he added, "I feel more relaxed. Less guilt."

"Okay. Now let's look in the last box. What *Action* will you take to back up your new thought and feelings?"

"I'm going to call Nate back and let him know how much I care about him," Richard said. "I'm definitely not sending that threatening letter. I'm going to tell him that it's best for both of us that he was let go, and that I'm willing to help him find a better fit somewhere else. I'll even offer again to hire a counselor or coach for him if he desires. And I can even do this process with him if he's willing. That could be really meaningful for both of us, especially if it helps Nate start to see how things could be different for him if he starts to move beyond some of his anger."

"How are you feeling about all this?" I asked.

"Relieved," Richard said, as if noting something unexpected. "It's a bit strange, but I'm looking forward to talking with Nate."

"Great, and going in with that energy and intention will make it easier for Nate to hear your real message. Should he not, well, we'll deal with it. But our work isn't as much about how others react to us, but about how we act toward others. That's where we have control.

"You've made another good step forward," I said, "The last section of our chart involves holding yourself accountable for your action. So when will you speak with Nate?"

"Today," Richard said, his natural leadership skills increasingly emerging.

"That's how Breakthrough Laser Coaching works," I said. "We quickly identify a thought that isn't working for you, then the feeling associated with this thought, and validate your inaction because of that thought and feeling. Then we create a new thought and feeling and get as much of an emotional buy-in as possible, which leads to new action. Even if the person doesn't have a huge buy-in immediately, acting as if there is one can often lead to positive changes."

Once mastered, I told Richard, this tool can be extremely effective. As the name "Breakthrough Laser Coaching" implies, quick breakthroughs to new growth can result. I asked Richard to practice using it with his employees between now and our next session, whenever anyone seemed blocked. Richard said that he thought Tonya might be a good place to start, since she seemed to have slid right back to Level 2 where Nate was concerned.

★ ★ ★

Richard reviewed his assignments with me:

- Call and talk with Nate;
- Use Breakthrough Laser Coaching with Tonya and, possibly, Nate; and
- Revisit his judgment journal with an intention of seeing the opportunity in all situations.

Although there had been dozens of signals that Richard had really turned a corner, it was reassuring to get one more: Richard couldn't wait to get started on the work he committed to complete, and he told me that he'd be on the phone with Nate about 10 minutes after we said our good-byes.

"If you want, I'll call you right after and let you know how it went," he offered.

"That would be great, Richard. I'll look forward to hearing about it." He'll do great, I thought, as I left the office to catch my train home.

# 12 | The Power of Partnership

*Writing the Success Script (Levels 6 and 7)*

*I Am Awareness. I Am Acceptance. I Am Knowing. I Am Presence. I Am Freedom. I Am white light refracted into all beings.*
—Bruce D Schneider, *Uncovering the Life of Your Dreams*

When Richard rang me a few days later, he explained that Nate had been difficult to reach but had finally taken his call just an hour ago.

Richard said that each time he picked up the phone, before he dialed, he took a moment to center himself and imagine being able to talk to Nate like they were friends again. It was better, Richard thought, that Nate wasn't available right away because it gave Richard the chance to visualize the conversation many times before it actually happened.

"So how did it go when you finally talked with him"? I asked.

"There were some bumps in the road," Richard reported, "but I couldn't ask for a better outcome."

"What was the key piece for Nate?" I wondered aloud.

Richard said he posed an important question and asked Nate to please give it sincere consideration: "Ultimately, what would you like to have come out of this?"

After giving it some thought, Nate told Richard that he didn't want to be angry anymore, and he didn't want to go back to feeling bad about himself, either. Nate had then brought the conversation to a turning point: "What I really want is some sense of peace regarding this and to get on with my life."

When Richard had asked him how well he thought he'd meet this goal by following his current line of action, Nate became silent, then confessed, "I don't really know."

So Richard posed this possibility to him: would Nate be open to a different line of action that would ensure the result he wanted?

That was when they really turned the corner, Richard said. At that point and without realizing it, Nate gave Richard signals that he would go for a Level 3 approach. With Nate's newfound perceptiveness, Richard knew he could help Nate find a way to forgive him, and perhaps even for Nate to forgive himself. Before he called him, Richard had already decided to give Nate whatever resources he had at his disposal. The rest was just details.

"So where does that leave you now?" I asked.

"Well, Nate's going to move forward with some counseling and career coaching that should help him regain his professional footing. And he's not pursuing the lawsuit."

"Congratulations. I'm sure that's a relief . . . and what's the status of your relationship with him?"

Richard took a deep breath, and I heard him exhale slowly. "You know what? I think we'll be resuming our friendship. I gave a lot of thought to this even before I called him, going through each of my options. And here's what I feel about it: I want to engage with him at a higher level. I want my response to him and my relationship with him to be driven by Level 6. Because the truth is, Bruce, he doesn't really need my 'help.' In so many ways I *am* like this guy. Now that I understand the levels of energy, and have experienced many of them, I can see that I'm no better or worse than he is. And we all go through the same stuff. Also, there's no reason for me to judge Nate as 'broken.' Nate's on a journey, just like I am. Maybe we can learn a bit more from each other."

He stopped abruptly and forced a laugh. "Now who's all touchy-feely, right?"

He sounded self-conscious and awkward.

"Richard, come on!" I urged him. "Aren't we beyond all that? This is awesome! Don't downplay it just because you're in unfamiliar territory. You're to be congratulated here: You truly *have* been up and down all the levels, and you are consciously choosing a Level 6 experience now. That's an amazing thing . . . think about how much you've grown in these last few months."

"I am a giant of a man," Richard said, gently chuckling at himself. I could hear both warmth and humility in his voice, and when we said our good-byes later, I couldn't help but marvel at the transformation taking place in this brilliant human being.

\* \* \*

When I saw Richard about a week and a half later for our regular appointment, he ushered me into his office and closed the door softly. He sat down in his usual chair, and I did the same. This routine had taken on an air of ritual lately, and this morning Richard and I seemed especially aware of it.

"So, Richard, what's up?" I began.

"To start with, profits," Richard responded. "If we keep this going, we'll meet our goal well before the six-month mark. Morale is higher, too. I'm happy to report that the only thing that's lower is my golf score."

Our day was off to a great start.

\* \* \*

The time had come to address in more detail the final two levels of the Energetic Self-Perception Chart. Richard had already beautifully demonstrated Level 6, so I decided to build on that. Level 6 is the start of the third circle of awareness, which is called self-Transcendence, I reminded him, and it's right where he'd been operating in his most recent conversations with Nate. The word *self* is written in lowercase, because it is the small self that you're transcending to allow the powerful leader within you to rise.

The core thought for Level 6 energy is synthesis, which is the blending together of people and everything else as one. When Richard reflected about Nate and how he saw himself in him, "In many ways, I am this guy," he was echoing a Level 6 perspective.

At Level 3, Richard might have elected to *forgive* Nate, to move on and let Nate move on. At Level 4, he might have looked for ways to be of greater service to Nate in his transition. At Level 5, he might have decided to take everything they'd experienced together as an *opportunity* to learn more about himself. At Level 6, no choices would be needed. Richard would experience all situations in business – as well as in life in general, not as good or bad – but only as situations.

At Level 6 there's little need, if any, to make judgments about yourself, others, or life's occurrences. Because of this, you encounter an ongoing joy within yourself – for no "reason" at all. While you can still feel the pain associated with everyday living, you don't judge that pain.

So as the diamond is within the coal, Level 6 offers a high potential for creativity and development of self and business, *because there are fewer blocks in the way of true potential.*

## Leaders with Predominant Level 6 Energy

While leaders at this level are highly active in their organizations and willing to do anything they'd ask anyone else to do, these individuals lead more by presence than by actions. They're role models who others look up to as wise, kind, and fair. These leaders seem to know all that's going on in their organizations without having to ask. They have a keen sense of intuition and use it on a regular basis to make decisions and to generate ideas.

At Level 6, leaders are powerful yet humble. They know their level of excellence and are still interested in growing. They listen to feedback from others about how they're leading and being perceived, and take action, without ego blocks, to improve.

Most leaders give minimal information to staff members about projects and company situations. Leaders with a predominance of Level 6, however, share detailed information about all aspects of the company on a regular basis. When it comes to keeping people informed, the Level 6 philosophy is: "The more they know, the more things flow."

As Richard illustrated in his recent actions, the main characteristic that separates leaders with a lot of Level 6 from others is their ability to see all staff members as equal to each other, and equal to them. Instead of believing they're more gifted than anyone else, leaders at this level recognize that everyone is gifted. Because of this, they can help others realize their true potential, in the process generating a team of genuine and deeply committed partners, instead of people who are only workers.

"Now, Richard, this is not to suggest that leaders at Level 6 believe in equal pay for everyone," I clarified. "They understand the nature of supply and demand and realize that people's specific talents should be compensated accordingly. Yet they also grasp a vital realization: without their staff to support them, these leaders themselves would achieve little."

"But with a staff like mine," Richard finished for me, "we can achieve some great things together."

Obviously moved by his own statement, he concluded, "In fact, we already are." Then he told me something about Tonya and Don that he felt proved it.

Richard told me of his work with Tonya recently, and particularly the helpfulness of the Breakthrough Laser Coaching process. He said he had been able to shift Tonya's perspective and feelings about Nate, and that she had been able to let it all go. She'd stopped pressuring him to respond to Nate with legalese and threats of their own. And then she'd made another shift that had given him an enormous boost. He took his time telling me about it.

Tonya was in Richard's office for their weekly meeting. "I have to hand it to you," she said to Richard, "Things are definitely looking good. Revenues are through the roof, the place looks great, and it's like coming to work with a whole new group of people these days. Nice work, chief."

Richard thanked Tonya and pointed out how important everyone else's contributions had been in the turnaround. He mentioned each person by name, from the committee they selected for redecorating to the team closest to him. "Christina, Don, and you have really come through for me and for the company. I want to thank you for that."

Although Richard was conveying a lot of emotion, and Tonya was clearly feeling it, her mind was on something else. When she changed the tone of their conversation, Richard thought that perhaps she did it to avoid feeling uncomfortable.

"Listen, Richard," Tonya began, all business. "That reminds me of something I've been thinking about. You know, Don's really proven himself in the last few months. I've completely changed my opinion of him – and I think I may have been mistaken about him before, but it's more than that. He's become an anchor around here.

"Anyway, here's what I'm suggesting: Give Don an official title promotion, confirming the new sales role. Make him a vice-president equal to me. He deserves it. He does just as much for this company as I do, and there's no reason he shouldn't be recognized for it. We can also clean up our 'chain of command' and make it more clear for people just who does what around here, and which teams need to report to Don, and which ones are accountable to me. This can take some of the pressure off of you, too. It seems like the best thing to do for everyone."

Richard was taken aback. He had been considering giving Don a promotion already but was reluctant to take action because he worried about fallout, especially from Tonya. Things were going so well that he hadn't wanted to create any source of friction. But there it was: Tonya clearly had made a major leap, moving from being so concerned with herself and her territory (Level 2) to seeing what would be best for the company (Level 4).

No doubt about it, this was an opportunity for everyone to win. And Richard was perfectly happy if Tonya took credit for the idea.

Tonya interrupted Richard's thoughts. "But don't tell Don I suggested it," she said. "I don't want him to feel like he owes me anything. This is about his merit and what he brings to the table. Let's not cloud the issue, okay?"

Surprised again, Richard agreed. He would talk with Don in the next few days and make the announcement to the company within the week.

★ ★ ★

"What do you think of that?" Richard asked me. "Our energy level just keeps going up around here. At this rate, we'll be averaging a Level 7 in another year."

He shook his head. "I still can't believe it."

"Believe it, my friend. This is the new reality you're creating."

★ ★ ★

When we moved on to a discussion of Level 7 energy, I had no charts to show, nor any dialogues or examples of leaders or organizations that have an average resonating energy at Level 7.

"That's because those things don't and will never exist, Richard. In this state, no words are spoken, no clients exist, and no business takes place. At Level 7, the three-dimensional world that you think you know and see becomes obscure and indefinable."

"This sounds like some of what I've been reading lately, stuff Jodi's recommended," he added, winking as he said it, "about Einstein's work. One thing he said that really struck me was that *fields of energy are the only reality*. I'm no expert, but from what you're saying, I'm getting that the true nature of energy is not stable or tangible, but instead, always changing and moving, right?"

Richard surprised me now, and I was delighted. "Yes, you've got it."

I reminded Richard about what he'd told me about his meditation sessions. "Didn't you say once that you sometimes feel as if everything turns 'liquid'? I think that's the word you used."

"Yes! But it lasts for only a little while. Actually, I'm not sure how long it lasts, because time feels fluid then, too."

That made sense. Level 7 is an energy that cannot be sustained; it can only be tapped into from time to time. "That's what you're doing, and the more aware you are of what this level is, and how to access it, the more you'll be able to use it. When you do, the benefits to you and your company could be phenomenal."

I expected Richard to get excited about this, but he seemed disappointed. "So I can never average Level 7?"

"No one can," I responded. "At Level 7, energy resonates at such a high vibration that the human form would not be visible."

"Okaaaaay," Richard said, lifting an eyebrow.

"Let's say you have a fan and it isn't plugged in. How much energy do the blades expend?"

"None," Richard said.

"That's correct. Now turn the fan to middle speed and think of the energy that's displaced, as well as what happens to the blades."

"There's much more energy and the blades seem to blend together."

"Good. Next, turn that fan all the way up. What happens to the blades?"

"They seem to disappear," Richard said, giving me another curious look.

"Right again, and there's much more power coming from the fan at that speed. So imagine what would happen for people at Level 7 energy if they were operating as high-speed fan blades. Level 7 is not something that we can sustain as an average. But when we tap into it, it does feel like you are not a part of this world, because you function fully in the moment at the level of pure power, the level of creation."

"I get it . . . I think," Richard said. "Are you describing our ultimate potential?" he asked.

"That's one way to describe it," I replied. "Honestly, the metaphysics of all this aren't as important as you understanding what the traits of Level 7 energy are and how accessing this kind of energy can benefit you. As they say, you don't have to understand how electricity works to flip the switch and turn on a light."

★ ★ ★

Those who learn how to resonate at this level, even for a few moments, have access to truth beyond illusion, and, in turn, they can engage their natural genius ability to consciously create their world. At Level 5, people create opportunities from challenging experiences. At Level 6, they create opportunities in *all* experiences. At Level 7, people's creative ability is constant and doesn't require an opportunity to present itself. In a sense, *life* is the opportunity.

"What do you think?" I asked Richard. "Fantastic or far-fetched?"

"Amazing," Richard said. His gaze shifted to that far-off yet very close place he often visited when we first began working together. Then he looked me squarely in the eye. "You're saying that if I can connect with this level of energy I can create solutions more quickly?"

"At this level, you can create *anything*. What's more, you can do it as quickly as you believe possible. Let's look at why. At Level 7, you experience no judgments. What comes to mind when you think of nonjudgment?"

"A real challenge," Richard said, sighing. "Given the entries I've made in my judgment journal, I'm not sure, with the stuff we face every day, that we can ever move fully beyond judging."

"That's an honest assessment," I responded. "Whether it's true isn't as important as recognizing that the more judgment-free we become, the happier and more successful we'll be. I asked you to do the judgment assignment because the less judgmental you become, the more ability you gain to access Level 7 energy. In fact, there is an inverse relationship to our level of judgment and our level of creation."

"I can see that. If I'm not clouding my head with lower energies, I have more clarity to create."

"Exactly," I said. "Now let's look at absolute passion, another aspect of Level 7. Absolute passion is not romantic. It's the essence of our core self and the nature of our true existence. The universe is a weave of nonjudgment and absolute passion. We are a single thread among this weave. Our own thread seems isolated, although in a meta-view we can see that we're actually part of an immense embroidery. The reason most people don't see this wider perspective is that they tend to see the trees but not the forest, or to use our metaphor, they don't see the tapestry for the thread."

"But isn't passion full of judgment?" Richard protested. "We have to love something to be passionate about it?" He was clearly probing the revolutionary perspective we were discussing.

"That's a perceptive question," I acknowledged. "I wish I could easily answer it. What you're wondering about reveals a paradox. The paradox is related to something we can call 'detached involvement.' This kind of experience means being totally engaged in a task or activity yet completely detached from the result."

---

**Energetic Principle #5**

## Detached involvement is the highest form of consciousness.

Detached involvement, the most challenging of all principles, offers us the opportunity to fully empathize and emotionally engage in life's situations, and yet, at the same time, "detach" from the judgment, the "story" we see, and the outcome.

When we connect with high levels of energy and employ the principle of detached involvement, we are the participant and the observer, seeing the world from both an objective and a subjective point of view. That is, we are simultaneously writing the scripts of our lives and acting them out. The ability to create the script that we want, hire the people to play the appropriate roles, and participate any way we like, is the mark of high consciousness and pure genius.

Few leaders are able to completely use their full genius ability. By learning to be totally engaged in whatever it is you do, intellectually and emotionally, and also remaining objective and detached from judgment as well as the result, you will unlock your true power and potential.

---

"To put it in context of the I Chart, look at the first circle of awareness in the chart and find the word 'need.' You'll see that it resonates with
Levels 1 and 2 energy. The most successful people in the world operate
with a kind of autopilot mentality, detached from their ego and from
judgment, yet they're completely passionate about what they're doing.
They want to experience everything, but don't need to experience anything. The result is that they don't feel like they have less if they don't get
what they want."

I referred again to the Energetic Self-Perception Chart. "Our diagram
shows the word 'absolute' in front of passion," I said. "Absolute means not
being limited by restrictions or exceptions – unconditional. Absolute passion, therefore, is complete passion for everything that life has to offer.
Level 7 is not about feeling passionate. *Level 7 is passion.*"

I studied Richard's expression. "How much sense does all this make?"

"Plenty, I think," Richard responded. "But let's see if I understand what
you're proposing. Let's use the example of a child who feels absolute passion
for his parents. The child experiences this emotion whether his parents are
'nice' or not. He loves his mother and father unconditionally and wholly.
Am I on the right track here?"

"You are," I said, "and you've offered a good example of what I'm talking about." Richard's scenario was a poignant reminder of how we can stray
from such childhood realities. "What you've said makes me reflect on what
happens to us as we grow up."

"Me, too," Richard said. "It seems that raising our energy level is like
relearning what we've always intrinsically known."

"You've got it," I told him. With this foundation laid, it was time to
explore this level of energy further.

★ ★ ★

Nobel laureate George Wald once said, "Mind, rather than emerging as
a late outgrowth in the evolution of life, has existed always as the matrix,
the source and condition of physical reality – the stuff of which physical
reality is composed is mind-stuff. It is mind that has composed a physical

universe that breeds life and so eventually evolves creatures that know and create . . ."[1] The higher we are on the Energetic Self-Perception Chart, the more quickly we manifest thought into reality. At Level 7, we are connected to an intelligence of the highest order. We can create our world as we choose.

Also at Level 7 energy, time becomes an illusion. This means that while at lower energy levels we may evidence a limiting belief about how long it may take to get something done, at Level 7 we can move quickly to create what we desire.

Earlier, I'd told Richard there was a more effective way to make good decisions than simply relying on intuition. This more effective technique arises from Level 7 energy, and it's potentially our highest level of functioning.

## Holographic Thinking

This Level 7 technique, called "holographic thinking," involves our ability to see multiple perspectives at once. Look at a photograph, and notice that it has only one dimension. That's how a camera sees it. Holograms, however, are created with mirrors to produce a three-dimensional image. Similarly, when you listen to music, you can hear it in mono or stereo, or even from multiple "surround" perspectives.

*When we think holographically, we can view a situation as a whole, taking in not just one of its dimensions, but all of them.* This wider aspect comes from our ability to incorporate our intuition, emotional awareness, experience, knowledge, and finally logic to whatever arises in life. We can think of this approach as including the best of both worlds of brain functioning: intuition and rational analysis. Once we master holographic thinking, we can employ it to ensure the greatest chances for success in every aspect of our business, and especially for making, both on a daily and a long-term basis, the very best decisions that we can.

---

[1]George Wald, "Life and Mind in the Universe," *International Journal of Quantum Chemistry* (March 12, 1984).

> *Holographic thinking allows a leader to see the sphere instead of the circle.
> In practical terms, this means being able to see short-, mid-, and long-term
> goals, as well as the strategies required to reach those goals, all at the same
> time. Leaders capable of doing this understand how all these goals and strate-
> gies fit together. The average person uses only a small percentage of the brain.
> Thinking holographically allows our genius for genuine breakthroughs to
> naturally arise.*

"Imagine you're playing a game of cards with a few of your buddies,"
I explained. "Imagine it's five-card stud poker, but you're the only player to
have 10 cards instead of five for every hand. You understand the advantage?"

Richard chortled. "Deal me in."

"Seriously, when we use our whole brain, we not only have the advantage of perceiving multiple perspectives, but also the ability to apply those
perspectives however we desire."

Richard again evidenced his high intelligence. "So when we think
holographically, we can see both the problem and the solution simultaneously?" he asked.

"Yes, to paraphrase Norman Vincent Peale, 'Problems contain the seeds
of their own solutions.' But let's go one step more. Here's the key: if we
become truly able to see the whole picture, including the past, the present,
and the future of any situation, we wouldn't see anything at all as a problem."

Richard tapped his index finger on the desk in front of him. "You've got
me thinking about something, but I want you to finish before I bring it up."

"Okay, I'm intrigued," I said.

"The shoe is on the other foot now, isn't it?" Richard teased.

"Feels fine to me," I said.

We went on to talk about how holographic thinking offers us the ability to resolve paradoxes. In business, here are just some of the seeming
contradictions that present themselves: trying to satisfy the needs of both
employees and customers, improving product or service quality while keeping costs down, attempting to be more productive while avoiding burnout,
and trying to work less while earning more.

Although it would be easier to think that life is simpler than that, true power comes from accepting that life is often paradoxical and complex. Thus thinking holographically is essential to our survival and our success. When we use a holographic approach to life, we can address opportunities – and challenges – from many perspectives at once.

"Let's take a look at the age-old challenge of trying to fit square pegs into round holes. In this classic puzzle, when we see this situation in the traditional way, we view the pegs, the holes, or both as either wrong or broken. Thinking holographically, we use our creative abilities to explore modifying either the pegs or the holes."

"It does make sense," Richard acknowledged. "I can certainly see the paradoxes, the square pegs and round holes, and the benefit of addressing those challenges in a thoroughly creative way."

"Right: Creativity rules the day. Because Level 7 is without judgment," I told him, "we don't waste energy seeing things from only a right or wrong perspective. When we no longer focus on finding the 'right' answers, we can instead create powerful solutions.

"If you look for the right answer, you're using black-and-white thinking. When this happens, you're usually worried about making mistakes, concerned that your answer may turn out to be 'wrong.' Yet from a wider perspective, the reality is that for nearly all challenges, there isn't only one solution. Your best strategy is being flexible enough to devise something that *works*, instead of something that's *right*. It's this difference that leads to greater production in the workplace."

"The fog's lifting a bit," Richard said. "Give me a practical example."

"Sure, let's look at something that's been on your mind: customer service. Typical rational, linear, left-brained thinking would deduce that the quicker you can get a challenge resolved, the better, so when a customer calls to complain, satisfying the person's need in an efficient manner saves the company money."

But another approach is also possible. "At the highest energy levels," I continued, "instead of just satisfying a customer's challenge, a customer service rep would create a new opportunity from the call. This opportunity might entail 'upselling' the customer an additional needed product. It might result in the person's completing a survey that leads to future sales from this customer or others. Or, it might simply involve creating some goodwill so that the customer concludes the interaction feeling like they were genuinely respected and taken care of, rather than simply 'processed' or even largely ignored.

"If we take more time than it might initially seem is needed to discuss a challenge that's arisen with the customer, we can get to know the customer better. More, our attention to the customer's situation raises energy. Linear thinking would say that this approach to customer service is too costly. Holographic thinking, however, enables us to see the value of what often can't immediately be grasped. How clearly are you seeing the practical dimensions of this kind of approach?"

"This is applying directly to what I was thinking about earlier. You want to know what it was?"

"Only if you're ready to tell me," I said.

"Okay, we'll wait," Richard decided. "You'll find out in two weeks, the next time we meet."

# 13 | Raising the Bar

*The best way to predict the future is to create it.*

—Peter Drucker, business/management expert

That day, when I left, Richard had taken some time to reflect on his relationship with Joe Simpson, one of the principals of the account Nate lost when we all started working together. It was the one that got away.

A few years ago, they had played golf together regularly – and Richard had been trounced just as regularly, but they enjoyed each other's company and liked to bounce business ideas off one another while they shot a few rounds. Not surprisingly, Richard originally sealed the deal for the Simpson and Simpson account on the links.

So now Richard thought it would be worthwhile to check in with Joe and see if there might be a possibility of recapturing Simpson and Simpson's business.

Just as he had done with his call to Nate, Richard visualized calling Joe and his old friend cheerfully agreeing to play a round for old time's sake.

Richard centered himself, settled into the wonderful feeling that always seemed to come when he did this exercise, and picked up the phone.

★ ★ ★

Just a few days after Richard's invitation, Joe joined him at the country club where they used to play. While they were getting ready, Richard asked him how things were going with the new marketing company.

"They're okay," Joe reported blandly.

Richard, no longer one to hesitate, asked, "It sounds like you're not thrilled with their performance – am I sensing an opening here?"

Joe was noncommittal. "You never know," he replied.

Pulling on his glove, Richard challenged, "If I win, we talk about this some more and whether the new and improved O'Connell Consulting has something to offer you."

Joe laughed and said, "We both know you're not going to win, but we can talk about that anyway. If I win, you have to buy me dinner, though."

Joe was a man who loved a good steak and never refused fine wine, so Richard knew it would cost him to take this man out for a nice meal.

"You're on." Richard grabbed his clubs and headed out to the fairway.

★ ★ ★

By the time they reached the back nine, Joe knew he was in danger of missing out on the Porterhouse he had in mind. Richard was playing with a focus and determination Joe hadn't seen in him before. And Richard was having a good time. He felt loose but controlled, able to concentrate on the game when he was up and equally able to relax between shots.

Initially irritated to be falling behind, but now intrigued by his old friend's transformation, Joe teased, "Hey, buddy, what's going on here? Where's that hacker I used to enjoy beating every week?"

Now it was Richard's turn to laugh. He explained that a lot had changed since the last time they saw each other, and his golf game was just one of many improvements. "I'll tell you all about it over dinner tonight," Richard offered.

"But – "

"Even though I'm going to win out here, I'm still your meal ticket tonight." He winked at Joe. "I treat all my clients like royalty. Why don't we call Jodi and Claire to meet us in the dining room after we get cleaned up?"

Later, during dinner, the four of them enjoyed getting reacquainted, and Joe was riveted by what Richard had to say about the recent revitalization of his business and even his personal life.

When the time was right, Richard made his pitch. He proposed a strategic alliance, where he would help Joe Simpson market his law practice, not only with a new campaign designed by O'Connell Consulting's top people, but also by referring his own clients to the firm for legal work if Joe would agree to refer potential clients, too. Since both specialized in the small- to mid-sized business market, it was a perfect fit.

Joe didn't even blink before he gave Richard a solid handshake and welcomed him back into the fold.

★ ★ ★

When Richard saw Don at the office the next day, he pulled him into his office with a conspiratorial grin, then delivered the exciting news: Richard had won back one of the biggest accounts the company had ever served.

"Don, I'm asking you to handle this personally," Richard said. "I told Simpson that I would put my top people on this, and I want us to knock this one out of the park, okay?"

"Great! I'll cherry-pick my partners for the campaign and account management," Don agreed.

"Let's pull together a team meeting this afternoon. You gather your people and schedule it, and let's get started right away," Richard said.

"Oh, and by the way, I've ordered a new nameplate for your door. I don't like the looks of that old one anymore. The new one says, 'Don Taylor, Vice-President.'"

Richard was standing with his arms out, as if bracketing the nameplate. Don looked through Richard's "frame," the corners of his eyes crinkling.

"Congratulations, buddy!" Richard went on. "Consider yourself promoted. It's my way of saying thank you for everything you've done for this company, and especially for what's been happening lately."

Don's usual reserve broke, and he embraced Richard in a bear hug.

"Thank you, too, Richard. I can't tell you what it means to be coming to work each day and looking forward to it again."

"Believe me, I understand," Richard said as they broke apart and shook hands. "I really understand."

★ ★ ★

Back in his office, Don had a flash: *I know she's technically operations and not marketing, but Tonya would be a huge asset on this team.* After all, she had been a corporate attorney. She spoke the language and could lawyer it up with the best of them. He would still be involved — he'd be her "second chair," he'd tell her. So he called her to ask for her leadership and to meet with him to select the rest of the team.

When she arrived, they immediately got to work reviewing the personnel. Don suggested Christina right away and Tonya agreed, "I need someone who knows this business inside and out, someone with heart and personality to balance out my hard edge. She can do all the account servicing, be their day-to-day contact."

They chose two people from the creative department to round out the work team then scheduled their meeting with Richard for later that day.

★ ★ ★

With everyone on board, Richard was delighted with the unusual assembly of people for this job. It didn't follow the "rules" of who should comprise a marketing team, but it fit perfectly for this client. He could see Christina's not-so-secret smile over this development, too. In her proposal to him, she had suggested that she contribute more directly to the bottom line, and thus make her raise more feasible, by becoming involved in some aspect of account management. If things went well with Simpson and Simpson, he could tell she understood she would be able to write her own ticket.

Richard was feeling prescient. He could see in his mind's eye that this would ultimately result in a promotion for Christina and the raise she'd been wanting. Don would inspire the whole group with his new willingness to share not only the work but the glory. The team would become a power center, managing what would become one of the firm's biggest accounts again.

What he couldn't foresee was the offbeat "Love Your Lawyer" campaign they'd launch, a fun and self-effacing promotion of the Simpson and Simpson practice with the message that "We're not just lawyers; we're people too."

## Transforming the Business from the Core

Just what was going on with Richard and his staff? It was the opposite of a catabolic crunch: the rise of anabolic energy. Richard's own energy – elevated, focused, no longer distracted by destructive forces – was enabling the whole organization to rise with him. In essence, the company was playing a metaphysical game of "follow the leader."

Richard was using what he had learned. He employed holographic thinking in coming up with a unique proposal for Simpson and Simpson. He also put centering to use, not only in his business relationships, but also in his golf game. He had become perceptive about other people's energy and finely attuned to his own.

We had three more sessions, mostly to solidify Richard's current strategy and direction. I knew that there was so much more to share with my eager client, and yet we mutually agreed that it was a perfect time to stop with our sessions and let all of the work sink in deeper and continue to play out in his life. He knew that I'd be there for him if needed, which always brings up mixed feelings for me. I so enjoyed working with him that I'd miss that work, but not hearing from him would most likely mean that he was in great shape and living the life of his choosing.

Regardless of what transpired in the future, we agreed to stay in touch. He also promised me that when things settled in a bit, we'd get to enjoy that golf game we never got around to.

# II

# THE
# ENERGY OF
# PERFORMANCE

# 14 | One Step Back, Two Steps Forward

*Don't be afraid to give up the good to go for the great.*
—John D. Rockefeller, business magnate and philanthropist

Over the next year, Richard kept in touch. It was always nice to hear from him, and since his texts arrived infrequently and were very superficial, I took the lack of contact as a sign that things were going quite well.

So when I received a text asking me to meet him for coffee the following week, I knew it wasn't because he missed me. I arrived first and sat down in one of the more private tables. As I waited, I was flooded with many memories of sessions, along with the tough conversations that lead to breakthroughs. I loved all my clients, I really did, but I have to be honest, Richard was someone quite unique. I saw a lot of myself in him and learned so much from him, and I was very much looking forward to our getting together. I felt optimistic that whatever it was that he needed, we were a great partnership and could tackle just about anything.

I stood as Richard arrived, giving him a big hug. "Great to see you, my friend. How are you?"

"Overall, very well. Things are great in my personal life. Businesswise, we're now at 40 team members altogether, with six people under Don in the sales department. The energy in the company is vastly higher and for the most part, it's pretty calm on a day-to-day basis." He laughed, adding, "No more screaming matches in the hallways. Business is steady, though we seem to have plateaued – the sales team just doesn't seem as 'on fire' as they did a few months ago. It's probably to be expected, but I was hoping we'd continue our rapid increases.

"All in all, things aren't *always* very well, but I am. I think that's the biggest difference from our work. I just don't think the way I used to. In fact, sometimes, when I'm really in the moment, I don't even think. So much less stressed and so much more 'in the game,' if you know what I mean."

"I certainly do. Very cool and music to my ears. Sounds like you have integrated a lot of our work together."

"I have and I know there's a lot more I have to do."

"Perhaps," I said, "there's always something new to learn and there's always a next level. That said, there are no 'have-tos.' If you're happy and by your definition, successful, you can choose what you'd like to do next and sometimes, choose what NOT to do. It's always about what experience you'd like to create for yourself."

"Yeah, and that's really why I wrote you. I do get it, but I think I'm so close and there's something I'd really love to experience."

"Close?" I mirrored back to him.

"I'm close to being the leader that I never thought I could be. I do a lot of things really well, but as in the current situation with the sales team, I have trouble motivating people when they are underperforming, and I really believe that is not only holding my company back, but also me, personally."

"You believe you have the power to motivate people to do more?"

"Um. I don't?"

# 15 | The Energy of Influence

*Through every victory and every setback, I've insisted that change is never easy and never quick; that we wouldn't meet all of our challenges in one term, or one presidency, or even in one lifetime.*
—Barack Obama, 44th president of the United States

The following week, we sat down at "our" booth. When the waiter came over, I ordered a club soda with a splash of cranberry, and Richard chose a gin and tonic. I didn't ever recall seeing him drink before, and certainly not during the day.

"Tough week, Rich?"

"Eh, a little. I've been thinking about today and honestly, it's causing me a little stress."

"What's the core thought behind that?"

"I guess that I don't know if I can do it again, you know, make a ton of changes. As fantastic as those changes turned out, I wouldn't say they were easy."

"First, know that it's natural to be hesitant to change. Not many people enjoy all aspects of the process. Next, you worked very hard to get where you are and a possible core thought is that you might have to start over, which could be a crippling thought. Finally, it takes some energy to get back in the grind with me – and to me, that's the most exciting part. What do you think of all that?"

"Yep, I don't enjoy change and I really don't want to start over, which I'm sure is just an old residual catabolic fear. But I have to ask, what could be exciting about needing more energy that I don't have?"

"It's exciting because you do have it. It's in there just waiting for the right formula to appear. Also, it should be a ton easier than you believe to find it, and when you do, you'll always be able to tap into it to assist you in whatever you choose to do."

"Since I don't really understand what you're saying, I'm not sure how easy this will be."

"Just think of how much energy you're spending that's not serving you and what it would feel like to shift that energy toward what you really want."

He thought for a while on that and took a sip of his drink. The waiter arrived to ask how the drinks were and if we were ready to order.

Richard raised his hand; an effort to say, "not right now." I felt that some food might help him focus better.

"Buddy, can I order for you?"

"Uh, sure," he said, still deep in thought while taking another sip.

For both of us, I ordered the "fish of the day," branzino. I remembered that Richard loved fish.

I believed that he was working out whatever plagued him on his own, so instead of delving into it, I decided to ask permission to move the conversation forward.

"How about this?" I blurted out, surprising my client for a second. "Why don't you put any concerns on hold, once again have faith in this process, and if you can even remember those concerns later, we can deal directly with them?"

Richard tilted his head a bit and I could see a small grin forming at the corner of his mouth. "Okay," he said, still working on finishing his smile.

Just then another waiter came by and asked if anyone had taken our order. Richard looked confused. I wasn't sure if he didn't remember me ordering for him or if he was a little annoyed with the waiter.

"Yes, we're covered," I said, producing a full smile as I said it. Richard then smiled as well, which was my sign to get back to business.

"Okay, let's get back to Rory McIlroy, shall we? How did he do this week in the tournament?"

"Uh, he . . . didn't make the cut. Not one of his best efforts."

"He won his last tournament though, right?" I asked.

"Yeah, blew the field away."

"So what do you think was different for him this time?"

"Should have ordered a small rabbit hole shovel along with lunch," he said, now seeming like he was coming back to the present.

"Indeed!" I exclaimed, and then said nothing more for what felt like an hour. My tendency early on as a coach was to jump in too quickly to "rescue" the client, but that's a tendency I was well aware of and I'd since trained myself to just enjoy the purposeful silence.

"So I guess you really want an answer?"

"Kind of the process, if you recall. I handle the question part and the other part is your job."

"You'd think after a year that your jokes would have improved," he said with a full beam.

"I guess, unlike Rory, I'm a bit more consistent."

I was surprised when the meals showed up so quickly. "Looks great," I said to the waiter. "Thank you."

I started to eat and Richard did as well. "Wow, this is really good," he said. I just continued to chew while looking right at him.

"Okay, okay," he said. "I'm a little hesitant to say this because it's just too obvious, but maybe Rory was just off this week."

"Yep, he was off and while that might be a little obvious, know that that was the effect. What might not be obvious was the cause. What might you guess?"

"Hmm," he said. Now I had his full interest. He took another bite of his fish, followed it with a sip of his gin and tonic, and then spoke while he was still chewing. "I don't think he plays that great at Liberty National. Maybe he just doesn't like the design of the course?"

"Possible. What else could have gotten in his way?"

"I don't know ... he didn't sleep well or maybe he wasn't feeling great?"

"We don't know, Richard, but what we do know is that there is a reason why people don't perform consistently. It's all about energy and what influences theirs. And it's not just professional athletes, but guess who else?"

"My employees?"

"Yes, and everyone else on the planet, too."

"Let me back up and give you a quick overview – and then we'll get into some details.

"So far in our work together, we've mostly dealt with shifting *overall* energy from catabolic to anabolic levels. There is nothing more critical for you than that. We've made permanent internal, or core, changes. What we're going to work on next is something that's both simple and accessible, yet very advanced. It's the key to understanding what shapes your energy IN THE MOMENT so that you can perform better, now. This work helps you understand the factors affecting energy around any specific task, situation, or relationship. It will also help you more easily and deeply understand and accept people, which will help you in both your quests to be a more power-ful leader and to be able to further let go of the idea that you need to be as involved you are in the day-to-day stuff.

"Any time you are not performing up to the level of your potential, something is blocking your energy, and this is the key thing to remember: if something is blocking your energy, you don't have 100% of your energy available to you to use in a given moment.

"With me so far?" I stopped for a second to check in.

"Yeah," he said without hesitation. "It makes sense and I'm already beginning to see the potential here."

"Did you say see the potential? Oh man, I think you've just graduated to the level of pun master."

"Learned from the best," he said. "So what can block my energy?"

"There are six energetic influencers: physical, mental, emotional, social, environmental, and spiritual. The understanding of what exactly these influencers are, how they affect our performance, and how we need to deal with them when they are working against us, are keys to success.

"While you might be a little upset with the sales performance, know that this situation has offered you the opportunity to take the next step in your journey, and perhaps help you find not only the success that awaits you, but the peace you long for."

"Wow," he said, and he exhaled more air after he said it. "So you're saying the challenge was a good thing?"

"It's not good or bad, but it is an opportunity for growth," I replied.

"I get it and I'm ready. Tell me more about the influencers."

"Let's go back one more time to Rory's golfing," I said. "You thought maybe his non-stellar play last week was possibly because he didn't like the design of that course. What kind of influencer might that be?"

"I guess . . . environmental?"

"Of course, without asking him some questions, we really have no way of knowing, but environmental would be an excellent guess."

"By the way, it may be obvious, but the way Rory – or anyone – approaches any course, or any situation, is completely unique to him. This means that even if it was an environmental influencer that lowered his energy and therefore decreased his capacity, that wouldn't mean that everyone he played against responded the same way to the same environment. In fact, other people might not have been bothered at all by the course design and still others might have had their energy raised by it.

"To complicate things a little bit more, what affects your energy in one situation may not affect it in another and what affects it one day may not on another day. That's why this work is most effective when done as close to a performance as possible. And when I say performance – anything you do is a performance; whether it's having a conversation, working on a task, playing golf in front of a TV audience, playing with your kids, or in the case of your sales team, closing new clients and deals."

Richard nodded slowly, taking in my words. "So six factors that influence energy in anything we do . . . right?"

"Exactly. How about we go through the influencer categories one by one and then, once you know more about them, we can use that information to address what's happening in the sales department."

"Sounds great," Richard said, nodding enthusiastically, and obviously sounding more hopeful than he had the last time we met.

# 16 | A Body of Knowledge (Physical Influencers)

*Our own physical body possesses a wisdom which we who inhabit the body lack.*
—Henry Miller, author

"Let's start with physical, because it's probably the easiest to understand. How well do you think you'd do at leading an important meeting when you have a splitting headache, or if you didn't sleep well the night before?

"Not well at all, at least not at my norm."

"Exactly. If your body isn't able to function in the way that's optimal for you, or in the manner to which you're accustomed, it's going to detract from your energy and that lowers your capacity."

"What do you mean by capacity, again?" he asked.

"If you have an eight-ounce glass, what is its potential?" I questioned.

"Eight ounces?" he said, confidently.

"Yes, but what if you only poured six ounces into it?"

He thought for a moment. "So it has a potential of eight ounces, but since only six are available, its current potential is only six ounces. So that's its current capacity?"

"Very nice. You got it now. And while people always have 100% of their potential available to them, in each moment, we not only want to know their current capacity, but we also want to make sure they get THAT capacity in the moment. So if the glass had six ounces but you only poured out half of it, you're not even getting the current potential. If you come to a company meeting not feeling well, you might be an eight out of ten. So your capacity is now eight. We can now try to raise that capacity, of course, but we also want to make sure you're performing at least at the eight that you are currently capable of."

I paused for him to take it in, which he indicated was the case by his head nod, so I continued.

"Some of the physical factors that can detract from your energy might be any type of illness, an injury, lack of sleep, poor nutrition or hydration, a lack of exercise, or asking your body to perform well past the limitations of its physical capacity (for example, running a marathon, when you've never run a mile).

"For any given task, optimizing these factors can help ensure that you are able to utilize 100% of what your body is capable of providing you when you need it."

"Makes total sense," Richard said. "I certainly am more motivated and productive when I'm feeling fit and healthy." He paused, looking pensive. "What about someone who has a permanent physical disability? Will their energy always be depleted?"

"Keep in mind that we're not comparing one person to another; again, we're talking about taking whatever one person has available to them and getting the most from that potential. If someone can bench-press 300 pounds as a 'max' but only 260 on a given day, something is getting in their way. If they worked out hard and did all the right things, perhaps they could increase their max to say, 310. At that point, the process we're discussing would help them, on any particular desirable day, bench-press 310. As the potential for what someone can do changes, that becomes a new set point. So, you can help people increase their potential, but for performance, we're trying to help people get the most out of what they have available."

---

Some of the physical influencers on energy and performance include:

► Health

► Sleep

► Nutrition and hydration

► Breathing and oxygen level

► Exercise/body motion and movement

► Injury and illness

# 17 | Mind Your Energy (Mental Influencers)

*When walking, walk. When eating, eat.*

—Zen proverb

"Let's go onto the next influencer, which is the mental factor. This involves having the right "brainpower" for the task at hand. Brainpower includes being present to your task with clarity, concentration, and focus. Basically, it's the machine that's known as your brain, working in the most efficient and effective way it can. The brain also needs the right amount of stimulation, with the optimal degree of challenge. Too much or too little will cause a less than optimum performance.

"Your energy will be diminished when mental factors aren't ideal – like if you are multitasking and splitting your attention, stretching yourself too thin, you have conflicting demands or are distracted, or other factors that slow down or limit your brainpower.

"And before you ask, no two people have the same potential, because no two people have the exact same brain capabilities. Let me pause there – off the top of your head, when was a time when mental influencers depleted your energy?"

Richard thought a moment. "I remember before I met you, Jodi always complained that I was constantly distracted and thinking about work. I don't suppose I was present or energetically at my potential when I was talking to her, huh?"

"Exactly," I replied, "Great example. And it's one of the reasons that, as your stress at work decreased, your relationship dynamics shifted in a more positive direction."

---

Mental influencers on energy and performance include:

► Alertness

► Concentration and focus

► Acute awareness

► Ability to access creativity and intuition

► Clarity

► Memory access

► Degree of mental stimulation

# 18

## "You Gotta Have Heart" (Emotional Influencers)

*Let's not forget that the little emotions are the great captains of our lives and we obey them without realizing it.*

—Vincent van Gogh, painter

"Ready for the emotional influencer?" I asked, chuckling.

"What's so funny?" Richard asked.

"I was just thinking that when we started working together, you held the limiting belief that emotions didn't belong in the workplace – and here I'm about to explain why the exact opposite is the case."

I went on to explain that emotional influencers involve how well someone's unique needs and desires are being met by what they are doing – when people's needs and desires are met, their energy will be enhanced and they're going to be more excited, engaged, and enthusiastic about doing what they're doing.

"Another emotional influencer on energy involves whether you have the emotional control to be able to choose how to express yourself in an appropriate manner, as well as to respond, instead of react, to any given situation. As I'm sure you learned, a leader who can honestly express emotions in an anabolic way is a leader who is better respected and trusted."

Richard nodded, looking a little sheepish. "I remember when we first met, I was almost hopeless, dreading coming to work, and was anything but excited and engaged. And, I barely shared anything about myself with others in the company, much less how I actually felt about people and things. And yes, I learned that the opposite is indeed true. Besides being more respected, people just liked me more for being real, and . . . they seemed to want to enjoy work more and were definitely more productive. I learned a ton about energy, and I think this aspect of it had the greatest influence on my company."

"Absolutely," I replied, "The emotional influencer was probably one of the strongest in creating your energy level back then and had a lot to do with the challenges in the company. Actually, it's still a very strong influence, but now, in a more positive way."

---

Emotional influencers on energy and performance include:

► Emotional awareness and understanding

► Emotional expression

► Emotional control

► Creating the emotions that fuel performance (satisfaction, excitement, calm, etc.)

# 19 | The People Factor (Social Influencers)

*Let us be grateful to people who make us happy, they are charming gardeners who make our souls blossom.*

—Marcel Proust, novelist, essayist, and critic

"Moving on," I said, "let's look at social factors influencing energy. This is an often overlooked aspect of energy, but it's a very important one. Social influencers involve having the 'ideal' amount and type of interaction with others. This may involve being surrounded by like-minded people who are excited about the same things you are. Or, you may thrive in a culture that emphasizes individual effort over teamwork – or vice versa.

"Social influencers detract from energy when social conditions aren't optimal for you, and also when other people's catabolic energy affects your own energy. If you value a casual game of golf with friends, but find yourself in a competitive tournament with strangers, your energy will likely be depleted. And of course, the opposite is true; if you value competition, you might get a 'high' from that and not perform as well in a casual game. Also, even if you're excited about doing something, when others around you are catabolic, their emotions and reactions can affect your own energy and enthusiasm.

"Think about how the entire office was affected by Don and Tonya's fighting, and how Nate brought down the energy of those around him with his hopelessness."

Richard nodded again. "And when Kyle came on board, it was like a breath of fresh air that energized everyone."

---

Social influencers on energy and performance include:

► Your desired amount and type of social interaction

► Your attitude toward working with others

► The influence of coworkers – dealing with catabolic relationships and cultures

► Your ability to communicate with and influence others

► Presence of desired support systems/having someone to be accountable to

# 20

# The Whispers of the Trees (Environmental Influencers)

*Nature holds the key to our aesthetic, intellectual, cognitive, and even spiritual satisfaction.*

—E.O. Wilson, scientist

"Exactly," I said. "Now to another fairly easy one – environmental factors. In a nutshell, environmental influencers can directly affect how your body works, and, consciously or not, can also include a belief or feeling that your environment will allow you to complete or enjoy the task you're about to do in the way that you'd like to. If you believe that something in your environment will prevent you from functioning in an optimal manner, or in the manner to which you are accustomed, then your energy will most likely be depleted."

234

Richard broke in, excitedly. "So if Rory believes that he doesn't play well at Liberty National, his energy will be depleted, and he actually won't play as well as he could."

"Rory may not even be aware of any belief that he doesn't play well at Liberty. He may just feel 'off' when he's there. And someone else who feels that the same course 'fits them well' will likely play closer to his potential there – given that all the other factors are optimized."

Again, Richard interrupted. "And that's one of the reasons Christina's energy shifted after her workspace was spiffed up with the new desk and the clutter was removed, right?"

"You got it. Everything is energy, including her desk, the clutter around it or lack thereof, and the 'relationship' she has with that environment. Even something as simple as too much or too little light can influence performance.

"Only the very powerful spiritual influencer to go."

---

Environmental influencers on energy and performance include:

► Conditions/climate

► Setting/surroundings

► Equipment and clothing

► Availability and use of technology

# 21

## The Value of Purpose (Spiritual Influencers)

*Just as a candle cannot burn without fire, men cannot live without a spiritual life.*
—Buddha

"Spiritual influencers involve your purpose, beliefs, values, gifts, desires, and goals, in relation to what you specifically want to do and how you want to do it. So when we say spiritual, we basically mean anything that can't be measured or anything that doesn't fit into one of the other influencer categories. When what you're doing is in line with your spiritual preferences, you have a better chance at being at the top of your game. When they're not . . . when something causes you to question or comes into conflict with those factors, then your energy can be profoundly affected. In fact, even though it's often the last thing people look at, your spiritual alignment could be the most powerful influence on your performance.

"Remember at the beginning of our work together when you were about to give up? One of the factors influencing your energy was the fact that you lost track of why you did what you did – you lost your 'love of the game.'"

"And when Christina felt valued by me, something that's really important to her," Richard mused, "her energy skyrocketed."

---

Spiritual influencers on energy and performance include:

► Connection to purpose

► Alignment with vision, values, and goals

► Fulfillment of desires

► Ability to create life balance

► Having something to look forward to

► Conscious awareness/perspective

---

"You got it, Richard. Now, that was a really simplified explanation, because in 'real life' the factors don't work in isolation. For example, if you have a headache, a physical influencer, this may cause you to have a lack of focus – a mental influencer.

"Spiritual factors have a very strong influence on the other factors that influence energy. Without a sense of purpose, for example, how much focus or clarity could you have? How emotionally balanced or reactive might you be? How physically invigorated or drained might you feel? How much desire would you have to be with others, or to create an environment that fed your senses?

"Similarly, you can see the ripple effect that mental factors can have on the other elements. You may know how what you're doing is related to your purpose or even your goals, but without true clarity and the ability to concentrate, you may end up quite frustrated and feeling like you're not making progress. This could throw your emotions off balance, which flows through to your physical vitality, which might be affected. Likewise, your social relationships might begin to suffer.

"Anyone who has experienced grief can attest to the effect that emotions can have on the other areas of life. Similarly, those who have gone through major physical illnesses know that spiritual, mental, and emotional factors were affected along with their body. Those who have experienced the loss of a support network, or a major household move also can verify that those events can have wide-reaching effects.

"So it's both simple and complex, but even if you just concentrate on the six factors individually, you'll have great insight into what's affecting your energy and the energy of others."

After finishing dessert and paying the bill, Richard said, "I think that's enough for today. I have a ton to think about."

"Of course," I said, "we've covered an enormous amount. What would you like to do this week to reinforce what we've talked about?"

"How about I keep track of what takes away from my energy in different situations? I can journal that if you think it will help me. I remember how impactful the Judgment Journal was for me."

"You can definitely journal about that. Another thing you can do to begin to create some 'positive influencer awareness' is to start to create what I like to call a Success Formula – a list of the factors that help you maximize your energy, and thereby propel you to perform at your maximum current potential. Each person's Success Formula is unique, and you'll continually refine yours by keeping track of what does and doesn't work for you. You can keep a journal to track what affects your energy. How does that sound?"

"Sounds perfect."

We made plans to meet at the office the following week, shook hands, and parted ways.

## Richard's Assignments

- Be aware of negative energy influencers.
- Create a "Success Formula" journal.

Here are some examples of components of Success Formulas:

**Spiritual:** Remember how connected I am to the mission of my company.

**Mental:** Stay focused and undistracted.

**Emotional:** No matter what happens, I will remain calm.

**Physical:** Stay loose and relaxed.

**Social:** Remember to enjoy those I'm with.

**Environmental:** Take a moment to notice the beauty around me.

# 22 | Exploring the Core Issue

*I can only control my own performance. If I do my best, then I can feel good at the end of the day.*

—Michael Phelps, Olympic swimmer

When I arrived at O'Connell Consulting, I was surprised and pleased to see someone else at Christina's desk. I introduced myself to the new receptionist, Miguel, who told me that Richard was expecting me and that I could walk back to his office.

On my way, I smiled as I saw Christina's office, which had a sign with her name and Client Liaison title on it. After chatting with her for a few moments, I walked to Richard's office, nodding as I saw Don and Tonya who were in a meeting with someone I didn't know.

Richard greeted me warmly. "I'm glad you're here, Bruce, and I'm ready to get to work!"

*What a difference from the first time I was here*, I thought. "Excellent," I said, "Why don't you tell me how your assignments went and then we'll get down to business."

Richard showed me his Success Formula list. "It's a work in progress, of course, but it was eye-opening doing this and journaling about what depleted my energy."

"What was your biggest takeaway?" I queried.

"That I am energized when other people smile a lot and mean it. It's a social influencer. That's also why I've been a bit down; our sales team doesn't seem to be having fun anymore."

"That's a great insight. How would you like to move that forward today, and if you choose not to do so or prefer to hold off till another time, what else would you like to work on?"

"I definitely want to take a look at the sales team. I've thought long and hard about each of them. I'm sure that each one of them is normally very anabolic. I can't pinpoint any 'trouble people' and they all seem to have great attitudes. I think they're motivated, but they are all underperforming. So something is off.

"I'm guessing," he continued, "that because it's the entire team, that it's something either environmental or social."

"Interesting," I commented. "Why do you believe that to be the case?"

"Because our mission and vision haven't changed, so while it could still be a factor, I'm ruling out spiritual as the main cause of the trouble here. I also figured that if it were mental or physical, it would be limited to a person or two, so more individualized. And if it were emotional and they were all affected by it, the only way I could see that happening would be if something was really off with Don or if someone new who wasn't a good fit came into the group. I know it's just a guess, but I suspect that I'm right about this."

I congratulated him on the thoroughness of his assessment. We spoke for a while longer about it, and in the end, Richard was still sure of his conclusions. He decided that he'd like to meet with each of the sales team members one-on-one and ask them some questions. He added that he could listen for clues to confirm his assessment as well as try to home in on which of the two influencers it was, exactly. He might even find the solution right then.

"Unless you'd rather do those meetings," he paused and smiled, knowing full well that I'd say no. "Though I would like some pointers as to what to ask them."

"Fair enough," I said. "You can start the conversation by explaining what you are trying to figure out and by asking them to describe the most important task they have on their to-do list." I went on to suggest several questions Richard could ask.

---

### Questions to Ask to Assess Energetic Reasons for Lack of Performance

- Describe the most important task on your to-do list.
- How engaged are you in taking on this task?
- What would increase your desire to do it?
- When you think about doing it, what kind of tension or anxiety comes up?
- What would have to be different in order to have no tension or anxiety?
- When was the last time you felt really good about the task? What was different then?

---

"As you're listening to their responses," I finished, "allow your intuition to help you decide if would be beneficial to directly ask them what they believe the real challenge is. Then, you can continue to follow up with questions. All of these will hopefully give you the clarity you're looking for, and possibly the solution to the issue."

Richard wrote some notes, then said, "No time like the present. Would you mind sitting in on the meetings? I'll do them via video conference, as the sales team works remotely. I will lead them, but perhaps you'll see something I miss."

I nodded in agreement. Richard said he'd like to start with Jamal, who'd been moved over from the art department into sales. Jamal, usually very productive, recently had his first less than stellar performance review.

Richard started the conversation as planned. Jamal answered, and by probing a bit, Richard learned that he was having some marital issues and couldn't focus as well as normal. Richard asked what he thought he needed to move things in the desired direction, and Jamal said it might be time for counseling. He said he wasn't sure it would save his marriage, but he was going to try. Richard couldn't identify any other glaring issues. As the call ended, Jamal told Richard that he felt much better after venting a little and he felt much clearer. Richard thanked Jamal for his honesty and his trust and told him he'd check in with him in a month or sooner if he chose to.

After we ended the call, Richard asked, "Mental or emotional influencer, or both? I know, we can't really know with 100% certainty. Either way, maybe I was wrong about thinking otherwise."

I nodded. "Seemed to me that it was a little of both. I'm not sure you have enough information to change your belief that the core issue affecting the group is either environmental or social. How did you think the conversation went?"

"Well, I can see how his marital issues would affect his work performance. I'm kind of relieved that it was that and nothing to do with work itself, but I'm more confused about things regarding the team in general. But yeah, I don't have enough info yet. I'm ready for the next one."

Over the course of the day, Richard spoke to each member of the team individually.

One person had a technology issue with her new laptop which she felt was making her less productive. Richard called the IT department on the spot and made a plan to replace the laptop the following day.

At the end of the day, Richard and I debriefed. Other than those two people, the overall lack of sales production was still a mystery. To a person, they all raved about working from home. They liked the flexibility and the lack of commuting.

"I'm still not sure what's going on," said Richard. "I'm tending to want to rule out environmental, as they all seemed to flourish in their own environment. So maybe still social, but I don't get it. They all seemed so happy with the job and in working from home. Plus, they all seem to really like and respect each other – and Don says they work well together.

"Perhaps we should have a team meeting? Actually, even though it's only the sales team that seems to have an issue, I'd like to have the entire company at the meeting. I think you should run the meeting, Bruce. What do you think?"

I thought about challenging him on asking me to do things that we both know he should do, but decided instead to focus on the more current issue. Therefore, I just encouraged him to do it himself, if for no other reason than I could watch the room to perhaps see things that went unsaid. Richard agreed, and also said that he'd ask the sales team to come into the office so they could all meet in person. We set a meeting date for the following week, and he said that he'd work on the meeting agenda.

# 23

# A Meeting
# of the Minds

*Leadership and learning are indispensable to each other.*
—John F. Kennedy, 35th president of the United States

The following week, Richard stood in front of the room and began talking into a microphone securely positioned on its stand. I listened to him fully addressing the issue, which was the overall decline in sales production, and doubted it was a surprise to anyone. He made sure everyone knew that the meeting was not to find a *person* to be the "culprit," but rather to work together as a group to see if they could find the *energetic* culprit and solve the challenge. He then shared what he had learned, or more accurately, what he hadn't learned in the individual interviews. Jamal appeared a little nervous, I noticed, but Richard looked him in the eye, obviously reassuring him that he would not discuss his personal matters with the group.

Glancing around the room, I saw that most people seemed tense and probably a little uncomfortable. I couldn't assess whether the sales team or the others were most uncomfortable.

Richard obviously noticed too, because he then asked, "So what do you think is going on here?" I saw people looking around to see if anyone would reply, and no one did.

What happened next was why I became a coach in the first place. I saw Richard take a slow deep breath through his nose and blow it out hard through his mouth. He repeated it. He then slowly eyed the room and I could easily detect a Mona Lisa smile that told me that he had just shifted to a more meta view of the situation. He wasn't judging, complaining, or even observing as he gazed around the room. Instead, he had put the issue on hold and was now in a state of deep appreciation. He was masterfully shifting his own emotions to shift the group. I know this because I felt it. I was sure of it.

I could also feel — and what I was observing confirmed this feeling — that the room was lightening up. People began to breathe more in rhythm together, and their body movements began to mimic one another. Like a bunch of grandfather clocks synchronizing their pendulums, this was the process of entrainment, as they too must have observed and felt Richard's energetic shift and, consciously or not, become more emotionally engaged and connected to him on a deeper level.

Richard seemed in no rush as he took the microphone from its stand with one hand and moved the stand to the far end of the room. He grabbed a chair that had been placed against a wall, dragged it to where he had been standing, sat down, and looked out at his team.

What I would normally have expected to be a very uncomfortable silence continued in what I could only describe as a group meditation, with eyes open.

Richard took one more deep breath and asked, "Why did you decide to work here?"

I thought it was an amazingly crafted and insightful question, at the exact time needed. I loved how he was addressing the group but using the word "you" as if he was talking to one person. I also liked the strategy of opening the question up to anyone, thereby addressing this as a company and not a team issue.

After what seemed like a few seconds but was probably more like a full minute, Don finally spoke. His resounding voice made it unnecessary for him to stand or need the help of any amplification, and he remained seated as he shared his thoughts.

"I think I've been here at least as long as anyone, and so my answer might be very different than some of the newer family."

*Family . . . nice touch, Don*, I thought.

"When I first joined O'Connell Consulting, it was because I loved marketing. I took this job because I could not only do that here, but also because the company was new and I believed there was a great opportunity for me to advance. I didn't want to build my own company but I figured I could sort of make this my own company."

He then stood and continued. He was now better able to see everyone behind him. "When I now look back and see myself, I can hardly recognize that person. He was the one who wanted – no, needed – to be a leader; needed to be in control and while very opportunistic, his goals were to seek and . . ." – he paused and smiled – ". . . only if he had to . . . destroy to get what he wanted. I'm sure a couple of you old-timers remember how Tonya and I used to converse in a very professional manner." He comically used air quotes for the word "converse."

I thought I might see a big reaction from the people in the room, but other than a few nods and smirks, I didn't.

"But that Don is no longer around," he continued, "and I'm happy about that, although I do appreciate who he helped me become.

"So that's why I joined, but again, unlike a lot of you, I had the opportunity to join for a second time. O'Connell went through a whirlwind of change not too long ago, and it was then that I believed we started a new company. I had a choice to engage, and I made it, but my reasons were very different than the first time.

"I wanted to be part of a family. That's it. Nothing more. After our shift as a company, I never saw business or the people in it the same way again. It was no longer about me; it was about us, and I shifted my goals from something down the road to a much more manageable and simple one: I was going to enjoy each moment I worked with each person I worked with. My new definition of family."

As he sat, everyone else rose and applauded. Richard did too.

When the applause subsided, Richard waited and then asked in a matter-of-fact way, "Okay, who's next?" which caused an eruption of laughter. Even I was thinking, *So glad I don't have to follow that!*

People still beamed as they began to sit again, and without too long of a wait, Kyle remained standing.

"When I was first hired, Don told me that I was going to be one of the new and improved models, or at least that was my interpretation of what he said," which led to some head nods and more, albeit softer, laughter.

"Seriously," he said, "I love what Don said honestly, I think I *just* got what a 'new and improved model' means. He was talking about the evolution of the company and a new and improved energy, not about me specifically, DAMN IT!"

The group laughed again, and this time it was uncontrollable. At that very moment, I don't think anyone even remembered why they were called to that meeting.

Kyle continued. "When I interviewed here I felt an excitement; an energy, unlike that of any company I'd been in. I just wanted to be a part of it. I felt energized every single time I came into the office. And if I have to be honest, today . . ." He paused as if he didn't want to finish the sentence. "Today, I don't feel it as much. I just assumed because our numbers were flat, everyone was down a little too. Honestly, I'm also a little worried about possible layoffs."

BOOM! I got so excited by what I just heard that it was hard to resist jumping up and commenting. I had to take a deep breath and remind myself that this company was in good hands. So I just waited for my client, perhaps even my new and improved model, to take the lead.

"Thank you, Kyle!" Richard exclaimed. "That was interesting and insightful. Who here can relate to what Kyle just said?"

All six of Kyle's colleagues on the sales team, including Don, nodded and/or raised their hands.

"Huh!" Richard said. "Looks like the whole sales team feels the same way. Who can tell me when they think the disconnection began?"

It appeared that Richard's initial assessment was right on, after all. *Atta boy*, I thought.

I could see that people were thinking by how they tilted their heads and looked up. Some pursed their lips as they looked up, another telltale sign. I could also feel that we had made a huge shift away from the problem and into the solution, which was now obvious to me and excited me, as I knew it was no longer a matter of *if* the answer would be verbalized, but a matter of *when*.

"Before anyone answers, let me explain to those of you who don't know what Bruce and I have been working on," Richard offered. "It might help identify the source of the disconnection."

I was now convinced that Richard had the answer as well and was now deliberately getting a greater energetic buy-in by leading the team in the process of discovery.

Richard went on to describe the spiritual, mental, emotional, physical, social, and environmental influences on energy. When he got to the social influencer, I could see the sales team perk up and give glances to one another. Sure enough, when Richard finished his explanation, Kyle raised his hand and stood up.

"Though I love working from home, I think there was something about being in the same room with my team members that was much more energizing than our video meetings. I would never have thought that before because I love the convenience and comfort of working at home. But I just realized what that cost me, and us."

The other sales team members nodded vigorously.

Don stood up as well and asked Richard if he could meet with his team privately to brainstorm solutions.

"I think that's a great idea, Don." He thanked everyone for being there, and people left the room chatting and smiling.

When we got back to his office, Richard commented that it was strange that the issue hadn't come up in the one-on-one meetings.

"This was a very difficult issue to identify," I said. "After all, they were still meeting and brainstorming on video calls and saying so often how they appreciated the freedom of working at home. There was just one key element missing – how they all played off each other's energy in person. So while one desire was achieved by their working from home, another desire, and a deep value for each of them, was taken away."

Richard nodded. "How about we meet at Giuseppe's again next week and debrief a little more? I'll let you know what Don and the team decided to do. Also, I'd really like to know more about how to sustain the kind of energy we experienced at the end of the meeting today."

I nodded back, "Get ready for another rabbit hole! I'll see you next week."

As I left, I turned back and said, "That was an excellent meeting, Richard, well done."

# 24 | Practice Makes Conscious (The Core Disciplines)

*Life isn't about finding yourself. Life is about creating yourself.*
— George Bernard Shaw, playwright and writer

The following week, Richard reported that the sales team had decided to come into the office together one day per week. Obviously, there'd been no uptick in business yet, but he could sense the change in energy.

"So about that new rabbit hole," he said. "Are there any 'tricks' to maintaining a high energy level? I'd really like to sustain the energy level I've been experiencing this week."

"For sure," I said, "but maybe we should order first."

We ordered our lunch and then I began.

"As we've discovered, there are many influences on your energy in any particular moment. The work we've been doing on the influencers deals with changing energy in the moment so that your energy is at the highest possible level at that time. So, to make sure energy is high, you'll want to have your employees constantly look at the influencers and make a lot of adjustments. Having people do what you did with your Success Journal will help them learn what works best for them and to make those adjustments.

"The next part of the equation is where the rabbit hole continues and never stops, and it centers around building a life philosophy and way of being that automatically resonates at high energy levels – and thus makes you less likely to experience energy drains in the first place.

"That life philosophy includes continuing to practice everything we've worked on since we started together, including mastering your awareness and practice of the seven energy levels to continually raise your level of consciousness awareness.

"I can also offer you 10 energetic disciplines that highly conscious people practice. Before I share them with you, know that this isn't a quick fix. First, you will learn the 10 disciplines, then you will practice them, and finally, along with all the other work we just discussed, you will live them. In doing so, you will permanently shift your attitude and belief system, thus raising your overall energy for leadership and for life, as well as increasing the potential you have to perform." I then pulled out a variation to a famous line from the old movie *Jaws*. "So basically, you're going to need a bigger glass."

I'm sure he got the reference to both the movie and to my earlier example of the eight-ounce glass, since Richard laughed, lifted his glass, and offered a toast.

"The 10 disciplines of high potentiality and performance are:

1. Awareness
2. Acceptance
3. Conscious Choice
4. Trusting the Process
5. Authenticity
6. Fearlessness
7. Confidence
8. Connection
9. Presence in the Moment
10. 100% Energetic Engagement

"All of the disciplines are intertwined and, to some extent, dependent on one another. You need to be aware and to accept 'what is' before you can make conscious choices. Once you know how to make conscious choices, you must then trust that the process you've chosen will get you where you want to go.

"When you live the first four disciplines, you are much more able to be authentic, fearless, and confident, which will lead you to the mastery practices of being connected, present, and energetically engaged and committed. Live all of them, and you will be a master.

"As you embark on the journey of learning the disciplines, remember what I just said about this not being a quick fix – it's a process. In fact, it may take years, or even a lifetime; that's why you practice them, taking small steps each day toward higher consciousness and potential."

I took a printed sheet of paper out of my briefcase and handed it to him. "Here are the 10 disciplines with some explanation about how to practice each one."

## The 10 CORE Disciplines of High Potential and Performance

### ►Discipline 1: Awareness

When you practice this discipline, you constantly observe and assess yourself and everything around you. You understand that what is true for you is not necessarily the Truth. At any given moment, you are aware of who you are, why you are who you are, and how you are reacting to your circumstances.

### ►Discipline 2: Acceptance

When you practice this discipline, you accept what is. You don't beat yourself up. You accept all aspects, traits, quirks, etc., of yourself and others. You don't take things or people personally, and don't look at anything that happens as more than it actually is. Instead, you accept that what has just occurred has occurred as it did, and don't catastrophize any particular experience, circumstance, or action. You understand that everything is perfectly okay, just as it is.

*(continued)*

►**Discipline 3: Conscious Choice**

When you practice this discipline, you know that the more overall energy you have, the more present and sharp you are, and the quicker and better you are able to make the best choices. You practice discernment and nonjudgment and simultaneously use logic, emotion, and intuition to make quick and accurate decisions. You know that you are always at choice, and so, instead of reacting, you respond by adjusting to given circumstances.

►**Discipline 4: Trusting the Process**

When you practice this discipline, you know that while you always want to perform at your best at any moment, there's always a focus on long-term growth. You understand your true goals, so instead of jumping into the latest and greatest new/best thing, you have faith in your current plan, and work that plan to excellence. You look for the lesson in each experience as you constantly review your plan and makes shifts as needed.

►**Discipline 5: Authenticity**

When you practice this discipline, you understand that while we are always searching for the greatest and most powerful expression of ourselves as people, we are each a once-in-all-history unique person. As we masterfully walk to the beat of our own drum, we inspire others to do the same. By being no one other than ourselves, we automatically express high levels of energy and, instead of effortful output, our performances, and indeed our lives, are effortless works of art.

►**Discipline 6: Fearlessness**

When you practice this discipline, you embrace the unknown and take reasonable chances without worry or doubt. You realize that fear does not exist in the present moment, and that whatever is unfolding will ultimately serve you. You know there is nothing to lose, and therefore, nothing to fear.

►**Discipline 7: Confidence**

When you practice this discipline, you are a master in being. You know that confidence is an internal capability, and instead of waiting for something to happen to bring confidence, you choose to create it. Experience (and your attitude) has taught you to trust yourself and let go of any concern about what might happen. Because you know that you can handle whatever occurs and will grow and learn from it, you embrace all outcomes. You are able to summon up feelings of success, peace, power, and calm and use them to create any experience you choose.

►**Discipline 8: Connection**

When you practice this discipline, you are aware not only of the influence that each person, place, and thing has on you, but also of your influence on them. You are also aware that no moment occurs in isolation, in that each event is influenced by the past and connected to the future. You know that by tapping into the power of anabolic energy around you, you are never alone, and can play at the top of your game without trying to force anything to happen.

►**Discipline 9: Presence in the Moment**

When you practice this discipline, you focus on one action at a time. You cannot be distracted, as you are totally present to the task and experience at hand. Your intuition is alive and you are open to each moment as it occurs. Once that moment is over, you put all your energy into the next one.

►**Discipline 10: 100% Energetic Engagement**

When you practice this discipline, you play full out. You know that true power can only be achieved through powerful intentions, full commitment, and engaging 100% of your energy into action.

# 25 | Never Underestimate the Power of Energy

*Mastering others is strength. Mastering yourself is true power.*
—Lao Tzu, philosopher

Two months later, Richard and I met in his office for an update session in which he shared all that had been happening. The sales team in-person experiment provided near immediate and positive results. Richard felt much more relaxed and, in his words, "free." He accomplished so much and yet he was very humble. You might imagine that events like these would leave a man bursting with pride and feelings of accomplishment, but he gratefully attributed much of what had occurred to good fortune.

"How lucky am I to be working with these people? Sure, I've done my fair share of hard work, but what we've accomplished has been nothing short of miraculous. When we first met, you asked me to consider what 'miracles' I'd like to have occur, and back then I just didn't understand how miracles are the business of energy, not magic. Whether it's anabolic or catabolic, I guess we should never underestimate the power of energy."

"What do you think the biggest miracle has been?" I asked.

While Richard considered my question, he looked at the ceiling in his office. When he dropped his eyes to mine, he seemed shaken. "You know what it is?" he asked. "It's that I survived before, living my life the way I did."

He had come to acknowledge how powerful a leader he could be – and already was – on his own. At the same time, he valued every person who helped make his organization what it had become. He truly felt that they were a part of him, and he was a part of them. It was impossible for him even to imagine the divisiveness and chaos that had confronted him every day before our work together began. It was impossible for him to imagine living as his old self.

That was a miracle.

# 26 | A Lesson in Presence

*Find ecstasy in life; the mere sense of living is joy enough.*
—Emily Dickinson, poet

Lightly cloudy, barely any noticeable wind, and close to 70 degrees, it was a perfect day for our long-awaited golf match. We met at the clubhouse and sat down for a quick breakfast before heading out to the course.

I tried to remain objective and present to the moment, but I admitted to myself that I had a little attachment to seeing what effect, if any, our recent work would have on Richard's golf game. Of course, I also looked forward to finally being able to enjoy the game I loved with one of my all-time favorite clients. I was about to learn about the former, along with a life lesson, before we even hit our first tee shots.

"First," he said, after sitting straight up in his chair, lifting his chin and facing me at eye level, "let me state the obvious: that I am forever in your debt for what you've done for not only my business, but for me, my family, and pretty much everything else in my life. Nothing will ever be the same, and while I did learn a great deal from the past, I won't miss it."

I thought about my belief in the power of coaching and knew he deserved all the credit, but felt I would be diminishing his message if I stated it at that moment. I was also sure that he knew I was thinking it. So I grinned, said nothing, and allowed him to continue without any interruption.

"And before you tell me you deserve none of the credit . . ."

I couldn't help but laugh a bit.

"Just know that I am truly grateful." He then stood and offered his hand. I followed his lead.

We started to walk toward the practice green. That's when he really surprised me.

"So," he said playfully, but still seemingly very seriously. "I was thinking about our match, and I do remember the stakes. You win, I buy dinner. I win, I buy dinner, correct?"

"I believe those were our terms, Rich, yes."

"Well then, I think that this round offers us a unique opportunity.

"I'm game, Buddy." I replied.

"I was thinking about the Core Disciplines, and thought that instead of keeping score, we instead practice the discipline of being present in the moment, together."

As he'd done many times in the past, the student reminded me that he was also the teacher. As a serious golfer, I always keep score. I do so only for my purposes, not to judge, but simply to monitor my progress. That said, his proposal reminded me that there is something very pure about playing for the sake of playing. The purity of doing and being at the same time, observing myself in the game, experiencing all of my senses, and enjoying my experience without any need for comparisons or numeric measurements.

Richard embraced the silence and allowed me my thoughts.

The thought continued to sink in deeply as we grabbed out putters and walked onto the practice putting green. I used my golf glove to wipe away a couple of nostalgic tears as I remembered how life seemed much simpler as a boy and being in the moment was the norm. The goal then was to play; nothing more than to enjoy the essence of whatever game was at hand.

I remembered running around in the street in my hometown of North Brunswick, New Jersey, playing kickball, football, and when I was even a few years younger, playing a game of kick the can with my friends.

I took a deep breath as my mind continued to transport itself to memories of the past, all of them as fresh as if they were happening in that moment. I took another deep breath, smiled, and as Richard had said, realized that I didn't miss any of the past; I just appreciated it for what it was and how it helped shape who I had become.

After the game, I realized that I had never actually addressed or confirmed his proposal. I had completely forgot about it as I lost myself in one of the most enjoyable experiences of my life. Yes, being present in the moment truly works. Four hours and 15 minutes felt like no more than 30 minutes, and yet, as if I was recalling a great movie, I could replay every shot that either one of us hit in my mind.

I didn't know how either of us scored, nor was I even a bit curious. As we sat down for dinner, we laughed and celebrated each other's play, along with a very memorable experience. I stood to offer my hand for a shake. Richard stood and grabbed it with both hands. "Thank you," was all I said. It didn't matter if he knew what it was for.

# APPENDICES

# A | Energy Leadership: Key Words and Phrases

*Energy.* Energy is intangible; it is the very essence of who we are. A person's energy has everything to do with how they show up in every aspect of their life and is reflective of their degree of consciousness, awareness, potential, and power. It is the backdrop of mindset. When most people talk about energy, they're referring to "output." Unlike light bulbs, which have a specific potential wattage output and reach that potential consistently (a 75-watt light bulb always puts out 75 watts when lit), humans don't utilize all of their unlimited potential "wattage."

*Leadership.* Leadership is how you interact with everyone, including yourself. Leaders are quite visible within small and large businesses. We tend to think of them as business owners, CEOs, and managers at all levels. Traditionally, leadership also extends into politics and other global affairs. However, parents, therapists and health care providers, solopreneurs, sports coaches, consultants, mentors, partners in relationship, teachers, authors, and anyone who interacts with people on a regular basis are all leaders. ***Everyone is a leader either by choice or default.***

If you don't think of yourself as a leader, then I invite you to expand your thinking. Leading is the way we help move people into action, including ourselves. **The question is not whether you *are* a leader, *but how well you lead*.**

***Energy Leadership.*** Energy Leadership is the process that develops a personally effective style of leadership, one that positively influences and changes not only yourself, but also those with whom you work and interact, as well as your organization as a whole. Energy Leadership is also the ability to shift, or lead, energy to make it work for you, those around you, and your organization.

***Organization.*** An organization is two or more people in a relationship with a similar purpose or goal. Organizations are not limited to business. All the groups, teams, and people around you are organizations, too. It's the colleagues you work with *and* the family you go home to. Your organization includes all those who are grouped within your many circles of influence. Each of us is a part of many organizations.

***Consciousness.*** Consciousness is the level of your self-awareness, how fully you realize your True Self, as opposed to the self you have been "trained" to see and accept. True Self is unlimited and perfect. Your level of consciousness is determined by how you see yourself, the world around you, the people in your life, and life in general.

Your level of consciousness, and the energy it produces, will actually attract or repel desired or undesired people, events, and outcomes into your home and work life. The higher your level of consciousness, the more energy you have, and the more productive, peaceful, powerful, and healthy you are.

There is a direct relationship between consciousness and success. Visit www.iPECcoaching.com to see the results of research studies on consciousness and success.

***Anabolic and Catabolic Energy.*** Anabolic energy is constructive, and catabolic energy is destructive. When the mind perceives a threat, anabolic hormones, such as testosterone, decrease, while the catabolic hormones, such as cortisol and adrenaline, increase. The increase in catabolic hormones serves a short-term purpose by creating enough physical energy to meet the stressor. However, on a long-term basis, a constant release of catabolic hormones deteriorates the entire physical system.

Both types of hormonal releases stem from thoughts; therefore, thoughts are either anabolic or catabolic. Each of us has trained ourselves to automatically react to many of our life situations. These "default tendencies," if catabolic, actually cannibalize our entire system.

Anabolic leaders have the ability to motivate and inspire themselves and others to do extraordinary things. They have the ability to make energetic shifts in all levels of the organization. People who lead with catabolic energy are, on a long-term basis, destructive to themselves, the people around them, and their organizations.

*Average Resonating Level of Energy.* There are seven levels of energy (consciousness). Your energetic level is noted as your Average (the combined values of the energy of each thought we have) Resonating (how your level vibrates, attracts, and repels) Level of Energy (your inner energy, which manifests into your outer energy).

Your Average Resonating Level of Energy (ARL) is something we also call your "E-Factor," meaning your energetic indicator of success.

*Core Energy Coaching.* At the heart of Energy Leadership is the Core Energy Coaching process, which is a system that was formalized in 1999 to implement the various principles, skills, and strategies described in this book. It shifts energy and people to the highest levels possible.

It's called core energy because the focus of this work is on addressing the energy behind the core thoughts that drive people forward or hold them back. Core Energy Coaching deals with cause instead of effect.

# B | The Perfect Breath and Basic Centering Techniques

**Notes:** If you feel uncomfortable during these techniques, stop and try them again at another time. If you continue to have difficulty, ask someone with experience to guide you. Practice the techniques in a sitting position so that you do not fall asleep.

**Purpose:** A partial list of benefits to practicing these techniques on a regular basis includes: enhanced ability to effectively produce visualization and mental imagery; better oxygen circulation; improved digestion; increased energy; general relaxation; improved sleep; decreased physical and emotional pain; reduced fear and anger; a reduced effort of the heart; lengthening of life; and a pathway to feeling a personal spiritual connection.

## Technique #1: The Perfect Breath

**Procedure:** Close your eyes and breathe deeply and slowly – preferably through your nose – from the diaphragm (just above the stomach), trying to expand this area first as you inhale. You may want to imagine filling your stomach with air as if you were blowing up a balloon. After your diaphragm is full, begin filling your chest with a smooth rolling motion, remembering not to release the air in your diaphragm as your lungs fill. If it helps, place one hand on your stomach and the other on your chest while you breathe. As you breathe in, your bottom hand should rise. When you fill your lungs by "rolling" more air into your chest, your other hand will rise as well. Fill both your diaphragm and your lungs before exhaling through your mouth.

**How it works:** Breathing deeply from the diaphragm first allows you to take in much more air than breathing through the chest only. This allows you to relax more deeply than breathing into the lungs alone. Extra air helps you remove stress and "bad" air while life-giving oxygen cleanses your entire body. Concentrating on breathing also helps block out distractions around you.

**Additional comments:** Whenever you think of it, take a Perfect Breath during the day. It is one of the healthiest things you can do for yourself. Program some triggers, such as a ringing phone, to remind you to take this breath. And do it any time you feel the first signs of stress.

## Technique #2: The Basic Centering Technique

**Procedure:** Close your eyes and use the Perfect Breath technique to breathe in deeply through your nose (you can use your mouth if necessary), to a slow, silent count of three. Hold your breath for a count of one and release it through your mouth (or your nose, if you prefer) to a count of three. Repeat the process to a count of five, holding for a count of two and releasing to a count of five. Take a third slow, deep breath to a count of seven, hold for a count of three and release it to a count of seven. (Note: For a variation to the Perfect Breath technique, you can also try a "Box Breathing" technique: Breath in through your nose to a slow count of four, hold for a count of four, blow out through your mouth to a count of four, and then hold after the exhale to a count of four. Each cycle should be rhythmic, as if you are breathing in and out to each corner of a box. After you are comfortable with slow breaths and holds of four, you can increase the number to five, six, and even seven or more.)

Notice any sounds and let them go. Follow your breath for a few moments. Now breathe normally and think about the top of your head. Notice how it feels and allow it to relax. Try to create a feeling of warmth there, and release any tension or stress from this area. As the top of your head relaxes, begin to think about relaxing your forehead. Create a cool feeling surrounding your forehead by imagining it as the color blue and as smooth and cool as a piece of glass. You may even imagine a cool breeze caressing your brow. Allow this area to totally relax.

Now, imagine a beautiful white light. Creating a feeling of warmth and relaxation, breathe the light into the remaining parts of your body in this order: eyelids, mouth and jaw, neck, shoulders and upper back, upper and lower arms, elbows, hands, fingers, chest, abdomen and stomach, lower back, hips, thighs, knees, calves, ankles, tops of the feet, toes, and finally, the soles of the feet.

Once you complete this, relax and enjoy the feeling. When you are ready to leave this centered state, tell yourself mentally that you will count from one to five and open your eyes at the count of five, feeling alert, refreshed, and peaceful. Then count yourself out of this state from one to five. Relax and enjoy what you feel for a few moments before moving around.

# You've read the book.
## Now *experience* it . . .

Are you ready to explore how physical, mental, emotional, social, environmental, and spiritual factors influence your energy and impact your world?

Understanding energy in this way opens limitless doors—giving you powerful new ways to shift your own energy, understand the energy of others, fulfill your potential, and ultimately, raise the consciousness of the world.

Continue Your Journey By . . .

**Learning advanced skills** to create profound personal and professional change in your life, and the lives of others, by working with an iPEC-certified coach (or becoming one yourself!).

**Accessing the full anabolic potential of your organization** with our organizational coach training and consulting services so your leaders and teams are flowing with collaboration, creativity, and innovation.

**Joining our online community** where you'll participate in live, interactive conversations and workshops designed to harness the power of energy with others on this exciting journey!

Come explore by visiting us at
ipec.com

Awakening Potential